KOI

KOI

Living Jewels of the Orient

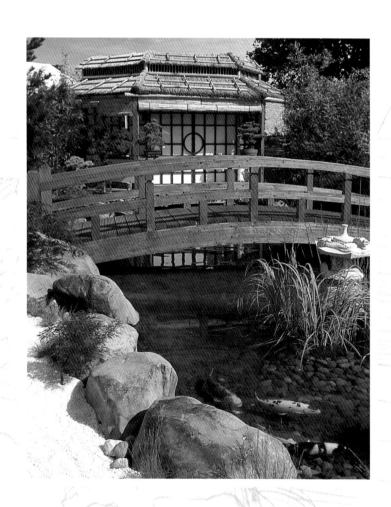

STEVE HICKLING • MICK MARTIN • BERNICE BREWSTER • NICK FLETCHER

BARRON'S

Authors

Steve Hickling is one of the leading authorities on koi in the UK today and has run World of Koi, a well-respected koi retail outlet in the South of England, since 1985. Steve and his team quickly built a reputation for constructing state-of-the-art koi ponds, incorporating innovative filtration systems that are now available worldwide. The company has recently been accepted by the Royal Horticultural Society as the first to construct a koi pond and garden at the Chelsea Flower Show 2002. Steve writes articles and answers readers' questions for koi magazines and gives talks to koi clubs. After 25 years in the koi world, Steve is anxious to share his experience and knowledge with a wider audience. He has contributed chapters on Filtration, and Pond Design and Construction, and has acted as the overall consultant on the project.

Nick Fletcher, former editor of the UK aquatic monthly *Practical Fishkeeping*, still regularly contributes articles to this and other fish-related publications. His interest in coldwater fish stems from his lifelong hobby of angling, which resulted in tanks containing native species, including pike. In the mid-1970s, on seeing a neighbor's koi, and being introduced to the late Hilda Allen of the British Koi Keepers Society, he was inspired to keep them himself. Nowadays, he prefers cosseting carp to catching them, and is actively involved in his local koi club. Nick has contributed the chapters on Buying Koi, Showing Koi, and the Koi Varieties Section.

Bernice Brewster first became interested in fish as a child, accompanying her grandfather on fishing trips. After graduating from London University, she worked for the Fish Section of the Natural History Museum before moving to a company dealing in Japanese koi. She now runs an aquatic consultancy business with a major interest in the koi hobby. In addition to writing articles for popular koi magazines, she has also contributed papers to scientific and veterinary journals on aspects of fish husbandry and management. Bernice has contributed the chapters on Water Quality, Physiology and Health Care, and Feeding.

Mick Martin has enjoyed fishkeeping since his school days, over 30 years ago. He has been an avid koi keeper for the past 20 years, gaining invaluable practical experience of koi husbandry through breeding his own koi, visiting Japan and buying high-grade koi on behalf of a major UK retailer, World of Koi. He has written articles for koi periodicals and has contributed the chapters on Koi Keeping – the Enduring Hobby, and Breeding.

First edition for the United States and Canada published by
Barron's Educational Series, Inc., 2002
First published in 2002 by Interpet Publishing
Original edition © 2002 by Interpet Publishing

All inquiries should be addressed to:
Barron's Educational Series, Inc.
250 Wireless Boulevard
Hauppauge, NY 11788
http://www.barronseduc.com

International Standard Book No. 0-7641-5448-6
Library of Congress Catalog Card No.
2001090609

Printed and bound in China.
9 8 7 6 5 4 3 2 1

Credits
Created and designed: Ideas into Print, New Ash Green, Kent DA3 8JD, UK.
Computer graphics: Phil Holmes and Stuart Watkinson
Koi variety photographs: Nishikigoi International (Nigel Caddock); Andrew McGill; Kinsai Publisher Co. Ltd., Tokyo, (Shunzo Baba)
Text adviser Varieties Section: Kate McGill
Production management: Consortium, Poslingford, Suffolk CO10 8RA, UK.
Print production: Sino Publishing House Ltd., Hong Kong.

Below: To help you become familiar with the terms used in the koi world to describe colors and varieties, panels such as this are featured throughout the Koi Varieties section.

KOI DEFINITIONS

Hi ~ Red

Kohaku ~ White koi with red markings

Kuchibeni ~ Red lips ~ literally "lipstick"

Magoi ~ Ancestral black carp

Maruten ~ A self-contained head marking, plus red elsewhere on the body

Tancho ~ Circular red spot on head. No other red on the body

Yondan ~ Four-step pattern

Contents

Part One

Introduction

Koi keeping is a hobby that generates obsession. Your starting point may be modest, but over the years, as your knowledge and understanding of these magnificent fish and their environment grows, you will find more and more to absorb you. And then you will be hooked.

The popularity of keeping koi has grown worldwide, spawning new clubs, shows, and specialized magazines and consequently more and more koi keepers. As a result, manufacturers are investing time and money in developing new foods, remedies, pumps, filtration systems, and all types of technical wizardry, which can only be a good thing for you, the hobbyist.

The hobby has changed tremendously over the past 20 years and this book reflects current thinking and the latest technical advances. The first part explores all the practical aspects of keeping koi, from understanding water quality and the filtration systems that maintain it to the decisions, difficulties, and triumphs of designing and building a koi pond in your own garden. Computer graphics reveal the working principles of the latest equipment in stunning clarity. This part of the book also features chapters on the physiology and health care of koi, how to feed them properly, and how to buy good-quality stock in the first place. The section closes with expert insights into the world of showing and breeding koi – providing an introduction to yet more exciting and rewarding aspects of the hobby.

Why are koi called "koi"? Where did they come from? How has an international hobby grown from naturally occurring color changes in carp kept as food fish? This is the subject of the first chapter in this part of the book and where our fascinating journey of discovery begins.

Koi keeping – the enduring hobby

Who would have thought that the rather ordinary black common carp (*Cyprinus carpio*) found in waters throughout Europe for centuries could have undergone such a transformation on the other side of the world? In just two centuries, the breeding of koi for the serious enthusiast and the hobbyist alike has become an international industry. Koi husbandry has expanded beyond all bounds in the home of Nishikigoi – Japan. This is how the fairy-tale story unfolded and became part of the Nishikigoi folklore.

Where did koi come from?

It is widely accepted that common carp were transported from Eurasia to the Far East more than 2,000 years ago and to Japan via China and Korea, where they were bred as a source of food. Carp are a very hardy breed of fish and could withstand the trauma of transportation by land and sea to far-off lands. There is evidence that the common carp, *Cyprinus carpio*, finally made it to Japan about 1,000 years ago.

But why were carp kept in captivity in those early years? It seems that Japanese farmers kept carp in mud ponds to supplement their daily diet of rice and vegetables. It is said they kept them in the paddy fields in which they grew their rice, but it seems more likely they were kept in the reservoir ponds above the paddy fields. Once any species is kept in a restricted breeding ground, sooner or later it will produce a mutation. In the case of carp, over hundreds of years these mutations caused

external differences, including a pronounced color change. The mutant fish were prized by the farmers and kept out of interest, instead of becoming food for the table. When these fine color irregularities were found, the farmers began producing "colored carp" as a hobby. This apparently occurred between 1840 and 1844, long after the early years of carp farming. From such humble beginnings, the keeping of Nishikigoi (brocaded carp) had started. Although koi are now bred throughout the world, only koi born and bred in Japan are true Nishikigoi.

The development of koi breeding

There are two distinct periods in the history of koi, the first being pre-1800. There is little documentary evidence about this era, since many of the references to koi actually concern wild carp.

Right: A stylized, nineteenth-century picture of a carp with a bogbean plant by Sadatora. Koi were often depicted in paintings and tapestries, indicating their importance in Japanese culture.

Above: This Ai Goromo was voted best in the Koromo class at the All Japan Show 2001. Koromo means "cloaked" or "robed." Matsunosuke first established this variety in about 1950 in Niigata.

Below: A mountain scene typical of the area around Niigata, with a terraced mud pond in the distance. Originally, the ponds were used for topping off the rice paddy fields and held carp to supplement the diet.

Above: The indoor koi pool at the Nishikigoi Information Centre, Ojiya. Displays promote the history of koi keeping, while the gardens feature traditional and modern pond designs.

The ancient Chinese and Japanese illustrations on silk showed koi, but without any bright colors. In fact, there is little evidence of colored koi before the early 1800s. At that time, Nishikigoi were kept as a prized possession by the noblemen of the time – the forerunners of today's hobbyists!

It is widely accepted that the true colored koi originated in Japan from the Niigata prefecture (similar to a small county) during the early 1800s. Nishikigoi originated in the villages of Takerawa, Hi-gashiyama, Ota, Taneuhara, and Kamagashima. Today, some of these villages have been enveloped by the expansion of the city of Ojiya, the home of Nishikigoi. In fact, there is a wonderful Nishikigoi Information Centre given over to the history of koi in the center of the city. Niigata is located on the west coast of Honshu Island, a two-hour

Where does the name koi come from?

The name "koi" dates back to about 500 B.C., when it was first mentioned and recorded to describe a wild carp presented by King Shoko of Ro to Confucius on the birth of his first son. The Japanese word for carp is "koi," which was later used to describe all carp, both the wild and the more recent, colored varieties. There appears to be no documentary evidence to show when the word koi was first used to describe the modern-day colored carp. Over the years, colored carp have been given many different names. When colored koi were first exported to the West, they were mainly red or red and white. In the early days they were known as flower carp (Hanagoi), brocaded carp (Nishikigoi), fancy carp (Moyoogoi), or even colored and colorful carp. Today, we tend to call them koi carp. In Japan they were originally called Hirogoi or Irogoi, meaning colored carp, but later they became known just as goi or koi. The preferred name in Japan for all single or multicolored carp is Nishikigoi, from the Japanese word "nishiki," used to describe an expensive cloth of many colors imported from the Indian subcontinent into Japan and China, hence Nishikigoi – "carp of many colors." Nishikigoi are held in such high esteem that they are recognized as the national fish of Japan.

bullet train ride from the capital, Tokyo. Niigata is revered throughout the world as being the best area for breeding koi. Some people say this is due to the quality of the mountain waters, while others claim the secret lies in the mud ponds that naturally contain montmorillionite clay, which is rich in vitamins and minerals. Whatever the reason, or as a result of the combination of both qualities, Niigata attracted the most famous names in koi breeding to the area.

There is no record of what was the first koi mutation, but it is thought to have been a red carp called "Hoo-kazuki," possibly from a mutant black carp. From this original red carp mutation the first white koi was produced. These were subsequently crossbred, resulting in the first red and white carp, originally called "Hara-aka," meaning red belly. The red and white carp is the oldest and still by far the most popular colored variety in Japan. It was not until much later, in about 1890, that it was officially recognized and named Kohaku. However, it is accepted that the Kohaku line was stabilized in Niigata in around 1930.

Although red and white koi were the most talked about mutation, other colored carp were being developed. It was not long before the true all-black Magoi was produced from the original two strains of wild carp: one brown/black, the other a blue/black. From this early mutation came the first known true blue koi, the Asagi, meaning "light blue." Much later, an Asagi Sanke was crossed with a Doitsu mirror carp and the first Shusui

Right: A wonderful Nidan Kohaku, "Nidan" meaning it has a two-stepped hi (red) pattern. The deep red is perfectly balanced over a pure snow-white body. The Kohaku is probably the most popular variety of koi in Japan today and also one of the oldest, dating back to the early 1890s.

The emergence of fishkeeping

Since the 1800s, there has been a massive expansion in the koi industry throughout the world. The Industrial Revolution in the Western world resulted in significantly better roads, transport, and communication, and an increased awareness of other nations across the world. With the spread of this knowledge, public zoos and aquariums displaying wildlife from the other side of the globe became very popular. As a result, people tried to re-create these habitats in their own homes and gardens, and fishkeeping began in earnest.

(meaning "autumn water") was bred. A Shusui is said to represent the reflections of red autumn leaves floating against a pure blue sky.

During this early time, before the science of genetics had been developed, breeders gained important knowledge of how to maintain these unusual colors and improve on them. But even now, with strong bloodlines going back over many years, it is still difficult to predict the resultant brood from a successful spawning.

Then followed what is known as the third mutation of early Nishikigoi. These are the Bekko varieties, comprising three types: Shiro Bekko (white fish with black spots – known as a tortoiseshell pattern), Aka Bekko (red fish with black spots), and Ki Bekko (yellow fish with black spots). The Bekko varieties do not produce natural metallic scales, apart from those bred with Gin-Rin (reflective silver) scales, unlike the similar Utsurimono varieties (black koi with white, red, or yellow markings). These original mutations became the founders of all the colorful koi to be bred later, with the exception of the Ogon variety (single-colored metallic koi) that was developed many years later.

One further color combination played a tremendous part in the history of Nishikigoi. A tricolored koi (white with red and black markings) called a Taisho Sanshoku, later to be referred to as just Sanke, was developed during the Meji era (1868-1912). No one knows who actually bred the first Taisho Sanke, but it was first exhibited in 1915, when the fish was about 15 years old.

Further developments

At the turn of the twentieth century, koi keeping became a very popular hobby within Japan. Another change in direction was to have an even greater impact on the breeding of future koi: Mirror carp were introduced into Japan from Germany. Their large shiny, uniform scales – five to six times larger than normal – proved very popular and the fish became known as Doitsu (Japanese for "Deutsch," meaning "German"). The Doitsu had a much heavier, deeper, and shorter body and was thought to be a hardier species than its Japanese counterpart, the Magoi.

As a result of more modern breeding methods, two kinds of Doitsu koi were perfected. Leatherback carp (Kawagoi) had few or no scales, while the mirror carp (Kamamigoi) displayed large symmetrical scales along its back, on either side of the dorsal fin. Some mirror carp displayed scales along their lateral line as well, and these are sometimes referred to as striped carp (Yoroigoi). Other varieties produced scales in irregular patterns reminiscent of ancient Japanese armor. The first successful crosses between the German carp and the Japanese carp were made in 1904. All varieties

Above: An Asagi with the typical uniform blue-gray scaling. This distinct reticulation is synonymous with the variety. The Asagi was one of the first Nishikigoi produced as a result of a mutation from a Magoi some 160 years ago.

Right: It is said that a good Taisho Sanke will support an excellent Kohaku pattern beneath smaller, well-placed patches of sumi (black). The Sanke, as it is more familiarly known, is another old variety, first exhibited in 1915.

Below: The category of Hikarimoyo includes one of the most popular koi varieties, the Ogon, a relatively modern variety, first produced successfully in 1946. Originally golden in color, Ogons now range from yellow through to a full red or orange. This unusual lemon Ogon displays excellent volume (size-to-weight ratio), with good, even scales.

were to be known as Doitsu Nishikigoi. These modern varieties contributed greatly to the expansion of Nishikigoi throughout the world. This breeding finally provided the last part of the puzzle – the Ogon.

Following on from the Taisho Sanke came the Showa Sanshoku Sanke (later called Showa), and along with it the end of the Taisho era. In 1927 the Showa Sanke made its debut, primarily a black koi with patches of red and white, unlike the Taisho Sanke, a white koi with patches of red and black.

In the early 1920s a wild carp with golden scales was crossed with a koi in a breeding program to produce the greatest amount of golden color. By 1946 the first Ogon (golden koi) was produced. The name "Ogon" initially referred only to the gold form, but today it applies to all single-color metallic koi. Ogons are included in the category Hikarimoyo (abbreviated from Hikarimoyo-Mono, "Hikari" meaning "shining" and "mono" denoting a single color). The exception to this category is the Matsuba Ogon. Although this koi variety is predominantly one color, its scalation is enhanced with black edging to the scales. This produces the famous "pinecone" pattern, so popular with hobbyists.

To put koi breeding into perspective, it is only very recently that modern varieties, such as Matsuba Ogon (1960s), Gin Matsuba (Platinum Ogon), Purachina (1965), Gin-Rin or Dia (wild silver reflective scales) varieties (early 1960s), and the Midorigoi (light green koi) in 1965, have all been developed. Thirteen colors and their numerous varieties are recognized for Nishikigoi and these are discussed in detail on pages 124-197

Enjoying koi today

Koi keeping enjoyed its heyday during the 1960s, when everyone in Japan appeared to keep koi. At that time there were more than 3,000 koi breeders, but today there are just over 1,000. Koi mainly originating from Japan are now bred throughout the world, including Thailand, China, Korea, Israel, South Africa, the United States, and Europe. As a result, Japan has tended to raise the quality of the koi it sells and now specializes more in the superior high-grade koi we have come to expect from the "Home of Nishikigoi."

Japanese hobbyists are well catered to by the Zen Nippon Airinkai, or ZNA, the world's largest koi society, which is now accessible on the Internet. Many countries have local koi-keeping societies run by enthusiastic volunteers eager to pass on their knowledge to new-found members. There is plenty of reading matter for koi enthusiasts, with monthly and quarterly magazines available throughout the world.

Surfing the Web

Today, koi enthusiasts can communicate with each other via the Internet. Log on to your web browser or any search engine, type in the word "koi" or "carp," and you will be offered numerous hits, or sites. Try visiting one of the sites and clicking on to a "link." This button is a shortcut option, enabling you to visit other koi-related companies or enthusiasts with their own web sites. These links contain text and/or photographs that have a connection with your original search profile. You will soon collect a mass of information on your chosen subject from around the world. Having acquired plenty of useful knowledge from your hits, you can download

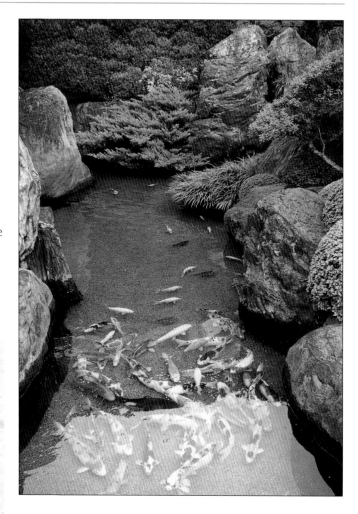

Above: A traditional koi pond in Japan. The large moss- and lichen-covered boulders at the water's edge and the pine and juniper trees in the background are typically used to create a Japanese landscape. Note the clarity of the water.

New varieties

New koi varieties are being produced by Japanese breeders all the time. With a greater understanding of genetics and an improved breeding program, new varieties are regularly being established. Obviously, it takes many years to perfect a new strain and ensure that it breeds true each season; only then can it be marketed as a new variety. The Pearl Scale Asagi is a good example of a recent addition. It features a reverse scale reticulation, where each scale is light blue edged with navy blue. Another development is the Kohaku/Goshiki. This is a Doitsu fish with the classic Kohaku pattern (red on a pure white background) for six months. However, it gradually develops Goshiki colors, which it retains for six months and then reverts back to Kohaku – two fish for the price of one!

One bizarre mutation reported in the koi press was of koi carp being bred with their eyes facing up toward the surface, instead of on the side of the head. Koi are natural bottom feeders, but because people like to hand-feed their fish, someone thought it would be an improvement if they could see their floating food quicker! Most koi keepers would not be in favor of such mutations, but that is exactly what occurred within the fancy goldfish breeding program.

However, it is good to see that the Japanese are not just producing the classic varieties, but are constantly searching for new and exciting colors and patterns, which must benefit the hobbyist in the long run.

the information and store it or print it out. This allows you to assimilate it at a later stage, in your own time. The web site for ZNA, for example, provides a wide range of information on keeping koi.

If you already buy dedicated koi periodicals, you will find that some have a web site of their own. This enables the Internet surfer to visit a particular site and be offered a full download of the current publication, along with shortcuts to all relevant information. Some have a facility for interactive chat lines that enable koi keepers from around the world, who may have made a "hit" on your particular site, to literally talk to each other in a conference situation. There is normally a help line section where you can request information concerning fish health, pond problems, or koi varieties, etc. If the web site cannot answer your problem you can be sure that someone, somewhere, out on the Web will be able to help you.

Keeping in touch

Interactive web sites allow koi retailers to offer state-of-the-art services to their customers. There are sites where you can plan your entire pond layout, including the location of all the pond accessories, using computer graphics. With the aid of the computer and photographs of the proposed pond location, a digitally mastered pond can be placed over the existing photograph. This allows you to view the completed pond project without committing yourself to a particular layout.

Another advance being tested is the web chronicle, a regularly updated computer magazine for koi enthusiasts. It will provide the koi surfer with a wealth of information on fish health, koi products, events, special offers, and even koi! The layout is very much on the lines of a regular koi periodical.

A family tradition

It is widely accepted that wine producers making a fine wine from a single grapevine have good and bad years, and the same principle applies to koi spawning; one season's brood can be much better than another produced the previous year. And, just as in fine wine production, koi breeding is often a family concern. Knowledge and experience are passed down from father to son and jealously guarded within the family. Young children and their mothers help out in the annual cull and sexing of Nishikigoi. Decades ago, some of the families were responsible for introducing completely new varieties to the world, and their descendants continue to specialize in them today.

Below: By contrast with the traditional Japanese koi pond, raised ponds such as this are popular in the West. In Japan, the koi pond is part of a traditional-style garden, whereas in the West the pond itself tends to be the main focus of attention.

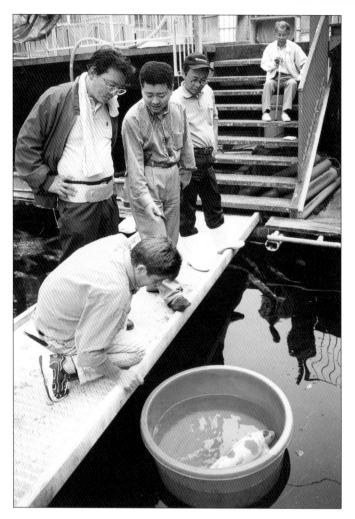

Above: The scene at a Japanese fish farm, where prime koi are "bowled up" for inspection by koi dealers from around the world. There is much competition between dealers during the spring and fall harvests to obtain the best deals for their customers at home.

Some surfers feel confident enough to hold a chat-line conversation with the aid of a microphone and web cam. It may even lead to surfers joining up, off computer, and forming another koi keepers society or arranging to meet at a mutually convenient Open Koi Show. Along with the competition aspect of these shows (see pages 108-115), there is something for everyone interested in the hobby. They are an excellent way of exchanging ideas and keeping in touch with new trends and products. Mini lectures or koi clinics hosted by a prominent koi expert are often part of the program.

E-mail is the easiest way of linking up with fellow koi enthusiasts. E-mails are fun and informative, and simply a matter of writing a letter or note to another enthusiast, sending it via your computer, and awaiting a reply. You will soon build up a list of contacts on your system and can forward a note to one or all of them at the press of a button. When sending e-mails, you can add any attachment to your message, in the form of pictures or even text obtained from another source, that you wish to impart to your friends. Not only is it a cheap method of communication, but you only have to compose the message once before sending it out to several people.

Your questions answered

You can already interact with your computer on the subject of fish health. Some web sites allow you to pose a specific question to which you are given multichoice alternative answers. You continue interrogating the computer until it gives you a final answer. This is really useful if you are dealing with an emergency in your pond at a time when dealers or veterinarians are not available. Reassurance is sometimes all you need when you are dealing with a crisis in the pond. If you have a major fish health problem, some web sites have a live web cam facility where it is possible to show closeups of your fish health problem, or you can take a digital photograph or video. These can then be sent via an e-mail as an attachment to an experienced koi dealer or enthusiast who may be able to pinpoint the problem immediately.

Below: A typical scene at an Open Koi Show in France. The show vats in the foreground are attracting attention from visitors united in their enthusiasm for a truly international hobby.

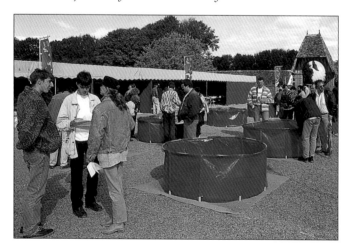

Water quality

Water – an extraordinary substance with unique properties – is essential to all living organisms. Compared with other liquids, water behaves in some very strange ways. For example, most substances shrink as they get colder, but at 3.94°C (usually rounded up to 4°C / 39°F) water expands, bursting pipes and tanks. In the pond environment, this means that at about 4°C (39°F), this denser but warmer water sinks and the least dense, colder water is at the surface, where it freezes. This is why ice floats.

The natural circulation of water

The total amount of water found throughout the world is constant, and it is continuously recycled through evaporation and precipitation in the form of rain or snow. The oceans are full of salt water and literally give rise to the world's supply of freshwater in the form of rain and melted snow and ice. The atmosphere is rich in the greenhouse gas carbon dioxide, which is very soluble

and simply dissolves into the precipitating rain, where it forms carbonic acid and thus makes the water mildly acidic. The atmosphere also contains an assortment of gaseous pollutants, such as sulphur dioxide from industrial processes and, increasingly, nitrogen oxides derived from motor vehicle exhaust fumes, which may also dissolve into rain, making it increasingly acidic.

On reaching the ground, some of the rain will simply evaporate, but the rest soaks into the surface and percolates down through the underlying soil and rocks, where it reacts with minerals and salts. The composition of the minerals and salts gives the water its chemical characteristics, and these vary according to the type of soil and rock through which it has trickled. The mineral content of this so-called groundwater can even include an assortment of metals. Granite substrates are impermeable to water, so few salts dissolve into the water as it trickles through the underground rock and it remains acidic and soft. In those areas where the water

The natural water cycle

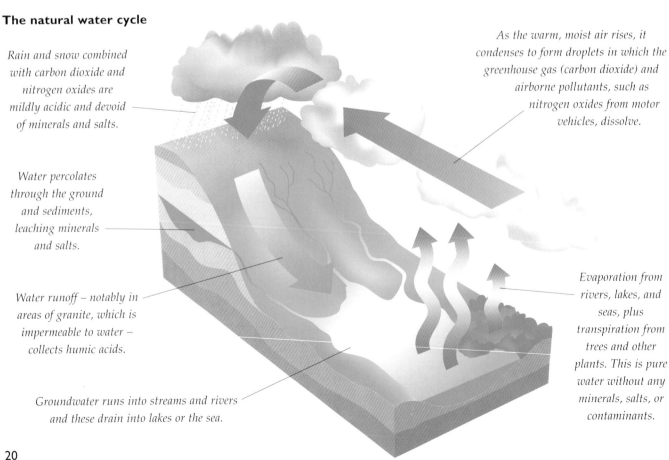

Rain and snow combined with carbon dioxide and nitrogen oxides are mildly acidic and devoid of minerals and salts.

As the warm, moist air rises, it condenses to form droplets in which the greenhouse gas (carbon dioxide) and airborne pollutants, such as nitrogen oxides from motor vehicles, dissolve.

Water percolates through the ground and sediments, leaching minerals and salts.

Water runoff – notably in areas of granite, which is impermeable to water – collects humic acids.

Groundwater runs into streams and rivers and these drain into lakes or the sea.

Evaporation from rivers, lakes, and seas, plus transpiration from trees and other plants. This is pure water without any minerals, salts, or contaminants.

Above: *Good water conditions are essential for keeping koi healthy. However, clear water does not necessarily mean it is suitable. Many dissolved pollutants, such as metals, chlorine, ammonia, and nitrite, are invisible yet cause sickness or death.*

filters through chalk, limestone, or gypsum, it is rich in calcium salts, which makes it alkaline and hard. Water hardness is familiar to most of us as the limescale found in kettles, pipes, and on water-heating elements.

The mineral sediments through which water percolates may contribute traces of heavy metals such as aluminum, iron, lead, mercury, cadmium, zinc, and bismuth. Dissolved metals can also find their way into the aquatic environment through mining, agriculture, forestry, and landfill practices. Some heavy metals, such as iron or zinc, are vital for living organisms in very tiny quantities, known as "trace elements." Many, however, are very poisonous to living creatures and are particularly soluble in soft water. In hard, alkaline waters, the metal ions are "locked up" as the salts of the metals, which makes them less harmful. In soft, acidic water, the metals are present in their most damaging form and are therefore poisonous to koi. The effects of metals on koi are various

and may affect only specific organs, or the effect may be systemic, causing significant changes in all organs and tissues, which means they no longer function properly.

Agricultural activities may also influence water chemistry. For example, in unpolluted waters, nitrate is found at very low concentrations, but through the use of agricultural fertilizers, some areas may exceed recommended drinking water levels of nitrate. Groundwater may also contain residues of chemicals such as pesticides and herbicides.

Natural waters are rich in biological material, ranging from microscopic organisms to large aquatic plants and animals, including fish. The presence of plants and animals in the aquatic environment means that there are also breakdown products of solid organic material from living or dead tissues. These breakdown products include humic acid, oils, waxes, assorted hydrocarbons, and fatty acids – all invisible residues that affect water quality.

Water treatment for human use

Occasionally, it is necessary for water main pipes to be treated with pesticides to eradicate insect larvae that can completely block the water system. These insecticides are pyrethrum derivatives and poisonous to koi. In most instances, several weeks advance notification is given that the pipes will be treated. Following such treatment, the water in the pipes is unsuitable for water changing for about a month.

The microscopic life found in water includes bacteria, algae, and single-celled organisms, technically called "protozoa." The majority of organisms found in natural waters are harmless, but some, such as the bacteria that cause cholera or typhoid, can cause outbreaks of disease in humans. At the turn of the twentieth century it was realized that adding chlorine gas as a disinfectant to drinking water reduced the incidence of waterborne disease in humans. Chlorine continues to be used as a disinfectant in water mains and koi keepers should be aware of its potentially harmful effects. In combination with ammonia, chlorine forms a range of substances known as chloramines, principally monochloramine (NH_2Cl), dichloramine ($NHCl_2$), and trichloramine ($NHCl_3$), the relative quantities depending on the concentration of the parent chemicals and the pH of the water. Although chloramines have a reduced

Below: Chlorine-based disinfectants added to drinking water are poisonous to koi. In soft water areas, the water can become contaminated with metals. And being mildly acidic, soft water causes any metals present to be in the most poisonous form.

Left: Water purifiers are commonly installed on the incoming water supply of many koi ponds. Modern purifiers have the capacity to remove contaminants such as metals, in addition to chlorine and its derivatives. There are many different types available, so be sure to select the right type of water purifier based on a water report for your local area.

Reverse osmosis

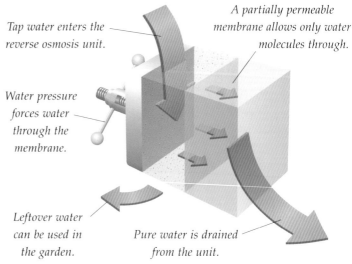

In normal osmosis (right), water molecules pass across a partially permeable membrane from a dilute solution to a more concentrated one. With reverse osmosis, water pressure is used to reverse this flow of water molecules.

Tap water enters the reverse osmosis unit.

A partially permeable membrane allows only water molecules through.

Water pressure forces water through the membrane.

Leftover water can be used in the garden.

Pure water is drained from the unit.

Right: *Water conditioners can remove chlorine and other harmful tap water contaminants. Many brands have a measuring device built into the container, enabling you to administer the exact dose. Mix the conditioner with pond water in a watering can and sprinkle it onto the pond surface or into the surface skimmer.*

disinfectant action on bacteria compared with free chlorine gas, the effect lasts longer in water and so there has been an increasing tendency to add ammonia at the chlorination stage of water treatment.

Both monochloramines and dichloramines are toxic to fish. Chlorine and chloramines present in water are measured as "total residual chlorine." For koi, the recommended maximum continuous exposure level to total residual chlorine is 0.002 mg per L, but even at this concentration there is evidence of toxicity and effects on the gill tissue. Chlorine at concentrations of 4 mg per L will cause koi to die within eight hours of exposure. New ponds should have the water treated with a water conditioner, which can remove both chlorine and chloramine, or alternatively, the water filling the pond can be filtered through a water purifier.

It is not necessary to use a dechlorinator when carrying out partial water changes of up to 30 percent of the volume of the pond because the chlorine will be diluted in the system. However, if you suspect that the water company may be flushing the water mains, avoid water changes or be sure to add a conditioner.

Maintaining water quality for koi

Koi keepers often say (as do all fishkeepers) that if you look after the water, the koi will look after themselves and, in many ways, there is much truth to this statement. Water quality varies according to its use; for example,

drinking water is of excellent quality, but the chlorine content renders it unsuitable for fish. As we have seen, numerous factors contribute to water quality and they interact with each other, so there is no simple definition of the term. With regard to koi keeping, water quality is almost exclusively concerned with physical and chemical characteristics such as temperature, dissolved oxygen levels, pH, the nitrogenous waste produced by the fish, alkalinity, phosphate levels, particulate organic substances, and dissolved organic substances. Here, we look at these parameters in more detail.

Water temperature

Water temperature is related to weather conditions, but it is important because it affects all physical, chemical, and biological processes and therefore has an effect on both koi and their pond system. For example, temperature directly influences both the solubility of oxygen and the toxicity of ammonia waste (see page 24).

Water temperature also has a profound influence on the physiology and health of koi. Increasing water temperatures cause koi to become more active, consume more food, grow, produce more ammonia as waste, and spawn. While any rise in temperature may have positive effects on koi, as the water warms, it also causes any dissolved contaminants or even treatments to become increasingly toxic to them. Decreasing temperatures cause koi to become less

Right: *Remember to monitor the water temperature routinely. There are several different types of thermometers available, from the floating model shown here to very sensitive electronic ones with remote probes.*

active, and their appetite and the efficiency of their immune system decline. However, many koi keepers now choose to heat the pond through the colder months of the year.

Over the last ten years or so, most koi breeders in Japan have installed sophisticated fish houses in which koi in their first and second years are overwintered in ponds with a minimum temperature of 16°C (61°F). Keeping young koi in heated ponds through the winter means that they have never experienced cold-water conditions. Therefore, in areas outside Japan that experience cold winters, it is better to either place these koi in heated pond systems or introduce them into the pond in the summer when the water is warm. After feeding and growing through the summer, most of these young koi should successfully overwinter.

Dissolved oxygen levels

Oxygen is an essential requirement for koi and should be regarded as the most important water quality parameter. There are a number of factors affecting the solubility of oxygen in water, but temperature has a major effect. In cold water, when the koi are least active and their oxygen requirement is minimal, this gas is readily soluble in water, but as the water temperature increases through the spring and into the summer, the

How temperature affects ammonia toxicity

% free (toxic) ammonia in total ammonia

Temperature °C

How temperature affects oxygen levels

Oxygen mg/L

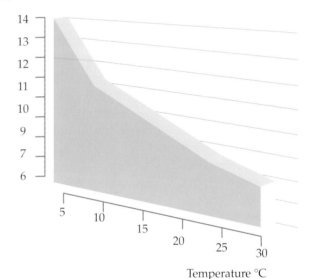

Temperature °C

Above: *As the water temperature rises, more of the total ammonia present changes into free ammonia, which is very poisonous to the koi.*

Above: *Oxygen solubility decreases with rising temperature. Affected koi are initially lethargic but as oxygen level plummets they rise to the surface gasping. To convert Celsius (centigrade) to Fahrenheit, multiply by 9/5 and add 32.*

Frayed fins

Fins clamped tightly against the sides of the body.

Koi gasping at water surface.

Gill cover flares as the koi tries to extract as much oxygen as possible from the water.

Heat exchanger for gas-fired boiler

Water heated in a gas boiler flows through the central core of the exchanger.

Warmed water returns to the pond.

Pond water is pumped through the wide bore tube into the heat exchanger.

Circulating water returns to gas boiler to be reheated.

Return to pond

Inlet from pond

Exchanger

Pump

Thermostat

Boiler

Above: *How the exchanger connects to a gas boiler. Vital safety valves and pressure vessels are not shown here.*

Heating the water

Although heating the pond is not absolutely essential, it does give you the ability to control the koi environment completely. If you do heat the pond, it is important to mimic the climatic conditions that prevail in the country of origin to help the fish acclimatize more readily.

One tried and tested solution is to heat the water to a minimum of 13°C (55°F) for 40 weeks and then gradually lower the thermostat by one degree each day until the water temperature is the same as the ambient temperature. Switch the heater off at this point and leave the fish in a torpid condition for six weeks.

After this period, switch the heater on again, making sure that the thermostat matches the water temperature. Gradually increase the thermostat by one degree each day until the temperature reaches 13°C (55°F) again. Japan experiences long hot summers, followed by short but severe winters, and this regime closely matches the climate there.

Some fishkeepers heat their ponds to a set temperature all year round, but experience has shown that if the fish do not have a resting season, they do not spawn as readily and tend to hold on to the roe.

Inline electric water heater

This unit controls the temperature setting and timer functions.

Heated water flows back into the pond.

Inside this stainless steel tube is an electrically heated element that warms the pond water as it passes through.

Pond water is pumped through the core. An arrow on the unit indicates the specified direction of flow.

solubility declines. Heating water from 9 to 15°C (48 to 59°F) reduces the available dissolved oxygen by 13 percent. From the table showing the solubility of oxygen at a range of temperatures, you can see that in the summer, when koi are most active and their oxygen demand is greatest, this vital gas is at a premium. The minimum dissolved oxygen concentration for healthy growth, tissue repair, and reproduction in koi is 6 mg per L of water, but ideally the concentration should exceed this value. The more koi there are in the pond, the greater is the demand on the dissolved oxygen. This parameter should be viewed as the limiting factor on the number of koi that any pond can hold.

Within a koi pond there are other factors that affect the dissolved oxygen concentration. Blanketweed grows prolifically in the summer and, like all plants in the hours of daylight, these algal strands produce sugars using the energy from sunlight and carbon dioxide dissolved in the

Oxygen in the pond – winter

Oxygen is readily soluble in cold water.

The koi are inactive at low temperatures and their oxygen requirement is minimal.

The koi are producing less waste and the lower temperatures inhibit bacterial activity.

Oxygen in the pond – summer

Less oxygen is available in the water as the temperature increases.

Blanketweed produces oxygen during the day, but consumes it at night.

At higher temperatures, the koi are increasingly active and need more oxygen.

More solid waste accumulates in the filter and this increases the demand for oxygen by the aerobic bacteria.

water, and liberate oxygen gas as a waste product during the process of photosynthesis. At night, respiration predominates, which means that the blanketweed uses oxygen and produces carbon dioxide gas as waste.

In addition to any blanketweed growth, the bacteria and other microbes that live in the filter system consume vast amounts of oxygen by way of respiration and yet more in the oxidation of ammonia to nitrate as part of the nitrogen cycle (see the illustration on page 30). In fact, 1 gm of ammonia requires 4 gm oxygen during its conversion to nitrate. The use of oxygen by the microbial flora is described as the "biological oxygen demand." Any aquatic system such as a pond will also contain a vast

amount of organic material from the koi, blanketweed, or other plant life, and from the microbial population. As this material accumulates in the mechanical filtration system and breaks down, it uses oxygen, and oxygen consumption increases. This is why it is important to clean this part of the filter regularly. The filter is therefore the biggest oxygen sink in a koi pond system. The filter bacteria are the most efficient at extracting oxygen from the water, followed by blanketweed, and finally, the koi can use what is left.

Many of the medications popularly used in koi ponds, such as malachite green, formalin, or a combination of formalin and malachite green, will strip the water of oxygen; do not use them if you suspect that the oxygen level is low. If you do need to add a medication to the pond, it is good practice to increase aeration before introducing any chemicals and to continue the aeration during the treatment.

In very cold weather, air is readily soluble in water and under certain conditions the water can become supersaturated with gas, leading to a condition known as gas bubble disease (see page 81). Although dissolved oxygen levels are elevated when water becomes supersaturated with air, it is the nitrogen content that gives rise to the symptoms of gas bubble disease. Supersaturation of water with air generally tends to occur when air under pressure is drawn into cold water. This can happen in a number of ways:

● A pipe or piece of tubing with a pinhole sucks in air and forces it into solution.

● Air diffusers in the deepest part of the pond may cause supersaturation. The pressure of water increases with depth and gases at high pressure dissolve more readily. In summer this is not a problem, as many gases are relatively insoluble in warm water, but in cold water, air readily enters solution from the air diffuser. Remedy the problem simply by raising any air diffusers to about 30 cm (12 in) below the water surface.

● Cold water already saturated with air heated in a closed, heat-exchange system becomes supersaturated as it warms up.

There are other ways in which dissolved gas levels become very high. For example, the photosynthetic activity of algal blooms can cause the water to become saturated with oxygen, and bore or well water is often saturated with nitrogen. Even air transport has been implicated as a cause of gas bubble disease in fish as a consequence of the changes in air pressure that occur during the flight.

Supersaturation of water can be detected by testing the oxygen content of the water;

Left: In hot weather, when oxygen levels can be very low, it is vital to add extra forms of aeration, such as airstones connected to an air pump. Aerated bottom drains (here) help to add oxygen and also create a good water flow to the drain. Excessive aeration, however, can cause problems.

Above: Venturis have been traditionally used to aerate koi ponds and can be very efficient, but the delivery of air slows or stops if the pump becomes blocked by a prolific growth of blanketweed.

Left: If you slide your hand into some supersaturated water, it becomes coated with a layer of fine bubbles. Gas supersaturation usually occurs at low temperatures, when air readily dissolves in the cold water.

Dissolved oxygen test

1 Stabilize the oxygen content with the first reagent, then add eight drops of the second (shown here), forming a cloudy precipitate.

4 Pour the 10 mL of yellow solution into a small beaker for the next stage of the oxygen test.

2 Add five drops of the third reagent and mix. The solution turns clear yellow.

3 Use the syringe to remove liquid down to the 10 mL mark on the test tube.

5 Add five drops of a fourth reagent to the yellow solution in the beaker, which turns black.

6-8 Gently swirl the black solution until it is an even color. Add the final reagent a drop at a time until the black solution is colorless. Each drop added is equivalent to 0.5 mg/L of oxygen in the sample of pond water.

readings above 12 mg per L are high. The gas can be seen venting at the surface of affected ponds, the water surface having the appearance of a fizzy drink as the tiny bubbles rise to the surface and burst. If you dip your hand into supersaturated water, it becomes coated in tiny bubbles.

It is important to identify the cause of supersaturation and rectify the problem. The affected water should be splashed and vigorously agitated to vent off the excess air. Oxygen levels can be monitored using simple test kits or electronic meters. Most of the meters available require frequent recalibration to ensure an accurate reading.

The pH value of water

The pH value of water is a measure of its acidity or alkalinity. The pH scale runs from 0 to 14: pH 0-6.99 is acid; pH 7.0 is regarded as neutral, and pH 7.01-14 is alkaline. Acid substances include strong battery acids, with a pH of 0-1; lemon juice, about pH 2; orange juice, pH 4; and milk, pH 6.0. Distilled or deionized water has a pH of 7 and is neutral, with no salts or minerals dissolved in it. Familiar alkaline substances include egg white, pH 8; antacid digestive remedies, pH 10; agricultural lime (calcium oxide), pH 13; and caustic soda (sodium hydroxide), pH 14. The extremes (pH 0-1 and 13-14) are the most corrosive.

Essentially, the pH is a measure of the hydrogen ions in a solution or substance and is based on a logarithmic scale, which means that each change in one pH unit reflects a tenfold increase or decrease. This is one reason why it is important to make any pH adjustments slowly; otherwise they can have quite profound consequences on koi physiology. In the koi pond there is also a close relationship between pH and alkalinity (see page 32). For optimum health, koi have a preferred pH range of 6.5 to 8.5. The pH of the koi pond is not a fixed value, however, and can fluctuate throughout a 24-hour period.

One of the most important reasons for monitoring the pH of the water is that in conjunction with temperature, increasing pH causes ammonia to become increasingly more poisonous to koi.

Broad range pH test

Above: It is vital to test the pH of the water routinely, as this affects the toxicity of ammonia. The ideal pH range for the koi pond is between 6.5 and 8.5, so a broad range test kit is ideal. Here, a small tablet is mixed with 10 mL of pond water and the color compared to a chart.

pH 4 *Too acidic – koi unwell, not feeding. Hard water: increase pH by water changes. Soft water: partial water changes, add marble chippings, oyster shells, or chalk-based minerals/clays.*

pH 5 *pH still too low – koi will be lethargic. Increase pH as described above.*

pH 6.5 *Preferred pH range is 6.5-8.5, but even at this level, it could be increased.*

pH 7 *Pure or distilled water is pH 7, but unlikely to be achieved in the koi pond. Distilled water is devoid of minerals/salts.*

pH 8.5 *Top value recommended for koi. Does not cause them any major problems.*

pH 9 *In planted ponds, or those affected by algae blooms, pH can rise above 9 to about 11 during the day, but causes few welfare or health problems.*

High range pH test

pH7.3
pH7.6
pH7.9
pH8.2
pH8.5
pH8.8

Above: You can use test kits for low range and high range pH values for greater accuracy. Here the result shows a pH of 8.2.

Ammonia, nitrite, and nitrate

Koi produce nitrogenous waste in two forms: ammonia and urea. Ammonia – NH_3 – is the main form of waste and is excreted through the gills. Urea – $CO(NH_2)_2$ – is shed in small quantities in the form of dilute urine and is broken down through microbial activity into ammonia. All the ammonia produced as waste is oxidized by beneficial, oxygen-loving bacteria to nitrite (NO_2) and then to nitrate (NO_3). These conversions are essential steps of the nitrogen cycle.

Ammonia is extremely poisonous to koi, causing changes to the gills and affecting the chemical composition of the blood (see page 82). When dissolved in water, ammonia exists in two forms: free ammonia (NH_3) and ionized ammonia (NH_4^+). Free ammonia is the most poisonous form and its relative concentration (as a proportion of total ammonia) increases in alkaline water and with rising water temperature. In mildly acidic conditions, however, more of the total ammonia will be in the ionized form. The maximum recommended continuous exposure level for free ammonia is 0.02 mg per L of water. The test kits available for monitoring ammonia levels measure the total ammonia concentration, including both free and ionized ammonia.

Free and ionized ammonia

Free ammonia (NH_3) consists of one atom of nitrogen and three of hydrogen.

The nitrogen atom of ammonia attracts a hydrogen atom from water (H_2O).

The hydrogen atom attaches to the nitrogen atom, conferring a positive charge on the newly created ammonium ion (NH_4^+).

Without one hydrogen atom, the water molecule becomes a negatively charged hydroxyl ion (OH^-).

How the nitrogen cycle works

Water returning to the pond from the last stage of the filtration system may still contain some nitrate. Nitrate is one of the nutrients responsible for promoting the growth of blanketweed.

Water changes are an important aspect of pond management, especially if ammonia or nitrite is polluting the pond. Regular water changes can also help to reduce nitrate concentration in the water.

By adding an oxygen atom into each molecule, aerobic bacteria (Nitrobacter spp.) convert nitrite into nitrate (NO₃). Nitrate is the final breakdown product of ammonia in the nitrogen cycle and far less toxic than ammonia or nitrite.

Protein supplied in food is used by koi for tissue repair and maintenance, growth, and reproduction. Any excess protein cannot be stored and is excreted as ammonia. The protein in any uneaten food also ends up as ammonia.

By removing the hydrogen and adding oxygen into each molecule, aerobic bacteria (Nitrosomonas spp.) convert ammonia into nitrite (NO₂). Although not as harmful as ammonia, it is still poisonous to koi.

Ammonia (NH₃) is released into the water by the gills. The small amount of urea voided in dilute urine breaks down to form ammonia. Ammonia is very poisonous to koi.

Activated charcoal and ion-exchange resins such as zeolite can be used to reduce the concentration of ammonia in the water. The ion-exchange resins work rather like a chemical trap, locking onto the ammonia and removing it from solution. However, it is important to realize that substances such as common salt (sodium chloride) added to the pond are more attractive to these resins, which will in turn release the ammonia back into the environment. Even where ion-exchange resins are used, it is very common to find ammonia still polluting the pond water, so they are not an effective substitute for partial water changes.

The secondary breakdown product of ammonia is nitrite, which is also poisonous to koi. The maximum recommended continuous exposure level for nitrite is 0.1 mg per L for soft water regions and 0.2 mg per L for hard water. Nitrite can build up in a koi pond, either because bacteria are converting ammonia at a faster rate than it can be broken down into nitrate (which is very common in new koi ponds), or because a different group of bacteria convert nitrate back into nitrite and nitrogen gas. This latter process tends to occur when there is a problem with the filtration system that prevents adequate supplies of oxygen from reaching the bacterial populations.

It is important to monitor the water routinely for the presence of both ammonia and nitrite. Where either pollutant is present at detectable levels, undertake regular partial water changes to eliminate ammonia and nitrite from the pond. In some instances where the concentrations of ammonia and nitrite are excessively high, the toxicity can be reduced by increasing the salinity of the water through the addition of common salt, sodium chloride.

Nitrate is the final breakdown product of ammonia and the least harmful; the recommended maximum

Ammonia test

4 mg/L A serious problem; koi will die within days. Make water changes, up to three times daily.

2.0 mg/L Koi feeling very unwell, often swimming through water inlet. Respiration rate increases through damage to gills and changes to body chemistry.

1.2 mg/L Ammonia accumulating in blood and tissues. Koi probably stop feeding. Improve conditions quickly through partial water changes.

0.8 mg/L Gill tissue swells and cells proliferate, leading to clubbed gills. Continue testing levels daily and make partial water changes.

0.4 mg/L Koi produce more mucus in response to ammonia. Monitor water and make partial water changes. Check that filtration system is working well and not congested. Feed less.

0.1 mg/L Not harmful for a few days. Long-term and especially at high temperatures and in alkaline water, this concentration exceeds recommended maximum continuous exposure levels.

Nitrite test

Below: *Ammonia and nitrite are very poisonous to koi. Polluted water can be crystal clear but deadly. Routine testing is the only way to be sure water is free of both.*

Less than 0.3 mg/L Fairly low and not a threat to koi. If nitrite values rise, monitor frequently. In the summer, a sudden increase in nitrite could indicate oxygen levels are too low.

0.3 mg/L In soft water, nitrite is more poisonous and this level can affect koi health; make partial water changes. In hard water, this nitrite level should be frequently monitored.

0.8 mg/L At this level, nitrite is harmful to koi in both soft and hard water; make regular partial water changes. Koi will show signs of irritation, rubbing and flicking on surfaces.

1.6 mg/L Nitrite combines with red blood pigment, affecting ability of koi to use oxygen. Koi become lethargic and produce more mucus. Make daily water changes to reduce nitrite level.

Over 3.0 mg/L Nitrite pollution is now a serious problem and can kill koi. Blood vessels become relaxed and pinprick hemorrhaging occurs in gill tissue. Water changes essential.

Below: Where the water is soft and the alkalinity low, buffering capacity can be improved by adding oyster shells to the filter system, as shown here in a Japanese koi farm. The acidic water will erode the shells, releasing calcium carbonate into the pond.

continuous exposure level is 50 mg per L above that found in the main water supply for the area. Although nitrate is harmless to koi, it is a plant nutrient and will promote the growth of algae such as blanketweed. Nitrate rarely occurs at detectable levels in natural lakes and ponds, so it is best to control the concentration in the koi pond through partial water changes.

Water hardness

Water hardness is basically a measure of the calcium and magnesium salts present in the water, although other trace metals can contribute. Like alkalinity, the hardness of the water plays a role in acting as a buffer and often the measured values are very similar. Generally, hard water is alkaline and soft water is acidic. Soft waters are usually associated with low calcium content and other minerals necessary for koi health. Pollutants, toxic substances, including some treatments, and metals tend to be more poisonous in such water. You will therefore need to incorporate trace minerals and salts into the diet of koi living in softer water areas. The waters in Japan are naturally soft and are buffered by the koi breeders using oyster shells and coral. The minerals and salts dissolved in hard water reduce the osmotic pressure on koi (see page 79) and tend to bind to, or chelate, toxic metals and pollutants, pulling them out of the solution and thereby making them less harmful.

Alkalinity

As the name would suggest, the alkalinity of water is a measure of alkaline substances dissolved in it. The alkalinity of the water is due largely to naturally occurring hydrogen carbonates (bicarbonates, HCO_3^-), carbonates (CO_3^{--}), plus mineral hydroxides (OH^-) in the water. In areas where the water is soft, it is acidic and therefore devoid of any alkalinity. The alkalinity of the water is very important because it acts as a natural buffer, preventing wide fluctuations in pH, which can occur naturally as a consequence of respiration from the koi and microbes in the filtration system. Excessive plant or algal growth, such as blanketweed, can also affect the pH of the water, which is buffered by the alkalinity. Through its buffering action, the alkalinity of the water is used up, and in the absence of water changes in hard water areas, the pond water can become increasingly acidic and subject to wide variation in pH. Where the water is soft and acidic, the pH and alkalinity can be increased by adding marble chippings, oyster shells, or the ceramic rock used as a filter medium (rich in calcium

Carbonate hardness (KH) test

1 Add the KH reagent a drop at a time to a 5 mL sample of pond water and gently swirl the tube to mix. Count each drop of reagent.
2 Initially, the sample turns blue.
3 As more reagent is added, the water sample turns yellow. Continue counting the drops added until the yellow color is stable. Each drop added from the beginning of the test represents 1°dH, which is equivalent to 17.5 mg per L of carbonate.

Phosphate test

1 Add 5 drops of the phosphate reagent to a 5 mL sample of pond water and shake gently to mix.

2 Allow the sample to stand until the yellow color has fully developed and then compare it with the chart. Place the tube on the printed chart and look down the length of the tube to compare the color of the solution.

0 mg/L No phosphate, ideal. However, this reading is still possible if a prolific growth of algae is consuming the nutrient.

0.25 mg/L Even such low levels boost algae growth.

0.5 mg/L Low but enough to encourage blanketweed. Make partial water changes and test incoming tap water.

1.0 mg/L This level and above cause algae blooms such as green water and blanketweed.

2.0 mg/L At this level, blanketweed will thrive.

4.0 mg/L Very high level of phosphate. Control it with partial water changes and/or by installing a vegetable filter.

8.0 mg/L At this level, there will be an algae bloom in the pond to consume the nutrient. Take action as described above.

carbonate). The mildly acidic water dissolves these alkaline minerals, releasing carbonate and hydrogen carbonate into the water, which improves the alkalinity. Sodium hydrogen carbonate (sodium bicarbonate) has been used in extreme instances to improve the alkalinity, but treat it with caution as it has anesthetic properties when used with carp and therefore koi. Ideally, the alkalinity should be between 100 and 150 mg per L for adequate buffering of the pond.

Phosphate

Phosphate is released by koi into the pond water as a waste product. It is the limiting factor for growth of plants and in most situations is in rather limited supply. However, if there are many koi in the pond they will release considerable quantities of phosphate and this provides the essential nutrient for nuisance algae such as blanketweed to thrive. Using a vegetable filter (such as a bed of watercress through which water from the filter trickles before it returns to the pond) helps to remove

the available phosphate and reduce the growth of blanketweed. You can establish phosphate levels using a simple test kit as shown on this page.

Blanketweed

One of the biggest headaches for many koi keepers is the proliferation of blanketweed, which thrives in warm water with plentiful nutrients and can choke bottom drains, pumps, filters, and pipework. Like many other algae species, blanketweed periodically undergoes a form of sexual reproduction that results in the release of spores, which are the likely source of initial contamination in the koi pond. While ultraviolet filtration systems can control single-celled algae (green water), they have no effect on the growth of blanketweed. Various chemical treatments are available in the form of liquids, granules, or crystals, but they are all only temporary solutions, as the blanketweed inevitably flourishes again once the chemical becomes diluted beyond a specific concentration.

Above: Oxygen bubbles clearly visible among strands of blanketweed. The gas – a daytime by-product of photosynthesis – gets trapped, causing the tangled mass to rise to the surface.

Right: Blanketweed can develop rapidly in the warm summer months. It can block bottom drains, choke pumps, and shut down filters, causing low oxygen and high ammonia levels.

Blanketweed remedies

Pads placed in one of the filter chambers provide a slow release of a chemical to control algal growth.

Natural control methods include barley straw, here in netting packs, dropped into the pond. The dose rate of barley straw is 50 gm per 1,000 L of water (2 oz per 220 gal).

Barley straw has become a very popular natural method of controlling blanketweed. It decomposes in the water through the activity of microscopic bacteria and fungi that produce hydrogen peroxide as a by-product and it is this that inhibits the growth of both blanketweed and green water. Since the bacteria and fungi are oxygen-loving species, barley straw will be effective only in very well-aerated water. It takes several weeks for the bacteria to become established on the barley straw, so this is not a short-term remedy for blanketweed. As the release of hydrogen peroxide is based on a decomposition process, be sure to monitor the water routinely for the presence of pollutants, notably ammonia and nitrite. Some barley straw is treated with fungicides, which are unsuitable for the koi pond; use straw of a quality suitable for horses. Blanketweed begins to grow early in the year, as day length increases through late winter and early spring. Ideally, start any treatment at about this time of the year, when it will effectively control the growth of this nuisance algae.

In recent years, magnetic and electronic devices have been marketed for the control of blanketweed. The success of these devices would seem to be variable; in some cases, they certainly do control the growth of this nuisance algae but in others the blanketweed continues to grow. It is quite possible that the success rate of such devices is improved when they are installed on a new pond and before the blanketweed has become established. If you use an electronic device that emits magnetic pulses, be sure to turn off the unit in the winter months; otherwise the weed may mutate and build up an immunity to the specific levels of waves, rendering it ineffective. Some electronic blanketweed controllers produce randomly changing magnetic pulses that prevent the blanketweed from adapting to their effect.

Phosphate in the water is utilized by the algae and as the algae die back in the late summer and fall, the phosphate can become locked into sediment, typically

An electronic blanketweed controller

Electronic circuitry in this sealed weatherproof unit generates random electrical pulses.

Power lead

Aerial lead wrapped around pipe transmits pulses into the water flow.

Pond water after having passed through the main filter system.

the type of material with which many filters become congested. In the spring, bacterial activity in these sediments releases the phosphate into solution, making an available source of nutrient for the blanketweed, a process that proceeds rapidly under low-oxygen conditions. Well-oxygenated water helps to keep the phosphate locked into the detritus, but regularly cleaning and maintaining the filtration system is equally beneficial.

Blanketweed does not thrive so well in brackish water, so in extreme cases where the weed is out of control, you can introduce salt or aquarium salt at the rate of 1.6 gm per L (0.25 oz per gal).

Particulate organic substances

All the microscopic organisms in the pond system, plus koi debris, such as discarded skin cells, mucus, and feces, and decaying plant material such as leaves or treated algae, are described as particulate organic substances. These often form a matrix that causes the filtration system to block and allow the water to track through the system. They also provide a food reservoir for the fish parasite *Trichodina* (see page 86), which feed on organic material trapped in the mucus layer of the fish. The *Trichodina* irritate the koi, which respond by producing more mucus, which in turn traps more organic material, and so begins the route to a clinical infection of this parasite. The presence of *Trichodina* in samples of koi mucus indicates the presence of organic material in the pond, filtration, and associated pipework. Clearing the filters and removing the organic material is therefore important in controlling outbreaks of *Trichodina* parasites.

In the laboratory, particulate organic substances are usually measured as "particulate organic carbon," or POC. A sample of pond water is filtered, the material dried and then burned using special equipment to convert all the carbon within the material to carbon dioxide gas, which is then measured.

Dissolved organic substances

As organic material from the koi, microbes, and plant cells decays, it gives rise to an assortment of organic chemicals. Many of these substances are not especially soluble in water but can be removed using a technique known as foam fractionation, or protein skimming, which results in a stiff foam that can be collected and removed (see page 48). Air blowers and airstones, or even venturis, can mimic the action of a foam fractionator, causing a persistent foam on the water surface.

Filtration

Koi will eat almost anything and quickly process their food into waste in the form of feces and urine. These waste products, together with those excreted by the gills, create toxic substances that become totally dissolved in pond water and cannot be removed by mechanical filtration. These toxins consist of ammonia and nitrite, harmful chemicals that stress the fish, allowing bacteria to invade the soft tissues, such as fins. The toxins also disrupt the fishes' osmoregulation processes (see page 79), causing damage to the delicate gill structure. Without some form of filtration, the fish are literally swimming in their own excrement and eventually die.

In the natural environment, water is filtered as it passes over the gravel and stones of the substrate, and the toxins that are present are broken down by bacteria that flourish on the substrate surface. To keep fish in an enclosed system, we need to emulate their natural habitat as closely as possible, which means passing water through a suitable filter medium in order to cultivate colonies of the same oxygen-loving bacteria that will remove the harmful toxins. In this section, we look at how filter systems work and consider the practical options available for koi keepers to maintain the water quality in their ponds.

External filter – aboveground or inground?

Water pumped to filter system

Filtered water returns under gravity

Above: An aboveground filter system. Water pumped from the pond passes through the biofilter under gravity and returns via a waterfall.

Right: A gravity-fed inground filter linked to the pond by a bottom drain and pipework. Water is returned by a pump in the last filter chamber.

External filters

When early experiments with undergravel filtration proved unsatisfactory in the long term, it became clear that the filter system of a koi pond had to be sited externally for ease of maintenance, if nothing else. This meant devising a receptacle that could contain filter media with a large surface area to support beneficial bacteria and through which water could flow freely.

External filters can be either pump fed or gravity fed from the pond. They are available in various shapes and sizes, and the number of compartments required is relative to the size of the pond and the intended stocking levels. Of all the filtration methods available, the external filter is by far the best, as the chambers are easy to maintain for cleaning purposes, but they must be fitted

Above: The pond and filter are like an ecosystem, where the bacteria in the filter are totally reliant on the koi in the pond for their source of food, and the fish are dependent on the bacteria to break down their waste products. If the koi were taken out of the pond the bacteria would die, and vice versa.

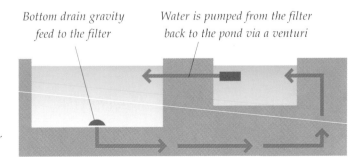

Bottom drain gravity feed to the filter

Water is pumped from the filter back to the pond via a venturi

with a drainage facility to remove waste products that settle beneath the media. Should the need arise, the system can be completely isolated from the pond simply by switching off the pump, if it is pump fed, or closing a slide valve if it is gravity fed.

If a system like this is installed belowground, it can be covered by decorative wooden decking strong enough to walk over. Alternatively, you could place a bench on top to act as an additional viewing area. Filters installed aboveground can be difficult to disguise, but remember that they do not have to be situated close to the pond. Providing the outlet is higher than the water level in the pond, water will run back to the pond under gravity even if it is 15 m (50 ft) away. Another important consideration is that the chambers should have a void beneath the media that is dished toward the base with an independent outlet (at least 4 cm/1.5 in in size) at the bottom, so that all the debris can be completely removed without having to disturb the media.

Choosing the right filter

You can choose from a number of filtration systems in a wide range of shapes and sizes, each with its own individual features. Choosing the correct system can be a difficult decision, especially if you are on a limited budget. Remember that this will be the single most important purchase that you are likely to make when constructing your dream pond and any mistake could be extremely costly in the long run. As with the design of your pond, research this aspect thoroughly before you decide which system is best for you. Make sure you understand the principles of biological filtration and that your chosen filter is sufficient in size to cope with the intended stocking rate and volume of water to be treated.

Hobbyists on a limited budget may be tempted to construct their own filter from concrete or use a converted cold-water storage tank. However, experience has shown that neither of these methods is particularly successful, as both materials have their limitations. Cold-water tanks have a tendency to distort and bulge over a period of time and, by their nature, have a flat base, making it impossible to remove the detritus that forms beneath the filter media. Without prior building experience, concrete filters can be extremely difficult to build and render completely watertight, especially around the areas where pipes enter and exit the chamber. Furthermore, it is almost impossible to mimic

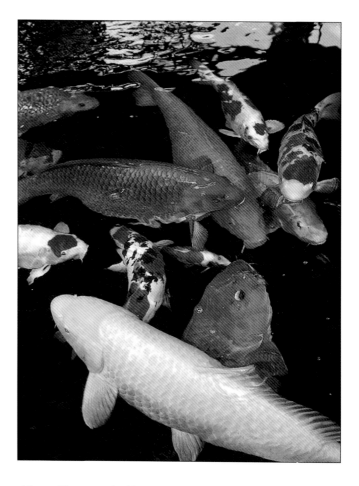

Above: If you get the filtration system and water quality right, the fish will look after themselves. Remember to test the water on a regular basis to avoid any problems. Keep a record for reference.

the cylindrical vortex or octagonal filter shapes that are the most effective in producing the maximum flow rates possible without dead spots occurring in the media.

A vortex filter

A vortex is a cylindrical, mechanical prefilter fitted before the main biological stage. It is connected to the 10 cm (4 in) pipework from the bottom drain in the pond. Water enters the center of the vessel at a tangent, causing it to spin gently within the chamber. Solids are taken to the base by centrifugal force and clean water exits at the top to the next stage.

As the water moves relatively slowly from the drain to the vortex, solids can build up in the pipework over a short space of time. These can become a breeding ground for harmful bacteria, so flush out the pipework on a regular basis, subject to stocking levels, feeding, etc. It is therefore very important to fit a 10 cm (4 in) slide valve before the inlet so that the supply to the vortex can be isolated and the chamber completely emptied when the slide valve or standpipe to the bottom drain is opened. Once the vortex is emptied, open the 10 cm (4 in) slide valve on the inlet and there will be a rush of water from the pond as it fills and equalizes the level in the vortex, bringing with it all the detritus that has accumulated within the pipework and around the bends. When this has settled at the base of the vortex, open the drain once again to ensure that all the waste matter is cleared. Alternatively, you can fit a T-piece and two slide valves, with one leading to the vortex and the other directly to waste. To flush the pipework, close the valve into the vortex and open the one to waste.

Multichamber filters

The bays, or chambers, in a multichamber filter are used for a number of reasons, but mainly as a means of separating different filtration media. The first chamber will take the brunt of the debris from the pond, so use a mechanical medium to trap this. At the same time, you must make sure that it will not clog quickly; otherwise

Filter system do's and don'ts

DO

Buy a filter large enough to cope with the volume of water and stocking rate.

Choose a very strong model, preferably made from fiberglass.

Ensure that the method of transferring water between chambers can cope with the flow rate for the pump.

Ensure that all waste products can be completely discharged individually from the base of each filter chamber.

Make sure that aeration can be introduced without disturbing the media.

DON'T

Skimp on size or price, as filtration is the most important consideration when setting up a pond.

Use cold-water storage tanks or attempt to build a filter from concrete.

Attempt to "do it yourself" until you have sought advice and professional help.

Use inferior filter products not designed for filter media, such as hair rollers.

Put too much filter media in each chamber; a depth of 23 cm (9 in) is sufficient.

How a vortex chamber works

This plan and side view show how a vortex chamber diverts some heavy particles to waste, preventing them from clogging the later stages of the filter system.

10 cm (4 in) exit pipe to brush chamber.

Waste from base of vortex to discharge box.

Water entering via the bottom drain in the pond.

Heavy solids fall out of suspension in the "still" center of the circulating water.

To waste

Some small particles will pass through to the next filtration chamber, where they are strained out by the brushes.

As the water "drags" against the edge, friction slows the flow and heavy particles drift down to the base.

Water enters the vortex at a tangent, causing it to swirl slowly within the vessel.

Gravity-fed multichamber filter

Vortex chamber, in which heavy solids such as fish waste, leaves, blanketweed, and general detritus settle out.

First biological/mechanical stage with brushes to remove particles that have passed through the vortex.

Preformed plastic honeycomb filter medium that provides a large surface area for bacterial growth.

Porous ceramic filter medium that acts as a biological filter and also strains out small particles.

Drain pipe leading to discharge chamber.

Airstones in each transfer port oxygenate water as it passes through without disturbing the bacteria. The airstones are not located so deep that bubbles pass through to the next bay and cause tracking.

This submersible pump returns water to the pond and sets up the flow of water through the filter.

Discharged water runs to waste under gravity through a 10 cm (4 in) pipe and "P" trap.

A 10 cm (4 in) slide valve is fitted to both the inlet and outlet of the vortex. When the standpipe is pulled and the water and debris are flushed to waste, these valves are closed to prevent water from tracking back through the connecting pipework.

Discharge chamber with four standpipes to flush the waste from the bottom of each chamber.

water will not be able to pass through to the next stage. The bays that follow will contain the main biological media, such as Japanese matting, plastic honeycomb material, semi-rigid graded plastic matting, etc. Use a dense material in the final stage to remove any fine particles before the water is returned to the pond.

Watch as water goes from one chamber to the next and ask yourself if it is capable of passing the total volume of the pond through the filter every two hours. If the size of the connecting pipe or ports between chambers is too small, the water will not pass through quickly enough to supply the pump in the final chamber, which could cause it to burn out. The transfer ports are also an ideal location to house airstones to reoxygenate the water as it travels between the bays without disturbing the beneficial bacteria contained within the media.

Pumps for koi filters and ponds

A good-quality, reliable pump is an essential and integral part of a pond and filter system, and must be capable of running continuously, 24 hours a day 365 days a year. All pumps are driven by an electric motor that rotates an impeller inside a casing. As it turns, the impeller draws water into the casing and expels it through the outlet. Generally speaking, the speed or flow generated by the pump depends on the size of the impeller and the amount of electricity the motor consumes, although in recent years, manufacturers have successfully produced high-output pumps that use a lot less power. Selecting the right pump for your system can be difficult, as there are several to choose from.

There are two basic types of pump: external and submersible. External pumps are used to draw water

A survey of filter media

Porous ceramic material

Manufactured by sintering selected fire clays at very high temperatures, resulting in a porous, foamed ceramic material. The rough surface with many open pores has a high surface area, making it ideal as a filter medium for aerobic bacteria. Its ceramic bonding provides strength and integrity when the water flow is reversed when flushing the bottom drains. Maximum depth of media 30 cm (12 in).

Advantages
Lightweight material.
Good mechanical filtration.
Easy to clean.
Does not deteriorate.

Disadvantages
Needs to be suspended in the filter.
Clogs over a period of time.

Plastic honeyoomb material

Relatively new to koi keepers, although widely used in the water treatment industry. It is made of lightweight polypropylene held in a three-dimensional matrix and installed in the filter chamber much like Japanese matting. This has a very large surface area for bacterial growth, together with an extremely efficient water distribution. As water enters the bottom of the media, it is channelled through the maze at a 15° angle to the center then back 15° in the opposite direction before exiting at the top. Water is thus kept in contact with the surface and the bacteria are able to break down toxins more efficiently. It is likely to become an increasingly popular filter medium.

Advantages
Inexpensive.
Lightweight.
No support tray required.
Easy to clean.
Does not deteriorate.
Large biological surface area.

Disadvantages
Can be used only in multichamber systems.

Sintered flint gravel

This medium has a good, irregular surface area on which bacteria can grow, plus an excellent mechanical "polishing" effect to help keep water clear. Do not completely fill the chamber with gravel, as this causes clogging. If this happens, water cannot find its way through the gravel and tracks up the sides of the chamber, bypassing the media entirely. Gravel should be 15-20 cm (6-8 in) deep and supported from the base on a uPVC perforated plate with a void underneath to encourage the heavy solids to settle on the base, where they can be discharged to waste.

Advantages
Inexpensive.
Does not deteriorate.

Disadvantages
Difficult to clean.
Water can bypass media over time.
Dense material that clogs quickly.

Filter brushes

Made from nontoxic polypropylene, with a stainless steel wire core. Normally used as a mechanical prefilter to the main biological stage to stop heavier solids, such as leaves, blanketweed, fish waste, etc., from entering the main filtration system. When brushes are left uncleaned they become biological. Rinse in pond water periodically (to retain bacteria) to remove solids; otherwise they become completely blocked. Arrange brushes so they just overlap in rows suspended from the top of the chamber. Leave a void under the brushes to aid further settling of heavier solids.

Advantages
Lightweight material.
Good mechanical filtration.
Very little maintenance required.
Easy to clean.
Available in a wide range of sizes to suit your filter chamber.

Disadvantages
Need to be suspended in filter.
Can be used only in multichamber filters.
Relatively expensive.
The chamber needs to be mass-filled.

These brushes are 40 cm (16 in) long and 15 cm (6 in) across.

Plastic pipe pieces

A non-clogging medium of cylindrical plastic pieces, ribbed on the outside with a smooth or spoked interior. Aerobic bacteria grow on the ribbed exterior and deal with ammonia and nitrite. Anaerobic bacteria on the inside help to break down nitrate.

Advantages
Lightweight material.
Does not deteriorate.

Disadvantages
Suitable only for multichamber filters.
Difficult to clean.
Tendency to float.
Water can bypass the media over time.

Perlag or Hortag

Baked clay spherical granules used in the final stage of filtration. This medium was widely used in the past, but has largely been replaced by porous ceramic rock.

Disadvantages
Clogs very quickly.

Foam

Open-cell foam, usually placed in three layers on top of ceramic rock in the filter. A dense material that tends to clog quickly and needs regular washing. Unfortunately, when the sponge is cleaned, any bacteria present will be lost, so its use is purely mechanical.

Advantages
Lightweight material.

Disadvantages
Little biological benefit.
Regular maintenance required.

Coarse, medium, and fine grades of foam used in filter systems.

Japanese filter matting

A polyester-based material supplied in 2 x 1 m (78 x 39 in) sheets. Cut into 23 cm (9 in) wide strips, with 5 cm (2 in) spacers in between to fit the filter chamber exactly; otherwise it will not function correctly. Install on a support tray so that water passes evenly through the holes. Bacteria will then develop on all the internal surfaces and will increase the surface area threefold. Because of the vast surfaces, the matting takes longer to establish the necessary nitrifying bacteria and other microorganisms that will remove the fish wastes. To speed up this process, introduce a live bacterial additive, which has the required bacteria held in liquid suspension. Introduce this to the filter system on a regular basis until the water is mature.

Advantages
Lightweight material.
Large surface area for bacterial growth.
Very little maintenance required.

Disadvantages
Solids pass through unrestricted.
Can be used only in multichamber filters.
Relatively expensive.

Semi-rigid graded plastic matting

Similar to Japanese matting, but supplied in 1.2 x 1 m (48 x 39 in) rigid sheets that can be installed vertically or horizontally. Water flows freely through its matrix of stiff fibers. The material is self-supporting in the chamber and there is no need to use a perforated plate. It is available in four densities: low (0.18 mm), medium (0.09 mm), high (0.06 mm), and super-high fiber diameter (0.045 mm), fitted in the first to last chambers respectively.

Three grades of graded plastic matting, the finest on top.

Advantages
Even adhesion of nitrifying bacteria to the filter mat fibers.
Lightweight.
Easy to clean.
Nontoxic.
Self-supporting.

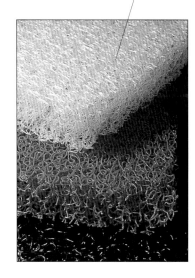

Disadvantages
Takes a long time to mature biologically.

Calculating the size of your filter

Step 1

In a pond of 16,000 L capacity a typical fish population might be as follows. (Use the graph on page 106 to estimate the weight of each fish based on its length.)

Six 50 cm koi at 2.4 kg each (21 in/5.5 lb).

Six 40 cm koi at 1.8 kg each (15 in/4 lb).

Six 30 cm koi at 0.5 kg each (12 in/1 lb).

Six 20 cm koi at 0.1 kg each (8 in/1/4 lb).

Total weight of fish in the pond is 28.8 kg (63 lb)

Double this figure to allow for growth and increased stocking rate and the total fish weight is 57.6 kg (127 lb).

Step 2

Use this graph to find the bacterial surface area required in the filter system to support the total weight of fish in the pond. In this example, the total fish weight of 57.6 kg (127 lb) needs approximately 177 m² of bacterial filter surface area.

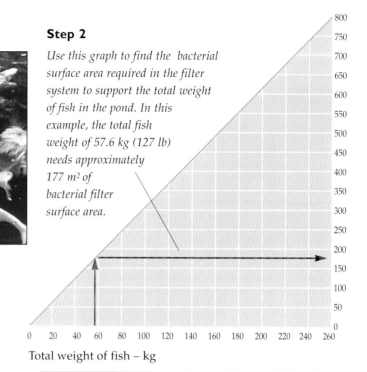

Bacterial surface area in square meters

Total weight of fish – kg

Conversion factors

Liters to English gallons, multiply by 0.22 | *Kg to lbs, multiply by 2.205*
Liters to U.S. gallons, multiply by 0.26 | *m² to ft², multiply by 10.76*
(Liters/English gallons are used in the text.) | *m³ to ft³, multiply by 35.3*

Step 3

In a four-chamber filter in which each chamber measures 60 x 60 x 30 cm (24 x 24 x 12 in), the volume of filter media in each chamber is 0.113 m³. The table below shows the surface area provided by different media and how the target of 177 m² is reached.

Ceramic rock
180 m² per m³
0.113 x 180 = 20.34 m²

Plastic honeycomb
709 m² per m³
0.113 x 709 = 80.12 m²

Japanese matting
531 m² per m³
0.113 x 531 = 60 m²

Brushes
160 m² per m³
0.113 x 160 = 18.08 m²

Total bacterial surface area: 178.54 m²

Above: This filter setup would be ideal for the proposed stocking rate. Add a fluidized bed for extra biological filtration.

through a surface skimmer (see page 72). Because skimmers are located remotely with an external fitting—they are not submerged in the pond but sit outside—it is necessary to connect solid pipework to an external pump with a suitable threaded inlet, so it pulls in water directly from the source. If the external pump is located below the water level, the pipework will be naturally "charged" with water by gravity and the pump will begin to operate immediately. However, if the pump is located above water level, it will be necessary to fit a non-return valve to stop water from tracking back to the pond when the pump is switched off and having to prime the pump again. Although most external pumps are self-priming, they cannot pull out the air in the pipework from the pond and will run dry unless the pipework has been filled manually through an access port or something similar.

Submersible pumps are designed to operate underwater either in the pond or in the filter system. If a submersible pump is located in the last chamber of a multichamber filter, all the dirt, algae, and general detritus

Top ten tips for a healthy pump

1 Fit the pump at the final stage of filtration so that all the detritus in the pond is filtered before it reaches the pump.

2 Clean the strainer housing and foam inserts on a regular basis and more often in the summer.

3 If the pump is placed in the pond you can prolong the intervals between regular maintenance by replacing the standard strainer housing with a larger prefilter.

4 Never pull the pump from the pond using its electricity supply cable. Instead, tie a string around the handle on the pump.

5 Place the pump at least 15 cm (6 in) from the base of the pond, as this will prevent it from becoming clogged by large objects.

6 If there are no bottom drains in the pond, vacuum it on a regular basis to

prevent the buildup of general debris that may impair the pump's performance.

7 From time to time, it may be necessary to descale the impeller/rotor assembly and soak it overnight in a domestic kitchen descaler.

8 Always fit a Residual Current Device (RCD) for added protection against possible electrical accidents.

9 Buy a cheap spare pump in case of emergencies. It makes sense to have one rather than risk losing all your fish.

10 Do not restrict the flow of water through the pump, as this will cause the motor to burn out and may invalidate the warranty. If you need to regulate the flow to a filter, fit a "T" piece before the valve and divert the balance of the water to a further venturi or waterfall.

Below: A typical submersible pump with a strainer housing to stop solids from clogging the impeller. Clean the sponge inside the housing regularly with pond water.

Typical external pump

This strainer basket prevents leaves and debris from entering the pump impeller housing.

Water outlet to UV sterilizer, fluidized bed filter, etc.

Water in from surface skimmer in the pond.

Mount this heavy pump securely in a dry, sheltered place.

will have been filtered out (or at least substantially reduced) before reaching the pump, which will make it perform more efficiently and extend its life expectancy and will involve less maintenance in terms of cleaning the strainer and impeller.

The widely used sump, or cellar, pumps are so called because they are designed to pump out flooded cellars, basements, and pits quickly in emergencies. They have been adopted by fishkeepers because they are cheap to buy and have a very fast turnover rate. However, by their very nature, they have a limited life expectancy as they are not intended for continuous use, especially if they are used in the "front line" in the pond, dealing with blanketweed, fish waste, leaves, etc.

Pump flow rate

It is important to understand that a pump should be capable of turning over the total capacity of the pond through the filtration system every two hours to ensure good retention time within the chambers and a healthy biomass. If the flow rate is reduced due to a blockage in the pump, the ammonia and nitrite levels in the water will rise and the oxygen level could fall below the minimum requirements of 6 mg per L, causing stress in the fish and potential losses. The ultraviolet sterilizer discussed later also needs to have a constant minimum flow rate and if this falls below the recommended level, the water may turn green due to an algae bloom.

All manufacturers state the maximum flow rate the pump is capable of producing at zero head (meaning at the surface of the pond without any pipework or fittings attached). However, it is important to take into account that flow rates can be significantly reduced by the height of the pipework above water level, otherwise known as "head." The head of pipework is calculated from the point where the pipework breaks the surface and NOT the depth of the pump. The flow rate would be the same at the surface whether the pump was 6 m (20 ft) or 1.5 m (5 ft) deep, because the pressure of water in the pipe is equal to the outside volume. In addition to the flow restrictions caused by the pumping head, the length of run from the pump to the filter or the return to the pond, the number of inline elbows, the bore of the pipe used, UV sterilizers, heaters, venturis, and other equipment can all adversely affect the flow rate. It is no good buying a pump for a 22,700 L (5,000 gal) pond that produces a maximum flow of 11,350 L per hour (2,500 gph) if there is, say, a 2 m (78 in) head, several elbows, and a long pipe run, plus several items of equipment, as the flow will fall below the minimum requirement.

Above: Submersible pump with a large strainer assembly that allows solids up to 8 mm (0.3 in) to pass through without clogging the impeller. The universal hosetail is attached to a swivel ball joint.

Coping with clogged pumps

The most common reason why pumps become clogged is the scourge of every koi keeper—blanketweed. The long strands of algae pass through the pump's strainer housing and entangle themselves around the impeller, causing it to slow down or come to a complete standstill. During the height of the season, when the weed problem is at its greatest, you may have to clear the pump twice a day to maintain the full flow rate. In the fall, leaves that are not removed from the surface will fall to the bottom of the pond, be drawn toward the pump, and sucked against the strainer. Fish feces, mud, newts, and frogs can all cause problems, especially if the pump is located in the pond. The best solution is to have a gravity-fed filter system and install the pump in the final stage. This way, all foreign objects will be removed before they can affect the pump.

The pumps that suffer most from clogging are the ones with relatively small strainer housings and foam inside. Because of the dense nature of the foam, it is not long before it becomes obstructed. Although sump, or cellar, pumps do not generally have foam inserts, they can suffer from the same problems because the strainer is still too small.

Choose a pump with an impeller that will allow solids up to 8 mm (0.3 in) to pass through, which can then be dealt with by the filter system.

There is a misconception that external pumps do not become clogged as quickly as their submersible counterparts. However, this is not true, as both take their

Left: A sump, or cellar, pump with an automatic float switch that turns the pump on and off depending on water level.

Universal hosetail for connecting pipe to return water to the pond.

Strainer to stop solids from blocking the impeller.

How a fluidized bed filter works

Water enters the base through a brass gate valve and a non-return valve at a high flow rate that causes the coral sand to "fluidize" within the chamber. The swirling grains provide an excellent medium for aerobic bacteria and also break down the toxins mechanically.

Water leaves the filter here and returns by gravity to the pond via a waterfall or other feature.

Sight glass

One-way flap valve prevents sand from draining back into the pond if the unit fails or is switched off.

Coral sand held in suspension ("fluidized") by the strong water currents within the chamber.

Water pumped in

Brass gate valve provides fine control of water flow.

feed directly from the pond and suffer the same consequences. External pumps are more difficult to install as they generally need to be placed in a dry chamber away from the elements and must be fitted with a non-return valve to prevent them from running dry, especially if they are above water level.

It is good practice to clean the pump regularly to ensure that the impeller within the motor does not become clogged, thus causing the flow rate to slow down or stop completely. This will help to maintain its full life expectancy and avoids the unnecessary expense of having to replace it.

If, after you have cleaned the strainer and impeller, a pump fails to operate, return it to your dealer for a replacement if it is still under warranty. If it is outside the warranty period, it may be possible to service the better-quality pumps.

If the pump should fail when the water temperature is above 10°C (50°F), you must replace it immediately. With the pump out of commission, the aerobic bacteria in the filter will begin to die and the oxygen content will fall to critical levels. If you cannot replace the pump right away, do not feed your fish until you have installed a new one and flushed the stagnant water out of the filter.

A fluidized bed filter

The concept of a fluidized bed filter is relatively new to koi keepers. While all biological filters rely on the same bacteria for ammonia and nitrite removal, it is how the filter operates that determines its efficiency. Remember

that with biological filtration it is the bacteria that do the work; the filter is simply a receptacle that provides a home for the bacteria to colonize. It is basically an open container filled with various forms of solid, stationary media and relies on water passing through it to keep the bacterial surface moist. Fluidized beds, on the other hand, are flooded cylinders partially filled with special granular media. The water flows upward through the media, causing it to expand and fluidize. The water that reaches the cylinder is oxygen-rich, which feeds the large numbers of bacteria that colonize the media and remove the nutrients present in the flowing water.

The result is a highly efficient filter bed that is no longer solidly packed, but in dynamic motion—the key to the fluidized bed filter's success. Water is evenly distributed as it flows through the cylinder and there are no anaerobic pockets in which harmful bacteria can develop. Because the filter medium is in constant motion, it cannot become clogged.

The filter bed is a mildly abrasive environment that is constantly cleaning and renewing itself as it moves quietly around inside the vessel. As a guide to the efficiency of the system, bear in mind that 0.03 m³ (1ft³) of coral sand medium is equal to 576 m² (6,200 ft²) of available surface area for bacterial growth. A typical standard filter measuring 90 × 90 × 90 cm (36 × 36 × 36 in) containing Japanese matting will only have about 2.8 m² (30 ft²) available surface area, so it is easy to see why a fluidized bed filter does not need to be as large as a conventional one. A fluidized filter will easily cope with the waste produced by 135 kg (300 lb) weight of fish, which is roughly equivalent to over 70 koi, each measuring 50 cm (20 in). Such a filter can be added to an existing system to enable the fishkeeper to increase stocking levels or to help if there is an ongoing problem with nitrite and ammonia readings if the filter is undersized.

Bubble bead filters

These filters use a medium consisting of small (3 x 5 mm), floating plastic beads. In normal running, the beads float in the upper part of the device, forming a filter bed that carries out biological filtration as well as straining out solid particles down to 15 microns (millionths of a meter) in size – a fine sand particle is 50 microns.

Several models are available, depending on the size of the pond being treated. All have the capability of being fitted with an integral UV unit to control green water. Cleaning the filter is made easy by a valve system that enables automatic backwashing, with collected wastes being flushed out on a regular basis.

Bead filters can maintain acceptable water quality with a loading of up to 8 kg of food per day per m^3 of filter media (0.5 lb per ft^3). This is equivalent to 23 kg (50 lb) of koi feeding at a 1 percent rate. For maximum water quality, this figure is halved to an upper limit of 4 kg of food per day per m^3 of bead media (0.25 lb per ft^3). These figures are based on standard bead media and typical pelleted foods with a protein content of around 35 percent.

Bubble bead filter

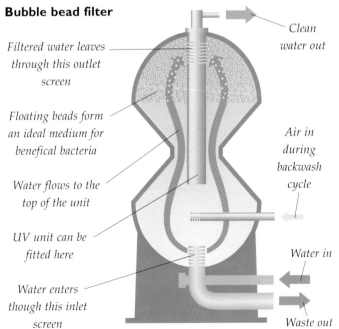

Filtered water leaves through this outlet screen

Floating beads form an ideal medium for benefical bacteria

Water flows to the top of the unit

UV unit can be fitted here

Water enters though this inlet screen

Clean water out

Air in during backwash cycle

Water in

Waste out

Providing sufficient aeration

The oxygen requirement of a biological filter, especially a fluidized bed and media in a multichamber system, is actually very high. If there is insufficient dissolved oxygen in the water, the filtration system can be affected, leading to an accumulation of ammonia or nitrite. To prevent this from occurring, multichamber filters should be fitted with airstone diffusers to provide extra aeration as the water travels through. This is essential because, as the water proceeds through each filtration stage, a certain amount of oxygen is removed by bacteria as they convert ammonia to nitrite and nitrite to nitrates (see page 30). Aerating the water in the transfer ports will create the optimum environment for bacteria to thrive on the surface of the filter media.

Other factors that influence the oxygen content of the water are the numbers and size of koi stocked in the pond. Large koi have a higher demand for oxygen than small ones, but a pond heavily stocked with small koi also places a high oxygen requirement on the water. It is easy to monitor the koi pond routinely for oxygen levels using a dissolved oxygen test kit (see page 28).

Below: An air pump suitable for a koi pond. These need to deliver a minimum of 40 L (10.5 gal) per hour to supply six airstones or an aerated bottom drain.

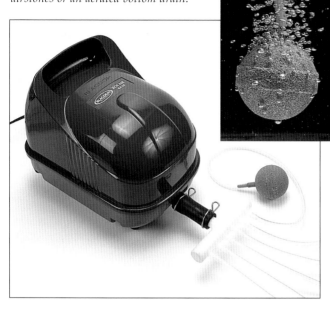

Airstones and air pump

Airstones, or similar bubble-forming devices driven by an air pump, should be standard pieces of equipment in the filtration system of a koi pond to provide supplementary air. As we have seen, they should be fitted in the transfer ports of the filtration system to ensure maximum saturation as the water passes through the chambers to feed the nitrifying bacteria contained within the filter media. If you do not have an aerating bottom drain, it is also a good idea to have a couple of air lines in the pond, so that if the main biological filter pump were to fail, the air pump would maintain oxygen levels and act as a backup. Do not place the airstones on top of or below the media, as this can cause unwanted tracking of water through the filter and disturbs the bacteria. In addition, too much disturbance within the filter chamber does not allow solids to settle freely on the base.

An aerated dome or adding a conversion kit in an existing pond will promote more efficient water circulation into the bottom drain, thereby improving the removal of solids from the pond bottom. It will also provide additional aeration when oxygen levels are low during the summer months or if treatments are introduced into the pond (see page 70).

The venturi

A venturi (devised by the Italian, G.B. Venturi) is a piece of equipment that injects air into the water. It is made from 2-4 cm (0.75-1.5 in) pipework, with a restrictor inside and an air tube that extends above water level. When water is pumped through the venturi, the restrictor forces air to be sucked in from the tube above water level and mixed with water inside the venturi to cause thousands of tiny bubbles that both aerate the water and improve circulation.

The working principles of a venturi

A venturi is an integral piece of equipment for a gravity-fed system, and provides excellent aeration and current in the water. It can be quite noisy, but a small piece of sponge inserted into the air line will silence it without affecting the flow.

A cone adaptor restricts water flow though the venturi, causing it to speed up. The resulting pressure drop draws in air through the attached air line.

The airstream mixing with the fast-flowing water creates thousands of tiny bubbles.

Air enters here

Plastic air line extends above the water surface, allowing air to be drawn into the venturi.

Oxygen-enriched water swirls into the pond.

How a protein skimmer works

The dissolved organic carbon sticks to the surface of the bubbles and is carried up and out of the tube as foam.

As the bubbles collapse, a yellow liquid builds up in the collecting cup and can be discarded.

Water from the pond flows downward into a rising stream of air bubbles.

Airstone connected to a powerful air pump.

Cleaned water returns to the pond.

Above: These are typical signs of a buildup of dissolved organic carbon, or protein waste, in the pond. Look for an oily appearance and long-persisting bubbles. Fitting a foam fractionator, or protein skimmer, will solve the problem.

Protein skimmers

If the surface of your pond takes on an oily appearance and bubbles from a venturi or waterfall take a long time to burst, then the problem is protein waste, or dissolved organic carbon (DOC). This can also give the water a yellowish tinge. The cause is decaying organic matter, including food, algae, blanketweed, and fish waste. The reason for the surface of the pond appearing oily is that the dissolved organic carbon is attracted to the water/air interface. In this effect lies the answer to the problem, which is used in a device called a foam fractionator or protein skimmer. In its simplest form, water from the pond is passed down a vertical tube against rising air bubbles from an airstone. The DOC sticks to the surface of the bubbles and is carried up and out of the top of the tube as foam. In more advanced units, water enters a vessel through a downward-pointing venturi, which ensures that the bubbles remain in contact with the water for a much longer time. With both of these types the critical factor is to keep the water level at just the right height so that only foam emerges from the top. As the foam collapses, the resultant yellow-brown liquid produced can be removed and discarded.

Mechanical filtration for water clarity

Mechanical filters are not essential items of equipment for the koi keeper, as they do not have any effect on water quality, only clarity. An efficient biological filter with good settlement and backwashing facilities should provide adequate clarity for you to view your fish and see to the base of the pond. An efficient biological filter will remove particles as small as 100 microns, and when you consider that one micron is one millionth of a meter, most people would be happy with that.

However, there are those enthusiasts who want their water to be as clear as drinking water and this is only achievable if the smaller particles are strained out by a finer, denser material. The only problem is that a dense medium will inevitably clog very quickly and require regular and frequent cleaning. If the mechanical filter were placed before the biological stage, it would probably need servicing every few hours, because it would have to deal with the brunt of the dirt coming directly from the pond. As most mechanical filters rely on water passing through them under pressure, they can be effectively installed only on gravity-fed systems after the water has passed through the biological stage, so that most of the waste products have settled or been strained out by the media in the filter bays.

The pump should also be capable of turning over enough water under pressure without affecting its flow rate; otherwise the biological filter's effectiveness will be impaired, especially if the volume of water passing through it is constantly fluctuating.

Some biological filter media, such as brushes located in the first stage of a multichamber biological system, have natural mechanical properties. However, they must be tightly packed, with each brush overlapping the next, so that the debris is trapped. It is no good having just a few brushes, as the water will take the easiest route, bypassing them altogether and taking the dirt into the next stage. Japanese matting and plastic honeycomb have very few mechanical properties, as water passes freely though the channels without restriction. Porous ceramic rock is very effective, because it is a fairly dense material,

Left: *A neat waterproof housing, featuring two 45 cm (18 in) sand pressure filters, multiport valves, electric heaters, pumps, ultraviolet sterilizers, and associated switchgear and pipework. Regular backwashing is essential to keep the system running efficiently.*

but even so, small particles still manage to pass through. You can see this happening over a period of time; the ceramic material becomes coated with a very fine dust, which is basically dirt that has managed to pass through the previous chambers and, as it is strained by the ceramic rock, settles on top of the stones.

Some filter systems incorporate layers of foam placed on top of the ceramic rock to prevent this from occurring, which is quite effective. Unfortunately, the foam has to be washed regularly; otherwise the water cannot pass through freely and the restriction causes the system to back up and overflow. A fluidized bed filter has a huge surface area for bacteria to colonize and, being in constant motion, the sand breaks down large solids very efficiently and never needs cleaning. However, small particles still manage to travel through.

So what is the answer to this problem? There are only a few proprietary systems suitable for a koi pond and choosing the right one will depend on the volume of water to be treated and stocking levels.

Sand pressure filters

Sand pressure filters are typically used for swimming pools, but can be useful to the koi keeper. They are effective at removing fine particles that pass through the biological stage, therefore enhancing water clarity. The main tank structure is made from extremely hard-wearing (injection molded) glass-reinforced plastic. The smooth, high-gloss internal and external finish ensures a free flow of water and easy cleaning. The side-mounted multiport valve configuration, together with the large, clear lid access, allows you to service the interior without any need to disturb the connecting pipework. The clear

lid also provides an excellent view of the water passing through, which is particularly useful when backwashing the filter, which should be carried out regularly.

Sand pressure filters are available in various shapes and sizes, ranging in diameter from 40 cm (16 in) to over 1 m (39 in). They can be installed at the final stage of the biological filter or plumbed directly from a surface skimmer. Water is pumped from an external, centrifugal, swimming pool pump into the multiport valve attached to the vessel, then travels through the sand into a series of fins at the base of the filter before being returned to the pond. Sand within the chamber removes any fine particles, but because it is so dense it tends to clog very quickly and has to be cleaned on a regular basis. To clean the sand in the filter, simply turn the lever on the multi-port valve to the "backwash" position for two to three minutes and dirty water is discharged to waste. Finally, move the lever to the rinse position, which settles the sand, before returning it to the filter position. This operation has to be carried out on a daily basis, but takes only a few moments.

Cartridge filters

These filters have been adapted from swimming pool technology and work in a similar way to air filters on a car. Water is pumped under pressure into either the base or the top of a cylindrical vessel, depending on the manufacturer. It then travels around the outside of the chamber and passes through a fine paper cartridge with several fins around the perimeter and a hole in the center, similar to a roll of paper towels. Cleaned water travels into the void and exits the vessel, still under pressure, so that it can be used to power a venturi or waterfall. Although these filters are extremely effective, they do require a great deal of maintenance and you cannot clean them by hosing them off. Invariably, the inlet and outlet are linked to a threaded lid, so unions have to be incorporated for easy removal if fixed pipework is used. The paper cartridge must be chemically cleaned over a period of time, then thoroughly washed and rinsed before it can be used again, so a spare is essential.

Plastic fin filters

Plastic fin filters are similar in design to cartridge filters, consisting of a reinforced plastic cylinder with ridged plastic rings acting as the filter medium. The filter body is fitted with a quick-release, snap-type metal fitting around the lid, which is simple to remove and does not require unions or special pipework. When the cartridge is removed, it can be washed with a hose and reinstated within minutes. The intervals between cleaning depend largely on the amount of waste the filter has to deal with, but it generally suits ponds up to about 9,000 L (2,000 gal). Fitted in an average pond it would probably need cleaning every five to seven days, so you should install a bypass if you are going away on vacation; otherwise the pond will grind to a halt.

Sieve filter

Another variation on the mechanical filter theme is a simple stainless steel box housing a fine sieve that physically strains out solids. The sieve consists of hundreds of laser-cut stainless steel blades arranged in rows at 90° to the water flow, and with aperture options of 50, 100, 150, or 200 microns (millionths of a meter). Water flows through but fine particles – including weed cells, fish parasites, and their eggs – are trapped.

Pond water is pumped or drawn by gravity over a weir in the body of the device. As it strikes the sharp edges of the blades, surface tension is broken. Dirt particles, or strands of blanketweed, are pushed away from the sieve because of the hydrostatic load created, and because the sieve fits into the body of the unit in a curved profile, the particles end up trapped at the lowest point. They can then be removed, either by hand or by turning off the pump, sliding out the sieve, and rinsing it off.

When water passes through the screen, a pressure drop sucks in air, so the blades act like mini-venturis, oxygenating the water. This device can be used in pump-fed or gravity mode with pumps of flow rates of up to 15,000 L per hour (3,300 gal per hour).

Plastic fin strainers

Filter body

Water travels from the periphery, through the filter rings, into the central core, and then out.

Dirt and trapped debris can be washed away through this drain port.

Water outlet

Lid attaches with a snap-on metal clamp.

Water inlet

Fine ridges on the overlapping plastic rings sieve out debris.

Above: *The plastic filter rings overlap onto a central core and form a mechanical sieve that traps particles as small as 105 microns (a micron is a millionth of a meter). Washing the stack with a hosepipe separates and cleans the rings.*

Sieve filter

Gravity feed from pond

Flap valve with float regulates inflow

Water cascades over weir and through sloping sieve of sharp-edged blades

Pump carries away cleaned water

Solids trapped by stainless steel blades are washed down to base of sieve

Cylindrical mechanical strainer

Another option for screening water earlier in the filter "chain" is a mechanical strainer fitted to the exit pipe from the prefilter or vortex on a gravity system. It is a cylindrical device with a stainless steel mesh around the perimeter that prevents solids larger than 100 microns from passing through. The screen is constantly cleaned by a pump that drives a rotor with two spraybars that clean the surface of the screen as they revolve.

Ultraviolet sterilizers

UV light is used in ponds to destroy algae growth caused by photosynthesis. Sunlight creates millions of single-cell, microscopic spores of green algae that tarnish the pond water, giving it a pea soup appearance with zero visibility. Ultraviolet radiation at a wavelength of 254 nanometers (billionths of a meter) is extremely effective in halting the reproduction of

algae. The algae readily absorb the UV light, which damages their DNA structure and makes them flocculate (clump together), so that they can be trapped in a mechanical filter.

At the heart of each UV unit is an ultraviolet lamp sealed inside a quartz glass sleeve. Although more expensive than normal glass, quartz glass is used because it is purer, will not filter out the UV light given off from the bulb, and maximizes the unit's efficiency.

UV sterilizers have no adverse effect on sensitive plant and pond life, and as no chemicals or other environmentally harmful processes are involved, there is no danger of pollution or overtreating the water. Providing the unit is installed in accordance with the manufacturer's instructions, and the unit is the correct wattage for pond capacity, stock level, and situation, all that is left is clear water. If you dose the pond with any treatment containing malachite green, turn off the UV sterilizer for 24 hours; otherwise the UV light will weaken the dosage.

Be sure to fit the UV before the biofilter to ensure that the pipework is fully charged with water. If you put it in after the filter in the gravity return, only half the pipework will be full of water and you risk burning out the electrics. Some hobbyists are under the impression that UV sterilizers help to reduce bacteria in the water and control some of the parasites. Unfortunately, this is

Cylindrical mechanical strainer

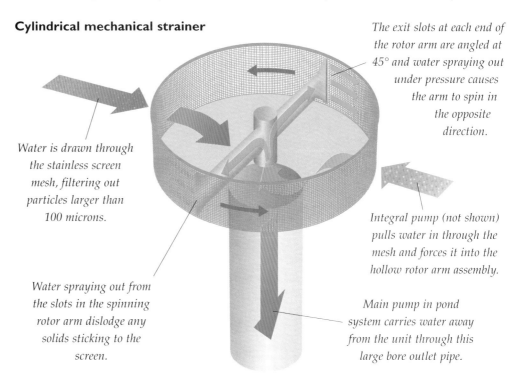

The exit slots at each end of the rotor arm are angled at 45° and water spraying out under pressure causes the arm to spin in the opposite direction.

Water is drawn through the stainless screen mesh, filtering out particles larger than 100 microns.

Integral pump (not shown) pulls water in through the mesh and forces it into the hollow rotor arm assembly.

Water spraying out from the slots in the spinning rotor arm dislodge any solids sticking to the screen.

Main pump in pond system carries water away from the unit through this large bore outlet pipe.

not true. Although a 30w UV may have some effect on bacteria and parasites in a 136 L (30 gal) aquarium, the same size UV on a pond of say 13,620 L (3,000 gal) would have little effect, other than on algae. All the water should pass through the UV sterilizer before teeing off to ornaments, waterfalls, and venturis, etc., to make sure it is treated.

Although most manufacturers state that a UV bulb will last between 8,000 and 10,000 hours, its efficiency will be reduced by anything up to 15 percent after 5,000 hours of continuous use (about six months) and water clarity will begin to deteriorate. To ensure that the pond remains crystal clear all year round, it is a good idea to replace the bulb before it loses its algal qualities. Do not be fooled if the bulb can be seen glowing through

Ultraviolet (UV) sterilizer

The top housing provides protection for the electrical circuit.

End caps supply power to the ultraviolet (UV) tube that runs through the center of the unit.

Water pumped in at one end circulates in a water jacket around the UV lamp and exits at the other end.

This quartz sleeve encases the tube but allows UV light to pass through.

The fluorescent tube in the middle produces ultraviolet light that is harmful to living tissue.

Translucent hosetails safely reveal the glow of the working tube.

Ozonizer and protein skimmer

Ozone generator

Ozone passes into the water flow through venturi

Protein waste

Water in from pond

Ozone reacts with water as it flows through the protein skimmer.

Water return to pond

Redox probe in pond ensures correct ozone dosage

the hosetails – it still needs replacing. Never look into an unprotected UV bulb, as this could seriously damage your eyes.

Over a period of time, the quartz sleeve may get dirty or a buildup of lime could prevent the UV light from shining through the water as it passes through the unit. To remove the bulb, pull off the end caps and carefully slide it out of the quartz sleeve. Carefully remove and wash the quartz sleeve in warm soapy water, which should be enough to clean it. To remove stubborn lime, use a long-handled bottle brush.

Ozone

Ozone (O_3) oxidizes everything it encounters, including viruses, bacteria, and fish parasites. This unstable and potentially dangerous "oxygen-plus" gas is a powerful sterilizing agent, requiring careful use in a pond context. It must never come into direct contact with koi or beneficial filter bacteria.

Modern ozonizers consist of two main elements: a generator (in which the gas is produced by a high-energy electrical discharge that literally bonds an extra oxygen atom onto each oxygen molecule) and a reactor vessel

Trickle tower

Spraybar

As the water trickles down over the plastic medium, anaerobic bacteria growing on the surfaces reduce nitrates to nitrogen gas.

Water in

Serrated plastic spheres act as the filter medium.

Depending on the flow rate, the static water level remains about here.

Return to pond

or skimmer (where it is mixed by venturi action with pond water, and protein froth and residual gas are removed before the water returns to the pond). A probe in the water flow constantly monitors the level of ozone, so there is no possibility of overdosing.

Ozone units supersaturate the pond with oxygen, kill blanketweed and single-celled algae, and allow filter bacteria to work more efficiently. The water achieves an unparalleled clarity, and koi are far less prone to niggling infections. Damaged tissue heals rapidly.

It is a myth that koi immune systems suffer when ozone is used. Rather, because the fish are not constantly

under low-level stress from resisting pathogenic attack, they become stronger and fitter than ever. Ozone units are not cheap, but are a worthwhile investment for people serious about keeping koi.

Trickle towers

After the final biological filter stage, treated water can be returned to the pond via a trickle tower to reduce nitrate levels. The plastic media inside the tower – literally a vertical tube down which the water cascades – promote the growth of anaerobic bacteria that strip nitrate (NO_3) of its oxygen atoms to produce nitrogen gas (N_2). Some trickle towers have a revolving spraybar at the top; others have a perforated plate through the water is sprayed.

Vegetable filters

Vegetable filters are becoming increasingly popular as a means of reducing the nitrate level in the pond and thus helping to control the blanketweed problem. All plant life readily absorbs nitrate and naturally removes it from the water, thus reducing the growth of blanketweed at the end of the nitrogen cycle. However, the vegetable filter has to be large enough to deal with the nitrate that the filter is producing and to date there are no figures available to indicate the pond-to-filter-to-vegetable filter surface area ratio that is required for maximum efficiency. Generally speaking, it would seem that an effective vegetable filter needs to be equivalent to 25 percent of the surface area of the pond.

Above: *A simple vegetable filter consisting of a "runway" with aquatic plants that absorb nitrates (NO_3) given off by the biofilter.*

A vegetable filter

Gravity return to pond

Vigorous moisture-loving plants, such as watercress, absorb nitrates as food.

Pump in last chamber

Multichamber filter

Gravity feed to filter

Above: *Install a vegetable filter after the biofilter to reduce nitrate (NO_3) levels and in turn reduce the effects on blanketweed.*

Designing and building a koi pond

Building your own pond following your design and carrying out or overseeing the work yourself is one of the most rewarding aspects of becoming a koi keeper. It is one of the few areas in which complete novices can express themselves, choosing designs that are imaginative, outrageous, conventional, traditional, or even Japanese – there is no limit to the possibilities. However, to succeed, it is vital to plan every aspect of the proposed pond before starting any work, because once the project is finished it will be very expensive to alter. Before putting a shovel into the ground, read plenty of books and specialized magazines and talk to people who have an up-to-date working knowledge of pond design and construction. There are plenty of koi clubs you can join, whose members will be only too willing to show you their efforts and share experiences, both good and bad, so that you can avoid making basic mistakes.

You will need to buy equipment that is usually carried in stock only by specialized koi dealers. Choose dealers very carefully; check that they actually use the equipment they sell on their own systems and can show you items such as pumps and filters in operation.

Choosing the location for your pond

The most suitable place for the pond has to be as close as possible to the house, so that you can view the fish all year round and in all weather. However, the excavation must be at least 1 m (39 in) away from the house; otherwise you risk undermining the foundations. If this were to happen, the property would have to be underpinned – a very expensive procedure that would not be covered by your household insurance.

The pond will become a major feature of the garden, so consider all the options before you start digging. Bear in mind the practical day-to-day chores, such as cutting the grass; will the cuttings fall into the water when you trim around the pond perimeter? Could any pesticides such as slug pellets pollute the water? Overhanging trees may become difficult to prune, especially if you intend to build a pond with a large surface area, and falling leaves can be a big problem in the fall, clogging bottom drain inlets and skimmer baskets. Roots from nearby trees and large shrubs can also become a problem, especially if you intend to build the pond using a liner, which could easily be punctured at a later date.

Place the pond in an area that enjoys the most natural light without too much shade from trees or buildings. The only disadvantage of this position is sunlight, which encourages the growth of blanketweed; you will have to use a treatment regularly to keep this unsightly filamentous algae under control.

Designing your new pond

It is vital to make a plan so that can visualize the shape of your new pond and how it fits in the garden. You can start by preparing a scale drawing of your garden on graph paper, so that one square represents, say, 30 cm (1 ft), 1.5 m (5 ft), or 3 m (10 ft), depending on the area to be fitted onto the paper. Measure any outbuildings and enter them on the plan. Then add permanent features, such as large trees and shrubs, as well as hard

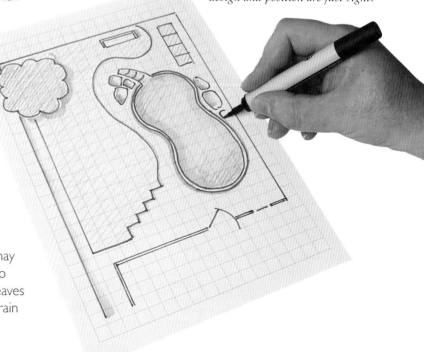

Below: Before you start building, make a simple plan to show how your new koi pond would fit into your garden. Changes are easy at this stage and you need to be sure that the design and position are just right.

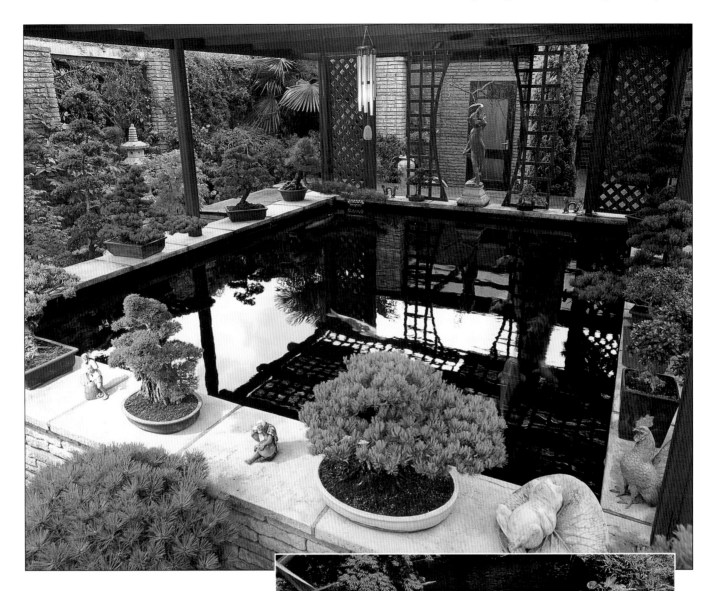

Above: *This is a good example of a formal pond raised out of the ground, with an attractive pergola built over the top to provide shade. Bonsai trees and ornaments have been placed around the perimeter of the pond to provide a Japanese atmosphere.*

Right: *A more natural pond, with plenty of mature shrubs and other planting to disguise the pond structure and filtration system. It is a good idea to leave one area open and accessible so that you can get close to the fish, especially when feeding.*

landscaping, including patios, pathways, raised borders, etc. Before sketching in the pond, make a few photocopies of what you have done so far, so that if you decide to alter the shape or position of the pond you will not have to draw in the existing features again. Alternatively, cover the paper plan with adhesive-backed plastic and use water-based felt pens to draw the shape of the pond. If you want to make any alterations, simply rub out unwanted lines with a cloth. If you have a computer there are some very good and relatively inexpensive garden design packages available that can help you create a visual of the finished pond and how it will look in your garden surroundings.

Spend plenty of time on the design and location of the pond. Show your ideas to fellow hobbyists and to your local dealer, who will be only too glad to offer you help and advice.

Pond designs

Anyone can have a pond, even in a modest-sized garden. In Japan, most hobbyists' gardens are quite small, but what they lack in surface area they make up for in depth to ensure a good volume of water.

The shape of the pond will be determined by a number of factors, such as the area it is intended to occupy, the existing hard landscaping, and the overall concept. For example, if it is to be built within or adjacent to a patio, the design is likely to be very formal – rectangular, L-shaped, aboveground with brick walls, etc. When designing a pond of this type, you need to consider "dead spots," which are areas where the water is almost stationary and does not circulate properly around

the pond and into the filter system. These areas can be agitated by aerated drains and additional venturis to regulate the flow of water.

Informal circular and kidney shapes are usually associated with a natural design and it is easier to control the water flow in such ponds because of the soft curves that allow a good flow of water around the surface. In addition, there are fewer areas where fish can damage themselves by "flicking" off sharp walls.

Sometimes it can be an advantage to have a natural fall in the garden, as it can open up all sorts of landscaping possibilities, such as streams, waterfalls, rocks, bog gardens, and raised patios. If the ground slopes toward the house, you could construct a very natural-looking waterfall or stream at the far end of the pond, with an impressive drop onto the water surface. The front of the pond could be raised out of the ground with decorative face brickwork or natural stone. You could install a window as an added feature. Never build a pond more than 60 cm (24 in) out of the ground, as it very rarely looks right.

An interesting concept is building a pond partly in the garden and partly in a greenhouse, so that you can enjoy the hobby all year. However, there are a number of potential problems associated with constructing such a

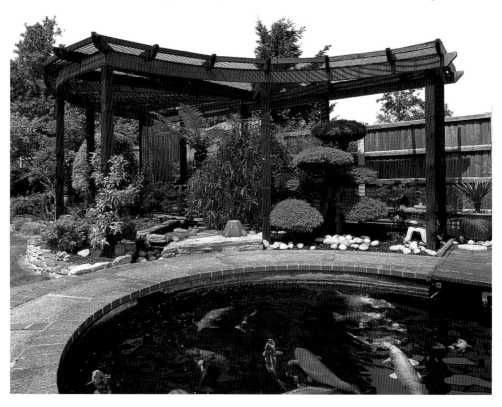

Right: A formal design in which brickwork has been used to achieve a circular shape with a Japanese-style backdrop and pergola. Granite ornaments, cobblestones, and shingles are also used to create the desired oriental effect.

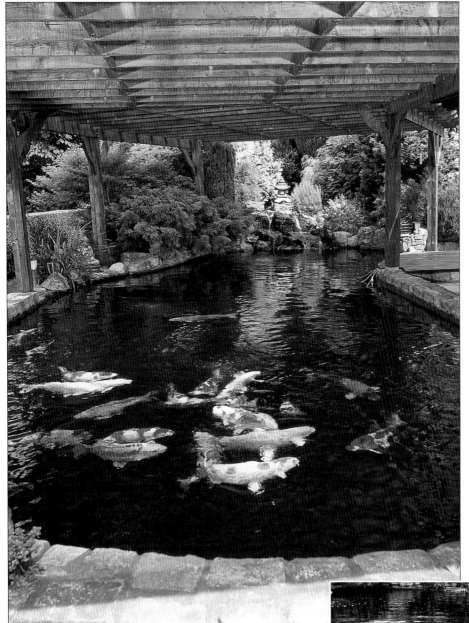

Left: *A large formal pond covered by a pergola. Make sure that the wood is treated with a nontoxic preservative; otherwise, the stain could leach out and pollute the water.*

Above: *A raised pond with a bridge over the center onto a decked area that hides the filter system. The water clarity in this pond is so good that the fish seem to be held in suspension.*

Right: *A natural-looking pond incorporating a window that provides an interesting viewing perspective. It is quite useful for checking the fish for damage and disease. Seek professional help if you contemplate fitting a window in your koi pond.*

Above and right: A raised koi pond that extends into a greenhouse. Two windows in the pond wall mean that your favorite koi are up close and personal the whole year.

advice, and if the proposal is feasible, the pond would have to be built using reinforced concrete and sealed with fiberglass. In such an elaborate design, the filtration system should be located in the garden, because you would not want to put up with the smells from the discharge chamber when purging the bottom drains. Also, pond filter systems tend to attract flies, which is the last thing you want in a greenhouse.

Condensation could be a problem within the greenhouse, but a space heater or dehumidifier will prevent a buildup of moisture. Consult the greenhouse manufacturer regarding the strength of the joists that span the expanse of water, and fit the glazing below water level to prevent cold air from entering the room.

Coping with the ground conditions

The type of soil found in your garden is mostly irrelevant, especially if you are constructing a cement pond, which could free-stand without relying on the surrounding backfill. This is the case even if the pond is constructed using a liner, because a liner pond has a ring beam (footing) to act as a stabilizer and does not require additional external support aboveground. However, the construction of a liner pond will rely on the state of the ground below the ring beam.

It is not really possible to predict where the water

pond and you should seek the advice of a construction engineer before undertaking the project. You will need to take into account such considerations as the depth of the foundations. If these are undermined, the side of the house could fall into the pond! Subject to the engineer's

Coping with a high water table

If you encounter a high water table, dig a dewatering pit to divert groundwater away from the excavation.

Ideally, pump ground-water directly to a main drain. If there is no drain nearby, make sure that you discharge the water well away from the excavation; otherwise water will percolate through the soil and back to the excavation.

Use a dirty water type of pump that will allow solids to pass through the impeller and away to waste. Choose one with a float switch so it will turn on automatically as the water rises, and off again when the level drops.

Do not backfill the dewatering pit until you fill the pond; otherwise water could build up underneath a liner, causing it to bulge and potentially tear the bottom drain connection.

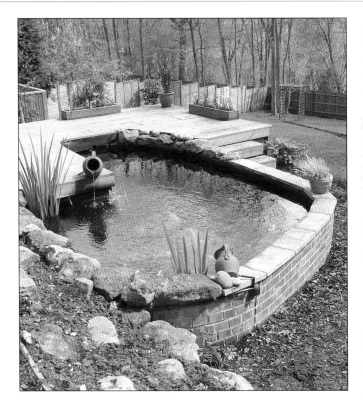

table is unless you dig pilot holes in strategic places in the garden. Although a high water table can cause certain problems, do not let it affect your chosen pond location because the difficulties can be overcome, although it may involve extra work.

If you are unlucky and hit the water table, the only way to ensure that the excavation remains dry is to dig a dewatering pit, or sump, close by. Make this about 60 cm (2 ft) across and 60 cm (2 ft) deeper than the pond. (A post hole borer is useful for digging this relatively narrow shaft.) Put a paving slab at the base of the pit and lower an automatic submersible pump on top – the slab will prevent dirt from clogging the strainer. Then run a flexible hose to a main drain or a lower part of the garden. As the pit is lower than the base of the pond, water will begin to fill the pit, causing the float switch on the pump to rise. This will activate the pump and the water will be drawn away to waste. When the pit is empty, the float switch will automatically fall and turn off the pump. Leave the pump in place until the pond is built and full of water, and then backfill the sump.

Most of the obstructions that you find during excavation can be overcome, but you may come across something totally unexpected, such as an unused

Pond building do's and don'ts

DO	DON'T
Thoroughly research and plan your proposed pond. Read books and articles, watch videos and talk to the experts before you start digging in your garden.	Dig a big hole and wonder what to do next.
Make drawings of the layout with cross sections and plans showing all pipe runs and dimensions, and keep this for future reference.	Take advice from amateurs who think they know everything there is to know about ponds. Talk to people who do it for a living – they don't want you to make mistakes because you are their future customers.
Work out the cost of the building materials and equipment and make sure you stay within your budget.	Cut corners or compromise on quality if you stray over your budget limit. Remember, you want to do this only once – get it right the first time and if necessary reduce the pond size and the material costs will lower accordingly.
Choose the right biological filter. Ask yourself the following questions: Is it manufactured from good-quality fiberglass? Can all detritus be removed without disturbing the media? Is it big enough to cope with your pond volume and intended stocking levels? Dealers should be able to demonstrate the filters on sale on their own systems.	Skimp on the filter system – this is the most important aspect of koi keeping. Savings on a cheap filter now could cost you more in the long run. Do not try to build a filter yourself. Manufacturers have invested a great deal of money developing efficient systems that you cannot emulate using domestic cold-water tanks.
Invest in a good pump. Most of the top manufacturers offer a three-year warranty.	
Show your proposals to your local koi specialist, who will check for any mistakes and give you practical advice and guidance.	Buy a pump with a high power consumption. This pump will be running 365 days a year so you want maximum output with a low wattage.

Pond liner materials

Mesh adds strength to this three-layered thermoplastic polyvinyl liner.

Polyester underlay. Use this under the liner to protect it from any sharp stones that may puncture it.

PVC liner 0.5 mm (0.02 in) thick. Suitable for watercourses and small ponds.

Composite liner 0.55 mm (0.022 in) thick. Thermoplastic polyvinyl layered with reinforcing mesh.

Butyl rubber 0.75 mm (0.03 in) thick. Long-lasting liner that can be welded.

EPDM rubber 1.0 mm (0.04 in) thick. Heavyweight liner with good strength and durability.

cesspool or the foundations of a building not shown on the deed to your property, and conclude that the additional cost of eliminating the problem is prohibitive. However, the usual obstacles are services leading to and from the house, such as electricity cables, sewage, and water pipes, which can usually be rerouted without too much trouble. The deed to your property may give you an idea of the location of any services near the proposed pond area, but if these are old and unreliable, the only sure way to find out is to start digging.

Access and waste disposal

Access is an important consideration, especially if you want a large pond and need a mechanical digger to carry out the excavation. Most are over 1 m (39 in) wide and will not fit through a standard garden gate, although it is possible to hire smaller machines without tracks, with sides that fold in and allow them to pass through narrow openings. Construction will be a bit trickier if you live in a terraced property with no access to the garden around the back, as all the excavated soil and building materials will have to be transported through the house.

If you are unable to dispose of the waste soil around your garden, you will need a backhoe. Most local authorities have a list of reputable companies that will be able to deliver the same day if it is off-road. If this is not possible, you will need a license. If large amounts of soil are to be moved it might be worth hiring a special truck that is capable of shifting large quantities and is cheaper to rent than a backhoe.

The cost involved

Remember, you want to carry out building work only once, so make sure it is done properly the first time, and stay within your budget. If you discover that you cannot afford to buy the best materials or filtration system, do not cut corners; wait until you have the money. When you have decided on the size of the pond, it is reasonably straightforward to calculate the cost. Throughout this section we will use the example of a pond measuring 3.6 × 3 × 1.2 m deep (about 12 × 10 × 4 ft), with a capacity of 13,000 L (about 3,000 gal) to help you calculate quantities, materials, and costs, etc.

Children and animals

If you have young children or pets, it is important to situate your pond carefully to avoid any accidents. Remember that a pond will contain deep water and is a potential deathtrap. If you are lucky enough to be able to construct a pond in a greenhouse, it should be fairly easy to keep children out of this area by fitting a self-closing mechanism on the internal door and positioning the catch high up. For outside ponds, it is better to build a raised pond and fit a decorative panel onto the wall around the perimeter. When the children are old enough to understand the danger, you can remove the paneling.

Construction methods

When building a new koi pond, the first consideration must be what material to use. Your eventual decision may be influenced by a number of factors, such as the ground conditions in the intended location, financial constraints, and the shape. Here we look at the advantages and disadvantages of the three most popular pond construction methods, so that you can choose the one that suits you best. These are: preformed fiberglass ponds, plastic liner ponds, and concrete ponds.

Preformed fiberglass ponds

The advantages of fiberglass ponds (glass-reinforced plastic/GRP) are that they are tough, made of a long-lasting material, and quick to fit. Little building knowledge is needed to install them and they are available in interesting shapes and designs from several manufacturers. There are no unsightly creases to deal with and no restriction on suitable sites. On the other hand, they are relatively expensive and most are too shallow to be suitable for koi. In shallow water, temperatures fluctuate very quickly. The only way to overcome this problem is to find a pond that can hold in excess of 4,500 L (about 1,000 gal), as this volume reacts more slowly to changes in ambient temperatures.

If you do decide to install a fiberglass pond, it is a good idea to add an inline heater to stabilize the water temperature. These heaters are available from most koi outlets and are very easy to fit. They are typically made of stainless steel with a 3.75 cm (1.5 in) threaded inlet and outlet and a digital thermostatic control (see page 25).

Plastic liners

Probably the quickest and cheapest method of building a koi pond is to fit a liner. You can buy these off the roll or prepacked. The three main options are PVC, butyl rubber, and EPDM rubber.

PVC (Plasticized Polyvinyl Chloride) liners are relatively inexpensive and available with or without nylon reinforcing. The material is generally manufactured in rolls 2 m (6.5 ft) wide and is sold off the roll or seam-welded by the distributor to be sold in prepacked form. It is typically 0.50 or 0.80 mm (0.02 or 0.03 in) thick and has a limited life expectancy. This material should be used only for smaller ponds or watercourses.

BUTYL (Isobutylene Isoprene Rubber) is 0.75 or 1.0 mm (0.03 and 0.04 in) thick and is produced by polymerization of specific fractions from the oil refining process. The manufacturers of butyl rubber sheeting will

not disclose their formulations except to say that 40-45 percent by volume of the finished sheet is butyl polymer combined with a small proportion of EPDM polymer to improve the end product's weathering properties.

The distributor uses a hot bond tape to vulcanize the butyl sheets together to form a perfect weld. This should not be seen as a weak point; in fact, it constitutes the strongest part of the liner. These liners are available in almost every conceivable size in prepacked form or off the roll and can be tailor-made with on-site vulcanizing for larger installations, such as lakes and reservoirs. For the discerning koi keeper who does not want to see any

What you need for a liner pond

To help you plan and budget for your own system, here is a typical 'shopping list' of the materials and equipment you will need to build a pond measuring 3.6 m long, 3 m wide and 1.2 m deep (approximately 12 × 10 × 4 ft) containing 13,000 L (about 3,000 gal) of water. The list can be adapted to suit a pond of any size.

Quantity	Description
3 days	Renting of mechanical digger
1	Insurance policy on above
36 m³ (48 yd³)	Spoil/waste removal capacity
1 m³ (1.3 yd³)	Ballast for ring beam and to encase bottom drain and pipework
7 × 25 kg (55 lb)	Bags cement powder
1	Liner 6.6 × 6 m (about 22 × 20 ft)
20 m (66 ft)	Polyester underlay off a roll 2 m (6.5 ft) wide
2	25 cm (10 in) bottom drains with flange seals
4 m (13 ft)	10 cm (4 in) PVC pipework from drains to filter
4	10 cm (4 in) PVC elbows
2	Venturi returns
2	3.75 cm (1.5 in) tank connectors for venturi
1	Fiberglass biological filter complete with media and pipework
1	Submersible pump to run system
1	30 W ultraviolet (UV) sterilizer

Optional extras

1	Surface skimmer with liner adapter
1	Pump for skimmer
1	Electronic blanketweed controller
1	Underwater light
1	Mechanical filter

pleats or folds, the liner can be box-welded (a method used to fit the excavation exactly) to your specifications, but this is typically twice as expensive as buying a flat sheet. A template would be required if the liner is intended to fit a more complex shape.

EPDM (Ethylene Propylene Diene Monomer) rubber is sold under various trade names. It is not supplied in pre-packed form but can be cut from rolls available in a range of widths, all 1.0 mm (0.04 in) thick. Although it does not contain any butyl, it has the same specification and is ideal for any pond size. The only drawbacks are that it cannot be box-welded and butyl tape will not adhere to it unless the surface is first prepared with gasoline and keyed. It is an ideal alternative to butyl.

Warranties for liners

When setting out to buy a liner, the temptation is to get the best price possible; after all, it's only a hole in the ground, isn't it? However, choosing a cheap liner could be a disastrous mistake.

Read any warranty carefully, as it does not cover all potential contingencies. Most offer only to repair or replace the product in the event of failure due to faulty seams, materials, or manufacture. There is no cover for consequential loss, excessive stretching, misuse, puncturing, or mechanical damage. Imagine this scenario:

A company installs a pond in accordance with the manufacturer's guidelines, but it develops a fault six months later. Who will bear the cost of removing the fish, providing temporary accommodation, draining the pond, taking out the faulty liner, returning it to the supplier, taking delivery of a new one, refitting it, and returning the fish? Meanwhile, one unfortunate but valuable koi suddenly dies.

The moral of this is that you should buy a liner only from a long-standing, reputable company that is more likely to honor the sale. Be wary of cheap liners; some are intended for roofing and may contain harmful fungicides that could be lethal to your fish.

Installing a liner pond

Try to keep the shape of the pond fairly simple; an informal kidney design or a formal shape such as a square or rectangle works well. The more complex the shape, the more you will be able to see unattractive pleats and folds that act as collection points for blanketweed and dirt once the pond is up and running.

When you have decided on the size and shape of the pond, do not dig it out right away. Remember that you need a firm edge around the pond on which to lay the liner, so that it can be disguised by the lawn, paving, brickwork, or decorative stone. To make this, you should construct a ring beam, or concrete collar as it is

How big a liner do I need?

To work out the size of the liner, simply double the depth measurement of the pond and add this figure to both the length and the width. For example, if the excavation measures 3.6 m long, 3 m wide, and 1.2 m deep (approximately 12 × 10 × 4 ft), you need a liner measuring 1.2 × 2 = 2.4 + 3.6 = 6 m (20 ft) long and 1.2 × 2 = 2.4 + 3 = 5.4 m (18 ft) wide. However, this does not allow for any overlap, so add 60 cm (2 ft) to each figure to produce a

30 cm (12 in) overlap around the perimeter. The final sheet size will be 6.6 × 6 m (about 22 × 20 ft).

Polyester underlay is normally sold from a roll measuring 2 m (6.5 ft) wide. To calculate the length needed from the roll for the above pond, divide the area of pond liner by the width of the roll. This works out as follows: 6.6 × 6 m = approximately 40 m² divided by 2 = 20 m (66 ft) off the roll. You can also buy underlay in prepacked form.

Measuring your pond for a liner

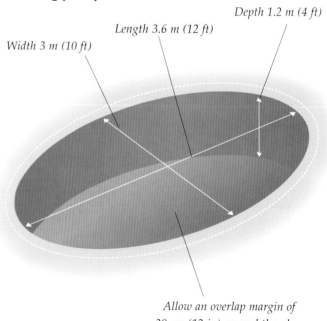

Depth 1.2 m (4 ft)

Length 3.6 m (12 ft)

Width 3 m (10 ft)

Allow an overlap margin of 30 cm (12 in) around the edge.

sometimes called. This acts as a foundation for the pond perimeter or a footing for brickwork if the pond is to be raised above ground level.

Mark out the ring beam using pegs driven into the ground about 60 cm (24 in) apart. Tie a string around the pegs to give you a better idea of how the eventual shape will look. If you are not totally happy with one particular area, simply lift the pegs and move them around until you achieve the desired effect. When you are satisfied, set out a second series of pegs 23 cm (9 in)

away from and outside of the first series to mirror the internal shape. Check around the perimeter using a spirit level. Dig out the area between the two peg shapes to a depth of 23 cm (9 in).

At this point you need to check that the top surface of the ring beam will be level. To do this, take out the wooden pegs that you have used to mark the shape and drive in a series of pegs along the center line of the trench all the way around. Make sure these are vertical and sticking up about 23 cm (9 in) above the bottom of

How to construct the pond

Building a concrete ring beam or collar around the perimeter provides a firm, level base for the liner and edging stones and prevents cave-ins during excavation.

1 Mark out the internal shape of the pond using string and then place pegs around the perimeter at regular intervals. Then measure out 23 cm (9 in) from each peg, mirroring the internal shape.

2 Dig out the trench to a depth of 23 cm (9 in) inside the pegged area. For uneven ground, drive pegs into the trench and check the levels with a spirit level.

The concrete forms a ring beam in the trench.

Position surface skimmers and pipework for venturis, etc., before filling the trench with concrete.

3 Fill the trench with concrete, completely encasing any return pipework and skimmers, etc. If you have used pegs to establish levels in the trench, lay the concrete up to the top of the pegs and leave them in position.

4 When the concrete has set, you can excavate the soil inside the beam without the risk of a collapse or cave-in.

5 Mark out the position of the bottom drain and 10 cm (4 in) pipe run, then dig a trench 38 cm (15 in) deep.

6 Encase the drain and pipework in concrete, ensuring that there is at least 15 cm (6 in) of concrete beneath the drain and pipe.

Liner offcut over edge

Concrete ring beam

Underlay

Leave a generous margin of liner around the pond edge.

Liner

Sand

7 Lay 5 cm (2 in) of sand over the base, and line the excavation and ring beam with polyester underlay. Next, put the liner into position and, if necessary, get into the pond (no shoes) and pleat and fold any creases, using double-sided tape if necessary. Then fill the pond with 45 cm (18 in) of water to settle the liner.

the trench. Using a long spirit level (or one on top of a piece of wood), check that the tops of the pegs are level all around the perimeter. Simply raise or drive in those that are not level as you go around.

The next step is to fill the trench with a 3:1 mix of aggregate/cement up to the tops of the pegs, which will create a level surface to the ring beam when the concrete has set. Leave the pegs embedded in the concrete. Remember to lay any return pipework and skimmers (see page 72) in the trench before filling with concrete. When the concrete has set, you can excavate the pond inside the ring beam without the risk of the sides collapsing.

Fitting a bottom drain

When the excavation is complete fit the base of the bottom drain, which is 25 cm (10 in) in diameter, with a 10 cm (4 in) pipe outlet on the side. (A domed cover fits on this to prevent fish from swimming into it, but do not

attach this now.) The 10 cm (4 in) pipework from the drain runs directly to the first chamber of the filtration system. The drain and pipe run must be totally encased in concrete and to achieve this you need to dig a trench in the base of the excavation. The depth of this trench depends on the exact dimensions of your bottom drain, but aim to have 15 cm (6 in) of concrete supporting the drain and pipe. For example, if the drain is 23 cm (9 in) deep, excavate the trench to 38 cm (15 in) and fill it with 15 cm (6 in) of concrete. When dry, position the drain and pipe on top of the concrete base and fill the entire trench with concrete.

Fitting the liner

Remove any sharp stones in the excavation, then line the entire floor and wall area with polyester underlay to protect the liner. (Do not use old carpet, as this will eventually rot.) Put the liner into the pond and add about 45 cm (18 in) of water, so that the liner is drawn

Calculating pond capacities

Using a flowmeter when you fill your pond is the most accurate way of registering the volume of water in the pond (see page 73). To estimate the capacity of various shapes of pond based on their overall dimensions, the following guidelines will be helpful.

To calculate the capacity of a rectangular pond, multiply the length by the width and the depth. Thus, our example of a pond measuring 3.6 × 3 × 1.2 m deep (12 × 10 × 4 ft) has a volume of 13 m³ (480 ft³). Each cubic meter is equivalent to 1,000 L (a cubic foot is equivalent to 6.25 gal). The capacity of the pond is therefore 13,000 L (3,000 gal).

To determine the capacity of a circular pond, use the formula πr^2, which is 3.142 (π) × radius × radius, to calculate the area of the surface. Then multiply this number by the depth. For a circular pond measuring 3.6 m (12 ft) across and 1.2 m (4 ft) deep, the surface area is 3.142 × 1.8 × 1.8 = 10.2 m² (113 ft²). This number multiplied by the depth of 1.2 m (4 ft) produces a volume of 12.24 m³ (452 ft³), and therefore a capacity of 12,240 L (2,825 gal).

For other shapes, divide the pond into easy-to-measure rectangular, square, or circular portions, calculate the volume of each, and then simply add them all together.

Right: *Slabs form a neat and stable edge for a koi pond. The underlay and liner overlap the ring beam and are covered by paving.*

Left: *If you place rocks around the edge, support them on a liner offcut to protect the pond liner.*

Right: *You can conceal the edge of the liner between vertical rows of bricks, as shown here. The concrete ring beam acts as an ideal foundation for the brickwork.*

8 *Place a pump in the bottom drain and pump the water away. Thoroughly dry the liner and connect the flange onto the bottom drain as shown on page 66. Fit the dome cover and all tank connectors.*

9 *Complete the edge of the pond with slabs, bricks, or stones and fill the pond using a flowmeter.*

The edge of the liner is secured and concealed by the slabs.

properly to the base. At this stage you should be prepared to get into the pond and fold and pleat the liner to remove as many creases as possible, as these will look unsightly when the pond is finished. You can pleat stubborn creases against the main body of the pond using double-sided butyl tape so that they do not protrude into the pond.

Sealing the liner around the bottom drain

Pump the water from the pond and fit the liner between the flanges around the perimeter of the bottom drain, using plenty of mastic to ensure a good seal. Most good-quality bottom drains are now supplied with a disk pre-drilled with holes at regular intervals around the perimeter. These line up with countersunk threaded slots built into the flange around the drain. Trim the liner inside the drain using a sharp blade, then apply a generous layer of a nontoxic sealant on top of the liner all around the perimeter of the flange. Put the flange on the disk, aligning the holes, and secure them with

stainless steel screws (usually provided), wiping away any excess sealant. Wait at least 24 hours before filling the pond to ensure that the sealant has cured and a skin has formed. Drill a 6 mm (0.25 in) hole in the domed lid of the bottom drain before you start filling, as air may become trapped under the dome, causing it to become dislodged and float to the surface at a later date. Over a period of time, the weight of water can distort the dome cover. To prevent this from happening, you can place "feet" (offcuts of pipe on their side) to support the edge of the dome.

Installing a venturi

The pipe that you laid across the ring beam now protrudes into the cavity of the pond and is covered by the liner. Cut a hole through the liner and solvent-weld a tank connector to the return pipe so that you can install a venturi, which injects air into the water. Once again, use plenty of sealant when fitting the flange and use self-tapping stainless steel screws to secure it firmly.

Fitting a bottom drain in a liner pond

Dome

This flange fits on top of the liner.

Drain casing

2 Apply a generous layer of nontoxic sealant on the underside of the flange. This should stay workable long enough for you to complete all the stages shown in this sequence.

1 Put the flange into position and line up the holes with those in the drain casing. Using a sharp knife, pierce a hole in the center and make four cuts toward the perimeter. This will prevent the liner from tearing beyond the flange.

3 With the flange in position, pierce holes through the liner and secure the flange to the bottom drain casing using the stainless steel screws supplied. The sealant will be squeezed out around the edge – you can clean this up later.

Fitting a venturi

4 cm (1.5 in) pumped return pipe

Venturi, with air tube attached.

Do not glue the venturi to this elbow. Fix it with a self-tapping screw for easy removal should it become clogged with weeds.

Fit and seal this flange to the connector in the same way as the bottom drain shown below.

Completing the surround

With the venturi installed, all that remains is to tuck the liner under your chosen surround. It is a good idea to place some "offcuts" of liner beneath any large rocks or boulders to protect the pond liner from piercing or tears. If the pond is raised out of the ground with bricks, lay the liner over the ring beam and construct the wall with the liner sandwiched between the two rows of bricks. Seal the internal pointing with resin to prevent lime from the cement from leaching into the water. If you intend to use paving slabs, again use offcuts of liner where the slabs are laid and bed them down on cement.

Filling the pond

When you fill the pond, use a flowmeter at the end of the hosepipe. You can rent one of these from your local aquatic center and it simply

4 With the flange firmly fixed, carefully trim off the excess liner around the inside of the opening. Use a sharp blade to create a clean edge.

6 Drill a 6 mm (0.25 in) hole in the dome to release any air trapped beneath it that may cause it to lift off.

7 The ideal gap between the edge of the dome and the pond just allows you to slide your hand underneath like this.

8 A side view of the bottom drain and dome. Note the even gap around the edge.

5 Fit the 4 cm (1.5 in) pipe in the socket in the center of the drain casing and push the dome onto the stem. Do not glue the dome in position in case you need to remove it later to gain access to the pipe.

registers the volume of water on a dial as it flows through. It is important to know the exact volume of the pond because in the future you may need to treat the water to remedy, say, a parasite problem, and precise dosing rates are recommended.

A concrete block pond

A concrete pond gives the greatest degree of flexibility with regard to location and design. These ponds are strong and there will be no unsightly creases, such as you might find in a liner pond. However, they are relatively expensive and time-consuming to install and not a project for an inexperienced, albeit enthusiastic, pond builder, as mistakes can be very costly to rectify. You may decide to use the services of a professional company that will provide you with plans and a detailed estimate. Remember that the pool will be a major building project similar to an extension on your home. If you intend to build it yourself, you must prepare or commission detailed drawings of your proposals and seek professional advice before you even think of getting out your shovel or renting a backhoe.

Building a concrete block pond demands a wide range of skills, including bricklaying, plastering (rendering), plumbing, fiberglassing, and carpentry, as well as a thorough understanding of electricity supply, loading, and

Above: For larger excavations, and where access allows, a backhoe can save time. This 113,500 L (25,000 gal) pond was dug in just four days.

wiring. However, once you appreciate what is required and have a good idea what you want, you could carry out some tasks yourself and call in the professionals when you need them.

The excavation

The excavation work does not require any specific skills, just a lot of hard work – so you can do this part yourself. If you are building a large pond, it is well worth

What you need to build a concrete block pond

To help you plan and budget for your own system, here is a typical shopping list of the materials and equipment you will need to build a pond measuring 3.6 m long, 3 m wide, and 1.2 m deep (approximately 12 × 10 × 4 ft) containing 13,000 L (about 3,000 gal) of water. The list can be adapted to suit a pond of any size.

Quantity	Description
3 days	Renting a backhoe
1	Insurance policy on above
36 m³ (48 yd³)	Spoil/waste removal capacity
2.5 m³ (3.3 yd³)	Ballast for pond base
22 × 25 kg (55 lb)	Bags of cement for pond base
140	Hollow concrete blocks 45 × 23 cm (18 × 9 in)
0.75 m³ (1 yd³)	Ballast to fill blocks and backfill
3 × 25 kg (55 lb)	Bags of cement for above
2 sheets	Steel matting measuring 3.6 m × 2 m × 6 mm (12 × 6.5 ft × 0.25 in)
2	25 cm (10 in) bottom drains
4 m (13 ft)	10 cm (4 in) PVC pipework from drains to filter
4	10 cm (4 in) PVC elbows
2	Venturi returns
0.75 m³ (1 yd³)	Sharp sand to render pond walls
13 × 25 kg (55 lb)	Bags of cement for above
3 kg (6.5 lb)	Glass fibers for render
10 kg (22 lb)	Clear resin
10 kg (22 lb)	Pigment resin
1	Fiberglass biological filter complete with media and pipework
1	Submersible pump to run system
1	30 W ultraviolet (UV) stabilizer

Optional extras

1	Surface skimmer
1	Pump for above
1	Electronic blanketweed controller
1	Underwater light
1	Mechanical filter

considering renting a backhoe. If you have never used one before, it may take you a lot longer to complete the excavation than it would a professional. Furthermore, the do-it-yourself pond builder is generally overenthusiastic and tends to excavate more than is required, which will result in extensive backfilling.

Some rental places offer a price for the equipment and operator, which is well worth considering. Most rental places do not provide any insurance while the equipment is rented, so you must arrange this yourself through your insurance agent. Ask the rental place for details of the make, model, and value of the equipment and insure it for theft and accidental damage; otherwise you could be faced with a huge unexpected bill if it were stolen or damaged.

The bottom drains and pond base

When the excavation is complete, and if you are installing a gravity-fed filter system, this is the time to install the bottom drain or drains. Place them evenly and centrally on the base and run the 10 cm (4 in) pipe to a convenient area where the filter is to be located. Mark out 10 cm (4 in) away from the drain and pipe and dig a

Constructing a concrete pond

Right: Begin digging in a methodical way, digging down to the required finished depth at one end of the area and working back. Where needed, use plywood sheets to retain the soil and prevent the sides from collapsing as you dig out further areas.

Below: Space the bottom drains and pipes equally in the excavation on top of a layer of steel reinforcing mesh.

Backfill the hollow section of the blockwork with steel rods and concrete, ensuring that they are completely filled.

Above: Place concrete blocks on top of the bottom drains to prevent them and the connecting pipes from floating up while the concrete base of the pond is setting.

Right: Begin building the walls using hollow concrete blocks measuring 45 x 23 cm (18 x 9 in) for the straight and slightly curved sections of the pond, and using bricks to create the tight curves.

trench 15 cm (6 in) deep along the entire run. Fill it with concrete to act as a base for the drains and pipe. Lay broken bricks, blocks, or hardcore on the remainder of the pond base, followed by steel matting across the floor area to reinforce the base. The matting consists of 6 mm (0.24 in)-thick steel rods joined together to form a mesh.

Once you are happy that the drain or drains and the pipework are spaced centrally, glue them with solvent cement, which melts the two plastics together. The pipework is standard waste pipe made from PVC. Remember to paint the glue over both surfaces to be joined and twist the pipe in the fitting to ensure that the glue covers the entire surface area.

The next step is to mass-fill the entire base with 23 cm (9 in) of concrete, completely encasing the drains and pipework. This must be carried out in one operation, using a strong 3:1 ballast/cement mix. If you prepare half the base one day and go back to it at a later date, there will be a weak spot at the join, which could fracture in the future. Remember that our sample pond measuring 3.6 x 3 x 1.2 m (12 x 10 x 4 ft) contains 13,000 L (about 3,000 gal) of water weighing approximately 13 metric tons bearing down on the base.

Another option is to employ the services of a cement truck to pump the concrete directly into the excavation. Although relatively expensive, you can be sure of an even mix of concrete that will be laid in a matter of hours.

In the past, pond builders would slope the base into the drains, and although this appears to be a good idea in theory, in practice, solids are drawn to the drain more effectively if the base is level. As the fish are constantly swimming around, they have a tendency to disturb any particles that settle, causing them to be mobile and naturally drawn into the drain.

Aerated bottom drain
Recently, more and more hobbyists have been fitting a bottom drain with an aerated dome, which promotes more efficient water circulation into the drain, thereby improving removal of solids from the pond bottom. It also provides additional aeration when oxygen levels are low during the summer months or if treatments are introduced. The most noticeable feature of this drain is the extra connection in the wall of the sump. This allows the air supply hose to enter the sump independently of the water outlet pipe, thus eliminating the possibility of

Perforated membrane creates a stream of bubbles

Air line valve

3.2 cm (1.25 in) inlet for air line

10 cm (4 in) outlet to filter

Above: *An aerated bottom drain with a separate inlet for an air line to connect to the valve visible beneath the dome.*

Right: *Air pumped through the membrane rises in a stream of bubbles that help to circulate the water into the bottom drain.*

restriction to the water flow and somewhere else for blanketweed to attach. A recess in the perimeter of the dome prevents the membrane from becoming detached when air is injected into it.

Building the walls
When the base is dry, build the wall using either solid or hollow 23 x 45 cm (9 x 18 in) concrete blocks. If you choose hollow blocks, fill the cavities with steel rods and backfill them with poured concrete from the base to the top of the construction.

Fitting venturi returns and a surface skimmer
As you get near to ground level, leave room for at least two 4 cm (1.5 in) pipes to fit through the wall for venturi returns from the filters. If you want to include a surface skimmer, now is the time to fit it into position. Skimmers are particularly useful for removing the leaves and general debris that fall onto the water surface into a

Completing the pond structure

Left: *The walls are complete and the cavities in the hollow blocks have been filled with concrete. Steel rods embedded in these cavities give the walls additional strength. Wait until everything dries out before applying sealant or fiberglass.*

Left: *The surface skimmer cemented in position. An external pump will draw water to a venturi or waterfall.*

Left: *All the internal surfaces of this pond have been lined with fiberglass and finished with a topcoat of black resin sealer creating a durable and attractive finish.*

Right: *A three-bay filter and vortex chamber with isolating valves.*

Above: *The aerated drain is placed so that the bubbles are visible through the window in the side of the pond facing the house.*

Right: *The basic construction is finished and the pond has been filled with water and is being tested for leaks. This is a vital stage before any fish are added.*

collection basket. The pipework from the skimmer is connected to the suck-side of a separate submersible or external pump. As the water flows into the mouth of the skimmer, the floating debris is trapped in a mesh collection basket. The return water from the skimmer can be run to another venturi, a waterfall, or an ornamental water feature.

An additional feature of a skimmer is that you can vacuum the pond by placing a cornea over the skimmer basket. This is a see-through, contact lens-shaped fitting with a 4 cm (1.5 in) thread in the center. Screw a universal hosetail into the female thread, then simply attach a flexible pipe to the cornea and the other end to the vacuum head, which is fixed to a telescopic pole to enable you to reach the bottom of the pond. Using this device, all the waste gathered by the vacuum head will be collected in the skimmer basket.

At this stage, you can also consider installing an underwater light into the wall of the pond. The best types are those commonly installed in swimming pools and jacuzzis. You can choose between small stainless steel fittings or a larger bowl-shaped unit secured in its own housing and connected to an umbilical cord. This in turn fits into an external deck box and a transformer before being plugged into the main electrical supply. Should the

bulb need changing, release the two locking screws on the outer casing, pull the bulb above water level, and change the fitting attached to the umbilical cord. Put the cord back into the casing, line up the bulb with the screws, and secure.

Completing the construction

Once the shell has been constructed, fill the void between the walls and excavation with a wet concrete mix to ensure that the soil does not subside onto the blockwork. When this stage is complete, you will have to decide how to waterproof the structure. Fiberglass is probably the best option, but it is expensive and should be installed only by a competent person. Two layers of 350-gm matting are applied to the walls and floor of the pond in sheets and a special gel coat is added to make them adhere to the cement. A tissue mat is then laid over the previous two coats to give the pond a smoother finish. When dry, all the surfaces are painted with the color of your choice.

Another popular option is to render the structure twice, incorporating fiberglass strands in the first sand/cement mix. This means that the cement content can be proportionately increased. This, in turn, will reduce the porosity of the mortar and increase its

How a surface skimmer works

This outlet can be plumbed into a sump to act as an overflow.

Water is drawn through the skimmer by an external pump and can be returned to the pond via a waterfall.

The mouth of the skimmer has a self-balancing, flap-type weir that skims the top layer of water.

Place a barrier in front of the mouth to prevent koi from swimming in and becoming trapped.

This removable strainer basket catches leaves and other floating debris.

Valves used in koi ponds

With a rectangular pond measuring 3.6 m long, 3 m wide, and 1.2 m deep (approximately 12 × 10 × 4 ft) calculate the total surface area to be covered, namely four walls and the floor, as follows:-

Wall 1:	3 × 1.2 m	(10 × 4 ft)	= 3.6 m² (40 ft²)
Wall 2:	3 × 1.2 m	(10 × 4 ft)	= 3.6 m² (40 ft²)
Wall 3:	3.6 × 1.2 m	(12 × 4 ft)	= 4.3 m² (48 ft²)
Wall 4:	3.6 × 1.2 m	(12 × 4 ft)	= 4.3 m² (48 ft²)
Floor:	3.6 × 3 m	(12 × 10 ft)	= 10.8 m² (120 ft²)

Total surface area:	26.6 m² (296 ft²)

1 kg (2.2 lb) of clear resin sealer covers about 1.8 m² (20 ft²) with three coats, so dividing 26.6 by 1.8 (296 by 20) shows that you will need about 15 kg (33 lb) of sealer for three coats, or 5 kg (11 lb) per coat. For a color finish, apply two coats of clear and two coats of pigmented sealer. Thus you will need 10 kg (22 lb) each of clear and pigmented sealer.

Gate valves, such as this 4 cm (1.5 in) brass one, provide precise control. This one is ideal for regulating the flow on fluidized bed filter systems.

5 cm (2 in) slide valves such as this would be used in pipework that provides a winter bypass and for closing off flow to waterfalls.

10 cm (4 in) slide valves such as this would be used in the main pipework runs of gravity-fed filter systems, such as isolating vortex units.

strength. When dry, apply a second sand/cement coat to cover the protruding fibers. When the rendering has cured, paint all the internal surfaces with at least three coats of a resin sealer. This is a moisture-cured, one-component polyurethane that forms a nonporous, tough, durable, but flexible seal designed for porous substrates such as cement. If you prefer a color finish, such as black or dark green, apply two coats of clear resin sealer, using rollers on the floor and walls and brushes to cut in around the edges, followed by two coats of pigmented resin sealer. Do not allow the resin to dry between coats, as any subsequent applications will not adhere correctly. Resin sealing can easily be undertaken by the DIY pond builder. The pond will be ready to fill after 48 hours. Remember to use a flowmeter so that you can record the pond capacity.

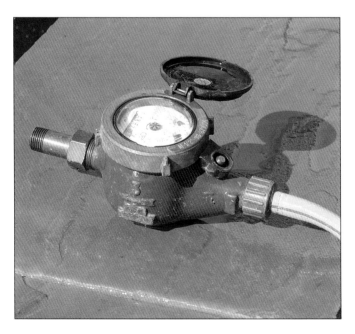

Left: *Fill the completed pond using a flowmeter attached to a hosepipe. Close the slide valve to the filter, fill the pond, and note the volume. Then fill the filter system and record its capacity. Add the two figures for the total volume. It is useful to know the pond volume in case you need to treat the pond with a medication and isolate the filter.*

The completed pond

This picture reveals how the filtration system and its associated pumps, valves, and pipework connect and function in the finished pond.

Two bottom drains connected to 10 cm (4 in) pipework draw water by gravity to the multichamber filter system.

One of two venturi returns that boost oxygen level and create currents. They point away from the skimmer.

The surface skimmer strains out any floating debris.

A window in the side wall of the pond provides a view of the koi from the house.

Autofill unit beneath the bridge introduces water through a pipe below the surface.

2.5 cm (1 in) brass gate valve to control water flow from the water supply.

2.5 cm (1 in) pipe takes water to an autofill unit located under the bridge.

As the plants grow and mature, they will soften the stark edges of the newly finished hard landscaping.

Multichamber filter system

These 10 cm (4 in) slide valves are normally closed. When opened (and the others closed) pond water can be flushed directly to waste via the bottom drains.

Standpipe chamber with four 5 cm (2 in) standpipes connected to the three filter chambers and the vortex. Removing each one allows that particular chamber to be flushed to waste.

Third filter chamber with porous ceramic media for biological filtration and "polishing." A submersible pump in this chamber returns water to the pond via a venturi.

Second filter chamber, with plastic honeycomb for biological action.

First filter chamber, with brushes to strain out solids.

When open, this 10 cm (4 in) slide valve directs water from one of the bottom drains to the first filter chamber.

Normally open, these two 10 cm (4 in) slide valves can be closed to isolate the vortex chamber when flushing it out.

Vortex chamber in which large particles settle out.

External pump draws water from the pond via the surface skimmer.

UV sterilizer helps to control green water.

5 cm (2 in) pumped return via venturi

5 cm (2 in) slide valve

Fluidized bed provides extra biological filtration.

5 cm (2 in) gravity winter return

4 cm (1.5 in) brass gate valve

One-way flap valve

5 cm (2 in) gravity return via stream

Physiology and health care

In order to understand how best to keep koi, it is necessary to become acquainted with some basic anatomy and physiology. It is only by learning how healthy koi function that we can understand what happens when they become sick, which in turn will help to us to implement an appropriate treatment.

Living in water

Life in the aquatic environment is presented with a completely different set of conditions from those experienced by animals living on land. Water is denser than air and more energy is needed to move through it, so a koi's body is elegantly streamlined to reduce drag. In addition to streamlining, koi conserve energy in the way they swim. The body musculature literally pulls the tail from side to side and it is the tail that provides the

Above: As the koi moves forward, the erect dorsal and anal fins prevent it from rolling from side to side with each movement of the tail. The erect pectoral and pelvic fins help to prevent pitching and are used to steer. The pectoral fins also control fine movements.

propulsive force that moves the fish forward. Because the water is forced in a stream behind, it creates minute vortices that act together to push the fish forward. The fins act as stabilizers, preventing pitching, rolling, and yawing. However, the pectoral fins have a further important function in controlling fine movements at slow speed.

For land animals, breathing air to extract oxygen requires very little effort, but the density of water means that koi use up a large amount of energy to perform the same function. It has been estimated that about 10 percent of the oxygen they extract from the water is required just to pump water across the gills. The intimate contact between the gills and water presents yet further problems of osmotic and ion regulation (see page 78).

In addition to the physical demands of the aquatic environment, microbes such as bacteria thrive in water and while most are harmless, a limited number are pathogenic, or disease-causing. In this section we not only examine how koi defend themselves against such pathogens, but also look at their anatomy and physiology. We then consider possible health problems in more detail and how koi keepers can recognize and treat them.

Skin and scales

One of the most characteristic features of any fish is the presence of mucus over the body surface, which makes it feel slimy to the touch. The mucus is not a living tissue but is secreted by the skin and acts as a lubricant as the fish moves through the water, so it is continually sloughed off and replaced. The second function of the mucus is to act as a primary barrier to microbes, including bacteria, viruses, fungi, and parasites. It succeeds in this role, not only because it is continually shed (and with it the microbes), but also because it contains natural antibodies, lysozymes, and bacteriolysins (enzymes and chemicals that literally dissolve bacterial cells). Mucus also plays a role in the release of pheromones and odors.

Koi skin consists of two layers. The outermost layer – the epidermis – is a very fine, delicate tissue that lies on the outside of the scales. The fact that you can feel the scales of a koi beneath the epidermis indicates just how

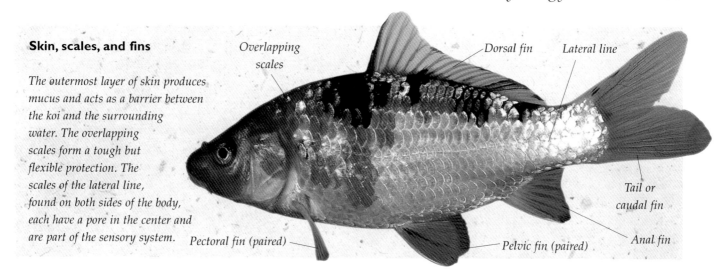

Skin, scales, and fins

The outermost layer of skin produces mucus and acts as a barrier between the koi and the surrounding water. The overlapping scales form a tough but flexible protection. The scales of the lateral line, found on both sides of the body, each have a pore in the center and are part of the sensory system.

Overlapping scales

Dorsal fin — *Lateral line*

Tail or caudal fin

Anal fin

Pectoral fin (paired) — — *Pelvic fin (paired)*

fine it is. This layer of living cells forms a barrier between koi and their environment and is responsible for secreting the mucus. The cells of the epidermis multiply on a continuous basis to replace older cells at the surface and repair any injury.

The second layer of skin is called the dermis and contains blood vessels, nerves, connective tissue, certain sense organs, and chromatophores – pigmented cells that give rise to the color patterns. The scales are formed in this layer of skin and if one is lost, a new one is produced by the cells of the dermis. Koi scales are described as cycloid and consist of a fibrous layer, or fibrillary plate, impregnated with calcium phosphate and calcium carbonate. With the exception of Doitsu fish, the scales overlap each other rather like roof tiles and provide a flexible, bony protection on the outside of the fish. They are more or less uniform in appearance and shape, apart from those that make up the lateral line.

The lateral line

All fish have a sensory system known as the "lateral line," a series of scales along each flank with an opening, or pore, visible as a row of dots. The pores open into a canal that runs along the flanks just beneath the scales. Positioned along the inside of each canal are a number of hair cells connected to nerve fibers that relay their impulses to the spinal cord and then to the brain. Any movement of water within the lateral line canals disturbs the hair cells and enables the koi to detect vibrations in the water, which may be reflected off other fish, obstacles, or even people's footsteps as they approach the pond. In fact, koi can distinguish between the footsteps of their owner and those of a visitor.

Muscles

Three basic types of muscle are found in all vertebrates: One is smooth muscle, found in the walls of arteries and larger veins and in the gut, where it is responsible for the movement of food; another is cardiac, or heart, muscle; and the third is striated, or striped, muscle. Striated muscle is associated with movement and is attached to the skeleton by gristly tendons. In fish it is formed into a series of W-shaped blocks called myotomes that encircle the body and provide the thrust for movement.

The skeleton

Overall, fish have far more bones than other vertebrates. For example, there are 28 bones in the human skull, but over three times as many in a koi skull. The skeleton is a complex structure with two main functions. The first is to provide support, forming a rigid structure for muscles to attach to, either directly to bone or via cartilage. The action of bone and muscle allows movement to take place. Second, it provides protection for delicate and sensitive tissues and organs, which are surrounded by bone. For example, the skull encases the brain and eyes.

The main skeletal elements are the skull, vertebral column (the backbone), pectoral and pelvic girdles, the numerous bones associated with the unpaired fins – dorsal, anal, and caudal (tail) fins – and finally the ribs, forming the lateral walls of the abdomen.

The digestive system

Instead of teeth in the jaws, koi have paired pharyngeal bones inset with a number of large, molarlike teeth and located just behind the gill arches. The pharyngeal teeth grind food against a cartilaginous pad at the base of the

Internal anatomy

The gills are the site of gas diffusion. Carbon dioxide is released into the water and oxygen is collected by red blood cells. Ammonia is shed by the gill tissue. Essential salts are absorbed by the gills. Water enters the body through the gills.

Sound waves in the water are detected by the swimbladder and amplified by a series of modified backbones, linking them to the inner ear of the koi, enabling it to hear.

The paired kidneys conserve salts in the body and produce vast amounts of very dilute urine to remove water and maintain an osmotic balance in the body.

The swimbladder is a gas-filled buoyancy organ that allows the koi to remain at any depth in the water using the minimum amount of energy. The gas inside is mostly oxygen, as this is taken from the blood supply. When the koi wants to reach the pond surface to feed, gas is added to the swimbladder. When swimming to the bottom, gas is removed.

Backbone

Koi have very good eyesight.

Brain

Barbels (two pairs)

The three-chambered heart (atrium, ventricle, and sinus venosus) pumps deoxygenated blood to the gills. The muscular section of the heart, the ventricle, receives oxygen-rich blood from the coronary artery.

Food is digested in the intestine through the action of enzymes and absorbed by the rich blood supply. Remaining solid waste is voided as feces.

The spleen stores immature red blood cells and produces cells of the immune system.

The vent describes the area of the body where the intestine opens at the anus and where urine from the kidneys is released and eggs or sperm (milt) are shed into the water through the urogenital opening.

The gonads, or reproductive organs, are situated on either side of the body. The ovaries produce eggs and can be very large. The testes produce sperm (milt).

In koi, the liver is a very large organ. All food digested in the intestine passes to the liver for storage or distribution to the tissues. The liver breaks down unwanted proteins into ammonia, processes damaged or old red blood cells to form bile, and breaks down any poisons or toxins.

skull. Koi do not have a stomach; the esophagus simply grades into the intestine. Food is digested in the intestine and absorbed through the lining before being transported by the blood to the liver. In koi, the liver is a large organ with a number of functions, but it is the main processing plant for all food and it is here ,that the components are further refined and sorted before being distributed to the tissues or stored. The liver also receives all the waste products from the tissues, breaking down damaged blood cells to produce bile, and unwanted proteins into ammonia. Any toxic substance accidentally ingested is also broken down by the liver.

Water and salt regulation

In fish, water and salt regulation – also known as osmoregulation – is a very important physiological process. The body fluids and cells of koi contain water and salts in specific amounts and it is important to maintain these concentrations on a continuous basis. The principal salts are sodium, potassium, calcium, magnesium, chloride, and sulphate. The body actually contains more salts than the surrounding water and the problem is that water readily enters the fish through osmosis. (Osmosis describes the movement of water from a weaker solution into a more concentrated one through a

Freshwater osmoregulation

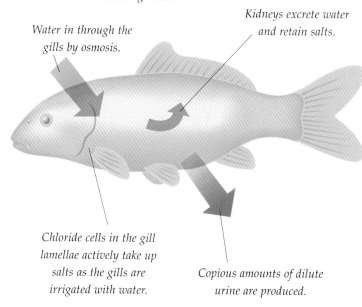

Water enters the koi's body by osmosis from the relatively dilute freshwater.

Salts readily pass out by diffusion.

The tissues and fluids inside the koi's body contain more salts than the surrounding water.

Water in through the gills by osmosis.

Kidneys excrete water and retain salts.

Chloride cells in the gill lamellae actively take up salts as the gills are irrigated with water.

Copious amounts of dilute urine are produced.

partially permeable membrane.) The surrounding water represents the weaker solution, the skin and gill tissues of the koi are partially permeable membranes, and the salt content of the blood and other body fluids represents the concentrated solution. This means that there is a tendency for water to enter the koi's body continually, primarily through the gill tissue, and for salts inside the body to leach into the surrounding water by diffusion. (This situation is helped to a certain extent by special cells on the gills called chloride cells that actively extract salts from the surrounding water.) Koi are able to overcome this problem because their kidneys extract

and retain salt from the blood, while removing excess water by producing copious amounts of dilute urine. Because water freely enters the body, koi do not need to drink.

There is also a compromise between the amount of gill tissue that the fish must "expose" in order to respire efficiently and the "danger" of exposing too much, thus allowing water to enter the body too freely. Forced exercise, such as that caused by continuously netting the pond, can cause a koi to absorb so much water that its body swells into a state of dropsy (see page 91), simply because it is using such a vast area of gill tissue to respire and letting in water during the process.

Gill structure and function

The gills are the principal organ of respiration and are of necessity very delicate, since they allow oxygen to pass from the water through the tissue and into the blood, and waste carbon dioxide gas to be released. Koi are remarkably efficient at extracting oxygen from water. The gill filaments, or primary lamellae, have a large surface area that is extended by outfolds of tissue, known as the secondary lamellae. The blood is in intimate contact with the water at the gills, the two being separated by a single layer of epithelial cells. In order to extract the maximum amount of oxygen from the water, the blood flow through the gills is in the opposite direction to the water flow, a so-called countercurrent system. Finally, as the blood cells pass through the secondary lamellae, they are literally stretched to increase the surface area and allow the maximum amount of oxygen to be transferred to the red respiratory protein hemoglobin.

The gills are an important site for excreting nitrogenous waste, with 82 percent being eliminated as ammonia and 8 percent as urea. The remaining 10 percent is excreted by the kidneys as urea in the form of dilute urine.

The fact that blood is in such intimate contact with the water at the gills means that it is either cooled or warmed, depending on the ambient water temperature. The oxygenated blood flow leaving the gills is divided into two branches, one to the brain and the other to the body tissues via the dorsal aorta, a large artery that runs beneath the vertebral column and therefore along the center line of the body.

The swimbladder

The swimbladder is a gas-filled sac that lies at the top of the body cavity, just beneath the vertebral column. In koi, the swimbladder is a two-chambered structure, with the posterior kidneys lying astride the constriction between the chambers. The primary function of the swimbladder is to control buoyancy and allow koi to remain at any depth in the water using the minimum amount of energy. In koi, the swimbladder primitively retains a connection to the gut and, indeed, the fish can top off the gas content of this organ by gulping air at the water surface. More usually, the gas content of the swimbladder is controlled by a number of blood vessels.

In koi (as in many other fish), the swimbladder fulfills a secondary role in amplifying sound and transmitting it to the inner ear via a series of small bones.

Health care

Keeping koi is a rewarding and enjoyable hobby, but whenever large numbers of animals are held in a captive environment, there are occasions when one or more becomes sick. It is very common to encounter outbreaks of disease as a consequence of poor water conditions and stress. Good pond management means testing the water regularly, ensuring that the pond and filters are free of organic detritus, observing the koi, watching and learning their normal behavior patterns, and offering a good-quality feed (see pages 102-107). In the event of any fish becoming sick, or even dying, it is important to determine the cause in order to effect an appropriate course of action.

In the event of any health problem, your immediate course of action should be to test all water quality parameters, if only to eliminate them as the cause of the problem, and to add supplementary aeration, providing symptoms of gas bubble disease are not indicated (see page 81). Increasing the aeration has two effects. The first is to make more oxygen available to the koi, which is important if they are stressed. Second, as the air passes through the water, it collects any volatile contaminants such as free ammonia. These are released into the atmosphere as the bubble bursts at the water surface.

When searching for the underlying cause of a health problem, look for a pattern in the

Koi herpes virus (KHV)

Recently a viral disease identified as Koi Herpes Virus (KHV) has been implicated as the cause of koi deaths. Contributing factors are stress caused by importation, transportation, or poor management, involving overstocking, low oxygen, or pollution with ammonia and nitrite.

Many diseases produce symptoms similar to those of KHV, but usually there is sloughing of the skin, accompanied by erosion of the gills and mortalities. The only way to identify the disease is by submitting samples of koi tissues from suspected infections for virology and histopathology. Koi will mount an immune response to KHV and can recover, but can suffer recurring bouts of infection. The genetic material of herpes viruses becomes integrated into the genetic material of the cell that it infects, so that under stress, the virus can become active and reproduce. Koi infected with KHV are infected for life, so they can become infective and spread the disease months and even years after the initial infection. As there is no cure for a viral infection, isolate all new koi before introducing them to the main pond.

numbers of koi affected. For example, if large numbers of fish of mixed sizes are affected, this may be an indication that there is a water quality problem, most commonly because of high levels of ammonia or nitrite, or low levels of dissolved oxygen. Outbreaks of infectious disease, such as those caused by parasites, bacteria, or viruses, tend to affect only a few koi initially, but the numbers increase steadily over a period of time.

Where only a single koi is affected and the problem does not appear to be spreading to any others in the pond, physical injury is the most likely cause. Most injuries to koi are incurred through poor or repeated netting and handling, so avoid routinely catching the fish in order to examine them. Not only do you risk injuring the koi,

Left: Stress is a contributing factor in outbreaks of koi herpes virus (KHV). Transportation is very stressful and can lead to the koi becoming vulnerable to infection.

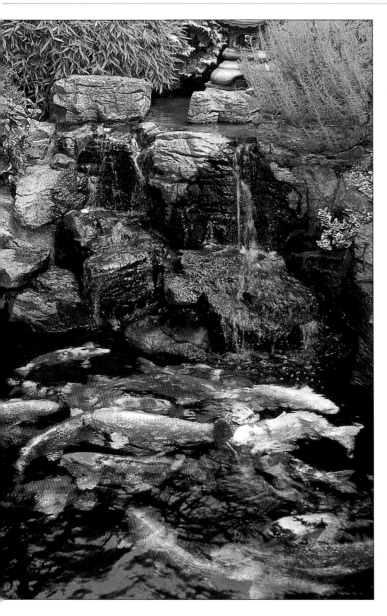

Above: If the dissolved oxygen level in the water begins to drop, the koi will become lethargic and stop feeding. At critically low levels, they will move to the aerated area of the pond and will be seen gasping at the surface. At this stage, extra aeration is vital.

but they will also be continuously stressed and subject to opportunist infections (see page 93).

There are situations where it becomes necessary to treat either an individual koi or even the entire population, but if in doubt, it is sensible to consult someone with experience in fish health matters, such as your koi dealer or a veterinarian.

Environmentally related disease

Poor water quality is the biggest cause of disease and mortalities in the pond and, unless the environmental conditions are improved through partial water changes, the koi are unlikely to recover. Exposure to poor water quality over a period of days to weeks causes koi to become increasingly stressed and subject to secondary disease and infections.

Dissolved oxygen

Oxygen is an essential requirement for koi, and in summer, when this vital gas is at a premium due to higher water temperatures, it can drop to critically low levels (see page 24). The minimum requirement for healthy growth, tissue repair, and reproduction is 6 mg of dissolved oxygen per L of water. Although koi will tolerate a drop to 3 mg per L for a short period of time, this does cause considerable stress.

In a koi pond, it is quite common during the summer months to find that the water has a consistently low dissolved oxygen level, which causes koi to become lethargic and cease feeding. It is frequently assumed that koi will come to the water surface and gasp if the oxygen level is low, but this really is a last resort. Fish gasping at the surface means that the situation is extremely critical and you must implement massive aeration immediately.

As we have seen on page 26, it is not only fish that use up the oxygen in the water, but also plants, algae, and bacteria. When the oxygen level crashes overnight, it is common to find the largest or most active koi dead in the morning and others breathing heavily at the water surface, even though they previously appeared to be in good health. Regardless of whether the oxygen level has been at a continuously low level or drops rapidly overnight as a consequence of algae or submerged plant growth, the koi will become stressed.

Gas bubble disease

In winter, when air is readily soluble in water, you may encounter gas bubble disease. The physiological effects of this condition closely match nitrogen narcosis, or the "bends" suffered by deep-sea divers, and, indeed, the affected koi suffer cramplike spasms of the lateral musculature of the body. Basically, the water becomes supersaturated with air, which means in effect that the air is in solution in the water. Air is primarily composed of nitrogen gas, which under conditions of air supersaturation means that the water is saturated with dissolved nitrogen and a small amount of other gases. It is the dissolved nitrogen content of the water that causes the symptoms of gas bubble disease, hence the similarity to nitrogen narcosis. As the koi breathes the water supersaturated with air, the dissolved nitrogen readily enters through the gills and into solution in the blood. Once inside the blood circulatory system, the changes in blood pressure allow the nitrogen to come out of solution as a gas, creating air bubbles in the blood flow, called air embolisms. These collect in the filaments of the fins and sometimes around the eyes, between the bony rays, the gill tissue, and membranes lining the mouth. Occasionally, air may become trapped between the epidermis and dermis, and when the pressure becomes too great, it simply lifts the entire outer layer of skin.

In most instances, once the problem has been diagnosed and remedied, the affected koi gradually recover without further treatment. You can deal with water affected by supersaturation of air by splashing it vigorously, say by pumping it against the wall of the pond or a solid object temporarily placed in the pond. The splashing action increases the water surface area, allowing the excess dissolved air to escape back into the atmosphere.

The effects of ammonia poisoning

When ammonia concentrations begin to increase in the water, the initial response of koi is to produce more mucus on the body surface and gills. If the ammonia level in the water continues to increase, the cells of the gills begin to swell and then proliferate, giving rise to a condition called lamellar hyperplasia. In the early stages, the tips of the gills are affected and the condition is often called clubbed gills. If the exposure to ammonia persists, whole areas of the gill filaments can become fused together. This causes the koi respiratory distress, osmoregulatory failure, and dropsy.

Where the water is free of any ammonia pollution, koi can readily shed ammonia from the body at the gills. Whatever the concentration of ammonia recorded in the water, the koi has the same amount in its body and

Left: When adding salt to the pond, it is best to dissolve it first in a bucket of water, rather than to add large volumes of salt crystals to the pond, which could burn delicate koi skin.

tissues. Where the water quality has deteriorated and become polluted with ammonia, the koi can only excrete ammonia in excess of the concentration found in the water. An accumulation of ammonia alters the pH of the blood, reducing the fish's ability to absorb oxygen from the water and utilize nutrients effectively, and reduces growth rates.

The toxicity of ammonia can be reduced by adding cooking salt (sodium chloride) or pond or aquarium salt (sodium chloride packaged for the aquatic trade) to the pond water. This converts free ammonia to the ionized form, which is less harmful. It is important to understand that the concentration of ammonia in the pond water must be reduced through regular, partial water changes. The volume and frequency of the water changes needed depend on the amount of pollutant present. Certain mineral substances, such as zeolite and ion-exchange resins, can be used to reduce ammonia levels by adsorbing the ionized form (see also pages 29-30).

Left: The normal structure of the gills is very delicate and the tiny, fingerlike lamellae that allow the blood to come into intimate contact with the water can be clearly seen here.

Left: Exposure to ammonia causes the structure of the gills to break down. The cells proliferate, causing the lamellae to become short and thickened – a condition known as lamellar hyperplasia.

The effects of nitrite poisoning

Nitrite is the secondary breakdown product of ammonia via the nitrogen cycle (see page 30) and is also poisonous to koi. Because nitrite is a skin irritant, it causes koi to rub and flick repeatedly on hard surfaces. This behavior may be mistaken for a parasite infection and treated inappropriately. Nitrite poisoning may also be called "brown blood disease," as nitrite binds with the hemoglobin in the red blood cells to form methemoglobin, which prevents oxygen from being absorbed and gives the blood a dark brown appearance instead of the characteristic red color. Nitrite is a potent relaxant of smooth muscle and a vasodilator (it causes the blood vessels to expand) and these effects can lead to failure of the heart and blood vascular system. Finally, there is evidence that nitrite acts as an immuno-suppressant (reduces the effectiveness of the immune system), and chronic exposure can lead to secondary infections, such as bacterial gill disease.

The effect of temperature on koi

Generally speaking, adult koi are tolerant of temperatures in the range 3°-25°C (37°-77°F), although as carp originated in southern Europe, the preferred temperatures are probably between 15° and 22°C (59°-72°F). In recent years, there has been a trend in Japan to overwinter koi in their first and second years in fish houses, where the water temperature is maintained at a minimum of 16°C (61°F) and more usually at 18°C (64°F). This means that juvenile koi are very sensitive to low temperatures and will develop symptoms of thermal stress when water temperatures drop below about 14°C (57°F). When exposed to low temperatures, young koi become lethargic and often lie on their sides, but will swim away if disturbed. Usually the integrity of the skin is affected, rendering the fish susceptible to fungal infections. Providing young koi are introduced into the pond during the summer months in temperate regions, they should adapt to the gradual fall in temperature as fall progresses.

The immune system of koi is influenced by water temperature and is most effective in the warmer summer months. This is followed by a gradual decline in efficiency through the fall and early winter and is largely ineffective during the coldest months. Traditionally, spring is regarded as the most difficult time for koi and this is probably because the fish are largely immunosuppressed, while the moderate increase in temperatures at this time of the year promotes the activity of parasites and other pathogens. The immune system is also affected by the nutritional status of koi and, given that they are largely unfed through the winter, this can also have a further impact in the spring months.

Koi will usually tolerate a rapid drop in temperature more readily than a rapid rise, although water temperatures may fluctuate by as much as 10°C (18°F) during a 24-hour period. Temperature increases can

Above: At temperatures of 18°C (64°F) and above, the immune system of young koi will be at its most responsive to invading parasites and bacteria. Once the water temperature drops below 10°C (50°F), the immune system is not particularly effective.

Taking and testing a mucus sample

1 Below: Holding the koi firmly, and using a small spatula or other blunt tool, gently run it against the body, moving in the direction of the scales, from the head toward the tail.

2 Above: With the slide close at hand, place the mucus sample in the middle of the slide, together with a small drop of pond water.

3 Left: Place the glass cover slip gently on the mucus sample, allowing it to spread over the slide and form a thin, almost transparent layer.

4 Right: Examine the mucus sample under the microscope. Start at low power and move the slide across, up, and across again to search for possible parasites.

lower the dissolved oxygen levels in the pond (see page 24), but the immune system of the fish takes time to catch up with any rise in temperature. However, many parasites and bacteria can take advantage of the warmer conditions, and thrive.

Parasites

A range of common parasites can infect koi. In order to resolve this type of problem, it is important to make an accurate diagnosis, as the presence of some species indicates that the hygiene and management of the pond need improving. Many of the parasites that infect koi cannot be seen with the naked eye and you will need a microscope to identify them. However, if you are a novice koi keeper you should seek the advice of your retailer or other professional, such as a veterinarian. You need some experience to determine the point at which

any parasite infection should be treated. If the infection is so low-key, for example, that it means searching through a mucus sample to find any parasites at all, then no treatment is required. It is perfectly normal for koi to have a limited number of common parasites associated with them. If large numbers of parasites are immediately apparent when a mucus scrape is viewed through the microscope, then it may be necessary to treat the fish, as well as attending to the management and husbandry of the pond. The parasites described here are those that commonly affect koi.

Microscopic parasites – protozoa

Most protozoa are free-living creatures, but a few species are parasitic on fish.

Costia (*Ichthyobodo necator*) is perhaps the smallest skin parasite of koi, being roughly the same size as a red

Above: Ichthyobodo necator, *or* costia, *causes intense irritation as it feeds on the skin. Infected koi may have a gray bloom due to the excess mucus produced as a response to the feeding* costia, *and a stressed "bloodshot" appearance.*

Below: A mucus sample showing many Chilodonella *parasites.* Chilodonella *tends to infect koi at lower temperatures and damages the skin as it feeds. Infected koi rub, flick, and jump in response to the irritation caused by this parasite.*

blood cell. Costia is bean- or comma-shaped, with two hairlike flagellae of unequal length that enable the parasite to swim. It survives in a range of temperatures between 2° and 30°C (35°-86°F), but prefers the cooler part of that range. Costia feeds by puncturing the cells of the skin and gills and sucking out the content. In large numbers they can cause considerable damage, weakening koi and allowing secondary infections of bacteria and fungi to take hold. The irritation caused by costia feeding may cause koi to increase the amount of mucus on the body, giving it a gray appearance. Stressed koi tend to be particularly prone to infection with costia.

Chilodonella piscicola is a heart-shaped parasite that infects freshwater fish, but is very tolerant of brackish water and therefore does not respond to treatment with salt (sodium chloride). It thrives at water temperatures of 5°-10°C (40°-50°F). In common with costia, chilodonella feeds by puncturing the skin cells and sucking out the content, which may lead to skin lesions, secondary infections, and compromise osmoregulation.

White spot *(Ichthyophthirius multifiliis)* parasites cause infected koi to break out in white spots, hence the common name. This parasite probably kills more captive fish worldwide than any other true fish disease. The

visible white spots are the mature stage of the parasite, and actually located beneath the epidermis. The mature white spot parasite ruptures its way through the delicate epidermis, leaving the skin literally peppered with tiny puncture wounds. In heavy infections, this entire layer of skin sloughs off. The wounds created by white spot parasites make it difficult for koi to regulate their water and salt balance and leave them vulnerable to infection by opportunist bacteria and fungi.

Once mature white spot parasites have left their fish host, they undergo a free-living stage, during which they reproduce and produce up to 2,000 infective swarmers that actively seek a fish to infect. At a temperature of 20°C (68°F), this life cycle takes seven days to complete. As the water cools, the cycle takes longer. The occurrence of white spot disease is generally stress related, and treatment should be started as quickly as possible. Medications kill only the free-living stages of the parasite, so it is important to control it before it develops into a full-blown infection.

Trichodina is probably the most readily recognized "parasite" found on koi, as it has a supporting ring of calcified teeth, or denticles. Strictly speaking, *Trichodina* is not a parasite, as it does not feed on the tissues of koi, but on the bacteria, skin cells, and organic detritus that become trapped in the mucus layer. A heavy infestation suggests a husbandry problem and although a treatment may be necessary to control the infection, the remedy lies in clearing the filters and pipework, where *Trichodina*

Above: *A common carp with a heavy infection of white spot disease, even visible on the eye. The larger parasites are mature and ready to rupture. The fish is sloughing mucus in response to the white spot.*

Above: *White spot disease also infects the gill tissue. Here an individual is surrounded by the delicate epithelium. The lesions created as the white spot ruptures out of the skin of the gill tissue reduce oxygen uptake and affect osmoregulation.*

White spot life cycle

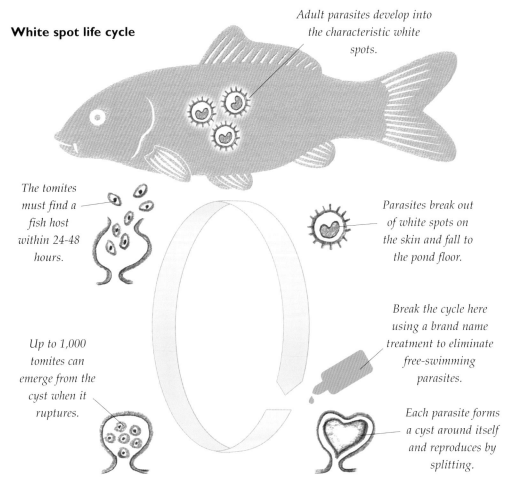

Adult parasites develop into the characteristic white spots.

The tomites must find a fish host within 24-48 hours.

Parasites break out of white spots on the skin and fall to the pond floor.

Up to 1,000 tomites can emerge from the cyst when it ruptures.

Break the cycle here using a brand name treatment to eliminate free-swimming parasites.

Each parasite forms a cyst around itself and reproduces by splitting.

Above: The gill flukes attach themselves to the tissue with hooks on the "foot," or haptor, and stretch out among the gill filaments to browse in the mucus.

Above: The characteristic appearance of Trichodina *with its inner ring of calcified teeth that support the structure of the parasite. The tiny hairs that* Trichodina *uses to move around are just visible around the outermost edge.*

Gill fluke life cycle

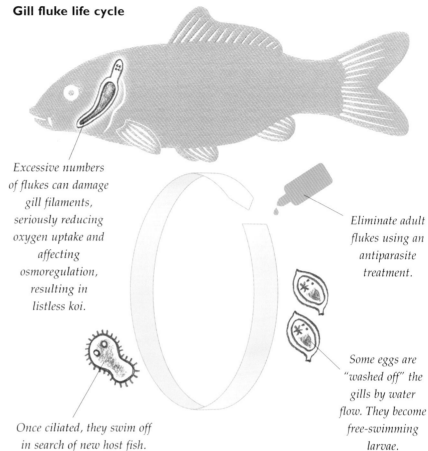

Excessive numbers of flukes can damage gill filaments, seriously reducing oxygen uptake and affecting osmoregulation, resulting in listless koi.

Eliminate adult flukes using an antiparasite treatment.

Some eggs are "washed off" the gills by water flow. They become free-swimming larvae.

Once ciliated, they swim off in search of new host fish.

can exist in trapped organic material. The presence of large numbers of *Trichodina* irritates affected koi, which respond by producing more mucus, thus trapping more particles on which the "parasites" can feed and thrive. It is quite common to find recently imported koi suffering from *Trichodina*. The reason for this is that salt is commonly used by shippers and retailers to ameliorate the effects of stress and this causes the koi to produce more mucus, which in turn traps food particles for *Trichodina* to feed on.

Flukes

Two main categories of fluke are associated with koi: skin and gill flukes. Heavy infestations of either indicate husbandry problems such as poor water conditions, including excessive amounts of organic material and low dissolved oxygen levels, or overcrowding in the pond. Flukes feed on the delicate epidermis of the skin and gills, causing irritation and excessive mucus production. For this reason, severe infestations of skin fluke are often called "gray slime disease." The rear ends of both gill and skin flukes are equipped with a pair of large hooks, like grappling hooks, plus a rim of tiny hooks. The hooks cause considerable damage to the skin and gills as the parasites move around and anchor themselves to feed. It is possible for flukes to transmit bacterial infections as they feed. Heavy infestations (in excess of 30 individuals in a single mucus sample) should be regarded as serious.

Gill flukes (*Dactylogyrus* sp.) are characterized by the presence of four tiny eyespots at the head end. Adult flukes attach to the gill tissue and reproduce by laying eggs, which are shed into the water as the gills are irrigated during respiration. The speed with which the eggs hatch depends on the water temperature, but the larval fluke is very active and quickly seeks a koi host to invade. It is quite common to find these larval flukes close to the operculum on the body of the fish. Heavy infestations of gill fluke cause the tips of the gill tissue to grow into trunklike appendages.

Skin flukes (*Gyrodactylus* sp.) are usually found on the body and differ from gill flukes in that they have no eyes and give birth to live young.

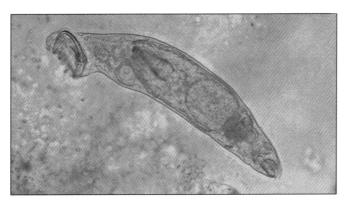

Above: The skin fluke gives birth to live young and here the "baby" can be seen in the central part of the body. Usually, large numbers are present feeding on the koi, which responds by producing more mucus, giving a bloom to the appearance, commonly termed "gray slime disease."

Large, visible parasites

The most commonly encountered clearly visible parasites of koi – anchor worm and fish lice – are crustaceans. This group of parasites is very injurious to koi and it is vital to eradicate any infestation quickly, before it can become established in the pond system. Any treatment for anchor worm and fish lice must take into account the water temperature and the length of time it takes for the young to develop.

Anchor worm (*Lernaea cyprinacea*) has a rather complex life cycle. Only the female is parasitic. Her thin, threadlike body, often with a pair of egg strings at the rear end, protrudes from beneath a scale on the affected koi. The eggs are shed into the water, and the rate at which the young hatch depends on the water temperature. Juvenile anchor worm stages bear no resemblance to the adult and are free living. At the point of sexual maturity, males and females congregate on the

Anchor worm life cycle

After mating, the female anchor worm crawls beneath a scale and burrows her head into the skin, where she transforms into the parasitic stage, held firmly in place by the anchorlike appendages.

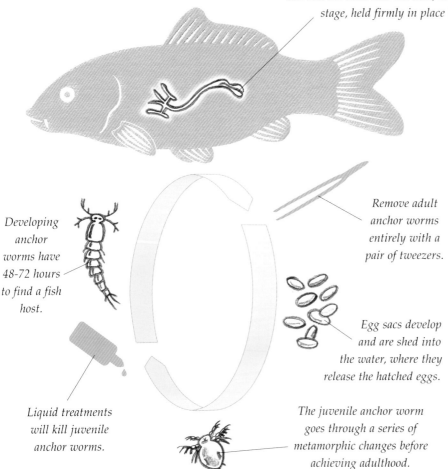

Developing anchor worms have 48-72 hours to find a fish host.

Liquid treatments will kill juvenile anchor worms.

Remove adult anchor worms entirely with a pair of tweezers.

Egg sacs develop and are shed into the water, where they release the hatched eggs.

The juvenile anchor worm goes through a series of metamorphic changes before achieving adulthood.

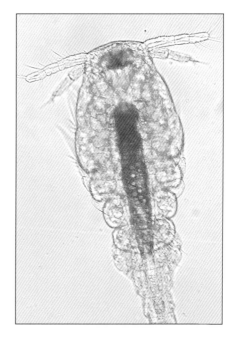

Above: An anchor worm before mating. Notice how the four appendages by the head are already in the anchor shape, These will harden to form the familiar anchor. Unmated females die at this stage.

Fish louse life cycle

Mating can take place both on the koi and in the pond environment. A single mating is enough to fertilize all the eggs ever laid.

Fish lice molt numerous times and mature individuals cover a range of sizes.

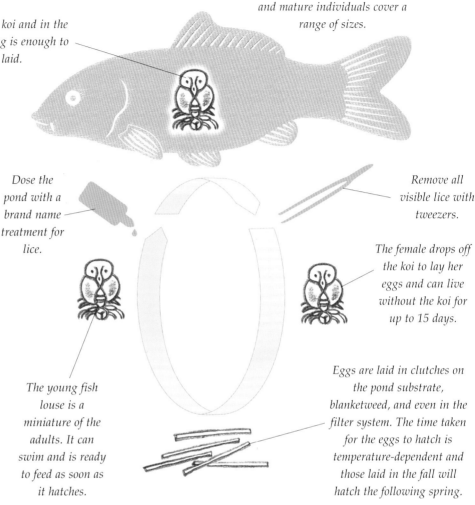

Dose the pond with a brand name treatment for lice.

Remove all visible lice with tweezers.

The female drops off the koi to lay her eggs and can live without the koi for up to 15 days.

Above: *The fish louse is very adept at swimming, although it prefers to remain on the koi to feed, holding itself onto the body surface by the two large sucker discs just below the head. The mouth is formed into a needlelike projection, which is used to pierce the host's skin. Then the fish louse sucks blood and fluids from the koi.*

The young fish louse is a miniature of the adults. It can swim and is ready to feed as soon as it hatches.

Eggs are laid in clutches on the pond substrate, blanketweed, and even in the filter system. The time taken for the eggs to hatch is temperature-dependent and those laid in the fall will hatch the following spring.

gill tissue, where mating takes place. The males die, but the female moves onto the body and searches for a suitable site, usually around a scale, to burrow beneath the skin. Once in place, she undergoes the most amazing transformation, with the head growing into an anchor device that will hold her in place for several months. During the time the anchor worm is attached, she feeds continuously on the blood and tissues of the fish. It is very common to find ulcers developing at the site of attachment.

Fish lice *(Argulus japonicus)* are saucer-shaped parasites about 1 cm (0.4 in) in diameter when adult. The young are miniature versions of the adults. All stages of fish lice will feed on koi, puncturing the skin to suck blood and juices, using a mouth that closely resembles a hypodermic needle. Unfortunately, this invasive method

of feeding also means that fish lice can readily transmit bacterial and viral infections. When the fish louse bites a koi, it also injects a substance that is an attractant to other lice, which feed at the same site. Over a period of time, this results in open lesions and ulcers.

Fish lice are active swimmers and the female lays her eggs on surfaces in the pond, on plants and blanketweed, and even in the filtration system. The rate at which the eggs hatch depends on the water temperature; at 16°C (61°F) they take six weeks to hatch.

Bacteria
Bacteria, usually including those species responsible for some disease in koi, are present in every aquatic environment. Preventing bacterial infections through careful management and good hygiene is far better than

trying to cure a problem once it has arisen, but infections can occasionally arise, even in the best systems. In most instances, only an isolated koi may be affected by a bacterial infection. Sometimes, koi will respond to name brands of antibacterial medication, but it is also possible that an antibiotic or antimicrobial treatment is necessary for the fish to make a full recovery. It is important that antibiotic and antimicrobial medications are used only as prescribed and when absolutely necessary, as bacterial resistance to these drugs is becoming a severe problem in both human and veterinary medicine. Since antibiotics and antimicrobials will be effective only if the immune system of the koi is functioning, the use of these drugs is inappropriate at low temperatures (when the immune system is at a low ebb). Finally, it is important to realize that antibiotic and antimicrobial drugs are not selective in the bacteria they target. They not only damage bacteria that cause disease, but also beneficial bacteria that may fend off other disease-causing species.

One of the most commonly encountered bacterial infections is caused by *Aeromonas hydrophila*, an opportunist pathogen that usually takes advantage of injured, sick, or weakened koi. It causes open lesions and severe ulceration. In recent years, it has become increasingly resistant to antibiotic and antimicrobial drugs and it is not uncommon to find it resistant to all drugs used in veterinary medicine.

Ulcers

Koi have three natural defenses against bacterial infection: mucus, skin, and scales. If any or all of these are breached, opportunist bacteria such as *Aeromonas hydrophila*, which are present in all ponds, will begin to attack the flesh. Left unchecked, a hole will develop and bacteria enter the bloodstream, causing popeye (exophthalmia) and/or dropsy. Ultimately, the fish will die. Ulcers result either from a parasitic infection or poor water quality and can be prevented by paying close attention to your fish behavior, regularly testing the water for nitrite and ammonia content and taking the appropriate action if anything is wrong. Given the value of many koi collections, it is sensible to invest in a microscope to check for parasites, as the majority cannot be seen with the naked eye.

Treating ulcers

When you first notice an ulcer, you must begin treatment at once, especially if the water temperature is above 15°C (59°F), as the problem will spread very quickly. The only way to carry out effective treatment is to anesthetize the fish first. It is virtually impossible to hold a fish still when it is out of water, especially if it is more than 30 cm (12 in) long, and in any case it would be extremely stressful for both owner and patient. Most dealers and hobbyists use an anesthetic containing tricaine methane sulphonate (MS222) at the rate of

Treating a koi with bee glue

1 A typical small wound or ulcer on koi.
2 Anesthetize the koi and carefully clean the affected site with a cotton swab.
3 Treat the cleaned area with bee glue spray until fully covered. This will now absorb into the surface tissues, not only disinfecting the area but also stopping bacteria from further penetrating the tissues.

Above: Allow the bee glue to dry, forming a protective coating over the area, before placing your koi back into the pond. Repeat every two to three days, or when needed. If problems persist, consult a koi health expert.

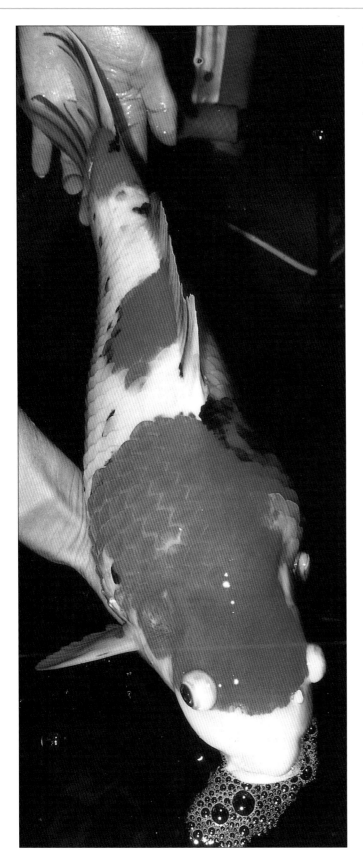

44 gm per 10 L (2 level teaspoons per 3 gal) of pond water mixed together in a large koi bag. Bear in mind that the law relating to the use of this and other suitable chemicals may vary around the world.

Net the fish into a floating basket and transfer it into the mixture using a koi sock (see page 111) to prevent further damage. After a few minutes the fish will roll onto its side as the anesthetic takes effect. Gently lift the fish out of the water, but do not remove it from the bag until you are sure it is completely sedated, because you do not want it to come to while you are carrying out the treatment. Transfer the fish onto a wet towel and cover its eyes, which will help to pacify the koi.

Using a cotton swab, apply pressure gently but firmly to the scales around the ulcer, following their direction from nose to tail. Dead scales will come away easily, allowing the surrounding tissue to regenerate. Work a cotton swab under the live scales around the ulcer to remove the

Above: *Many bacterial infections and ulcers arise from physical injury, such as on the koi pictured here. A small injury to the lower jaw has allowed secondary infections to occur, resulting in it eroding away as the tissue dies and sloughs off.*

Left: *A Sanke with symptoms of dropsy and popeye. The muscle and tissues have filled with fluid such that the scales cannot stay flat. This is often described as "pinecone." The skull is a solid bony case that restricts any swelling and as the muscle and tissues of the eyes fill with fluid, they bulge out of the head.*

Treating an ulcer

1 *Above: Once the koi has been anesthetized, place it on wet toweling to prevent any further damage to the skin. Usually the head and eyes are covered by the towel, which reduces the likelihood of the koi suddenly flapping, but leaves the ulcerated area exposed.*

2 *Above: Examine the area for any evidence of large parasites, such as anchor worm or fish lice, which might have caused the ulcer. Using a cotton swab, apply gentle pressure to remove dead tissue and clean the area. Remove any dead scales with a pair of tweezers.*

3 *Above: Once the area has been cleaned, apply an antiseptic solution. This can be covered with a thin layer of waterproof gel, which seals the wound and helps to prevent further secondary infections.*

4 *Above: Gently place the koi into a floating basket and provide aeration to help it recover from the anesthetic. It should soon be swimming normally, but continue to monitor it during the recovery period.*

bacteria, and dry the area with a tissue or paper towel. Clean the wound with an antibacterial product and apply an antiseptic solution to the affected area. Now apply a sealer over the antiseptic; otherwise it will wash off as soon as it comes into contact with water. The sealer should be capable of adhering to a mucous membrane; there are creams formulated for mouth sores in humans that are ideal for this purpose and these should remain on the fish for three or four days. When the treatment is complete, return the fish to the floating basket and put an airstone close to its head to speed its recovery.

It may be necessary to repeat the treatment after a week or so, depending on the severity of the ulcer. However, you should give the fish a chance to repair itself. If you notice a white skin starting to develop over the wound, leave it alone, as this means that the koi is recovering. Stubborn ulcers that do not heal may require more special treatment with the aid of antibiotic injections, but this should be undertaken only by an experienced professional.

Viruses

There is no cure for a viral infection, but fortunately, it is unlikely that any koi keeper will encounter a serious viral disease. Although spring viremia of carp (SVC) virus is a serious disease that can affect carp, koi must have been in contact with infected fish to become infected themselves. As spring viremia of carp predominantly affects wild carp, it is unlikely that most koi keepers will encounter the disease, unless fish are taken from rivers or lakes to stock the pond – a very unwise strategy and illegal in many countries.

The most common viral disease in koi is carp pox, caused by a herpes virus closely related to the one that causes cold sores in humans. Carp pox is visible on the body surface and fins as white waxy lumps that usually disappear once the water temperature increases through the spring and into the summer. Occasionally, a koi will suffer from carp pox for two or three years before the lumps suddenly disappear.

Fungal infections

Koi with a suppressed immune system generally tend to be more susceptible to fungal infections, although damage to the body surface – perhaps caused by water conditions, parasite damage, or physical injuries – may also lead to infection. Stressed koi are also susceptible to outbreaks of fungus because the integrity of the skin breaks down, thus allowing fungal spores to invade. Once a koi has become infected, the fungus appears as a cotton batting-like growth, often a dirty brown color as it traps pieces of dirt and detritus. In some ponds fungal growth can appear green, as microscopic algae become trapped in the fibers. Fungus spreads extremely rapidly and very invasively, entirely coating a koi within 24 hours and reaching deep into the muscle tissue.

Stress

Stress plays a very prominent role in outbreaks of disease in koi. How much effect stress has in rendering koi susceptible to outbreaks of disease depends on factors such as its severity, the period of time over which the koi is exposed to the stress, the overall condition of the koi, its reproductive status, and age. The effects of stress are cumulative and therefore it is easy to increase the stress experienced by koi. A short-term stress, such as the attentions of a predator or netting the pond, induces a "fight or flight" response, where hormones such as adrenaline are released into the circulation, initially causing the heart rate to increase and blood vessels to constrict. This is accompanied by the release of high-energy glucose to fuel muscles. The released hormones also stimulate ion exchange and gill perfusion, meaning that more of the gill surface area is in contact with the water, which is rapidly absorbed through the gills and could lead to dropsy. The overall effect of the hormones is to allow koi to respond rapidly to the cause of the stress and to escape.

Long-term stress, or a situation where a koi is subject to a variety of stresses, results in the release of the hormone cortisol. Cortisol induces the release of glucose and affects ion regulation, which under non-stressful conditions is primarily through the gills. However, stress causes the gut to become a site of ion regulation, and ions and salts are readily lost from the koi's body as a consequence of an increase in the production of urine. The main function of this hormone is to provide the long-term energy supply that enables the koi to survive the stress, but the side effects of its release are the suppression of the immune system, growth, and reproduction. The effects of cortisol on the immune system are significant, as they render any stressed koi susceptible to secondary infections and disease, which can then prove difficult to control.

Interestingly, stress caused by handling or cold shock results in the release of both adrenaline and cortisol, which have a synergistic effect, meaning that each enhances the activity of the other.

The fungus will spread over the entire body surface of the koi, even infecting the eyes.

Right: *Fungal spores are found in every aquatic environment but usually it requires koi skin becoming damaged through physical injury or exposure to pollutants to allow the fungus to become established.*

Above: *Under the microscope, fungus has a rather fibrous appearance as it grows with fine, interconnecting branches known as hyphae.*

Treatment table

Always take great care when adding any treatment to the koi pond. It is important to know the volume of water in the pond and filtration system. Follow exactly the directions supplied with name brands of medications. When undertaking any calculations to obtain the required dose, always ask someone else to check the figures; it is easy to make a mistake with the decimal point! Always measure any medication accurately and never add any extra. It will not make the treatment more effective and could be harmful.

Many chemicals used as treatments also have an antibacterial effect, so it is important to monitor the water quality constantly during the period the pond is being dosed.

Above: Measure any medication carefully and never add it to the pond in concentrated form. Fill a plastic watering can with pond water, add the correct amount of medication, and stir. Gently sprinkle on the pond surface.

Acriflavine

Application: Treating parasitic, bacterial, and fungal infections.
Dose: 5-10 mg per L, dissolved in water
Possible problems: As a result of frequent use, many fish pathogens have become resistant to this chemical.

Chloramine-T

Application: Treating *Ichthyobodo necator* (costia), *Trichodina* sp., white spot, and skin flukes, skin, and gill bacterial infections.
Dose: Dependent on water hardness, pH, and water temperature

pH	Softwater dose (mg per L)	Hardwater dose (mg per L)
6	2.5	7
6.5	5	10
7	10	15
7.5	18	18
8	20	20

Possible problems: Chloramine-T can be toxic to koi in soft water. It is advisable to use an alternative treatment. Do not use where there are exposed metal surfaces. High doses may be toxic to koi. Always start with the lowest dose and increase if necessary. Do not use in conjunction with formalin or benzalkonium chloride (Roccal).

Formalin

Application: Treating a range of protozoan and fluke infections.
Dose: 37-40 percent formalin 15-25 mg per L.
Possible problems: Formalin reduces the oxygen content of the water and is a gill irritant. Monitor dissolved oxygen levels before and during treatment with formalin. It is a good idea to install additional aeration, both before and during treatment. Formalin is more toxic in soft, acidic water. At higher temperatures, formalin becomes increasingly toxic. Do not use if a white precipitate of paraformaldehyde is visible. Formalin forms paraformaldehyde at temperatures of 8°C (46°F) and below. Avoid using formalin if koi are stressed, such as following importation or transportation. If koi are ulcerated or have open lesions, use an alternative, less harsh medication. Aquatic plants are sensitive to formalin and may be adversely affected.

Leteux Meyer Mixture

Application: Leteux Meyer Mixture is a combination of formalin and malachite green. The effect is more potent when these two chemicals are combined than when either is used on its own. A very effective treatment for white spot disease and other protozoan parasite infections.
Dose: 0.1 mg per L malachite green with 25 mg per L formalin.
Possible problems: Leteux Meyer Mixture will reduce oxygen levels in the pond and should be used only if the dissolved oxygen content remains above 5 mg per L. Increasing temperatures cause Leteux Meyer Mixture to become increasingly toxic. In some countries, the use of products containing malachite green is prohibited.

Malachite green

Application: Used for treating white spot disease and fungal infections. Zinc-free malachite green must be used for koi treatment. This chemical has some unusual properties; in acid conditions it is green in color and water soluble, whereas in alkaline conditions it is colorless, insoluble in water, but soluble in fats and oils. The use of malachite green in the aquatic environment is controversial, as this chemical is a known mutagenic (increases genetic mutations by directly affecting the DNA) and a possible cancer-causing agent. Its use has been prohibited for the food fish industry and some countries have banned the use of malachite green entirely. In others it is still available for use with ornamental fish.
Dose: 0.1 mg per L.
Possible problems: Malachite green is a potent respiratory poison for which there is no antidote and the effects are cumulative with regular, repeat treatments. The oxygen content of the water is reduced by malachite green; use supplementary aeration before and during treatment. As the temperature increases, malachite green becomes more toxic. Malachite green is more toxic in ponds with a low pH.

Organophosphate insecticides

Application: Used for the treatment of flukes, fish lice, anchor worm, gill maggots, and leeches. In some countries the use of organophosphates for fish treatment is illegal.

Dose: Follow the manufacturer's recommended treatment advice.

Possible problems: Organophosphates are potent neurotoxins and some have been implicated as teratogens. The effects of treatment with organophosphates is cumulative, even if repeated doses are weeks apart. Certain fish species are very sensitive to organophosphates.

Potassium permanganate

Application: Used for the treatment of protozoan parasites and bacterial infections of the skin or gills.

Dose: 2 mg per L.

Possible problems: Potassium permanganate is toxic in water with a high pH, forming a precipitate of manganese dioxide on the gills, so use it with caution. The presence of organic material in the filters and pond reduces the effectiveness of potassium permanganate. Do not use it in conjunction with either salt or formalin.

Quaternary ammonium compounds (Roccal)

Application: Has been used for treating bacterial infections of the skin and gills and is of particular use where bacteria are multiplying within the mucus. After treatment, place the koi in untreated water.

Dose: 10 mg active QAC per L for 5-10 minutes

Possible problems: Quaternary ammonium compounds are increasingly poisonous in soft water and with increasing temperatures.

Sodium chloride (common salt)

Application: Used for treating protozoan and fungal infections, as a mild bactericide, and to reduce osmotic stress.

Dose: Short-term bath, 20 gm per L for 10 minutes with aeration. For a prolonged immersion (pond treatment) use 3 gm per L.

Possible problems: Salt does not break down or evaporate and is removed only by partial water changes.

Using a salt dip

Below: It is very common for koi to become disoriented and lose their balance when first introduced into a salt bath. If the koi remains disoriented or becomes distressed it should be removed from the salt bath immediately and returned to the pond. Always use aeration, as shown here, when using a dip treatment of salt.

Right: Use a salt tester – basically a hydrometer with suitable scales on it – to check the concentration of the salt solution. Aim for a strength of 20 gm per L for a short-term dip.

Using potassium permanganate

Above: When preparing a potassium permanganate dip, measure the chemical carefully, ensuring that any residues are fully dissolved before introducing any koi. Time any dip or bath treatment carefully and never add a few more minutes extra exposure time, as the chemical could be harmful to the koi.

Above: Once the koi has been placed in the potassium permanganate solution, monitor its progress continually. If the koi becomes distressed, return it to the pond immediately and do not persist with the treatment. After treatment, place the fish in a tank or bowl of clean water to wash away the chemical.

Buying koi

Buying koi is both a pleasure and a commitment, as all ornamental fish – whether inexpensive or very valuable – deserve the same high level of care. Buying and accepting losses of cheap koi before filter systems are fully matured is indefensible. When fish go into your pond, they should enjoy a stress-free environment from day one. And only when you are certain that you can provide these conditions should you start to build your own collection.

Buying koi is not as time-sensitive as it once was, thanks to improvements in shipping techniques and overseas holding facilities. And, if you heat your pond, you need no longer fear that newly imported koi will struggle to adapt to a change in climate. Options have widened in other directions; today, it is possible to fly to Japan to select fish at their source from their breeders, or even to buy koi over the Internet. However, a visit in person to a reputable dealer is still the first choice for most koi keepers. This chapter advises on choosing and buying your fish, how to get them home safely, and whether or not to quarantine them.

Country of origin

It makes sense to buy the best koi you can. Long-term, the cost of fish will be small compared to the outlay on their pond and the ongoing bills for food, medications, and electricity.

Japanese koi are the finest in the world, and in real terms represent the best value for the money. Fish from Israel, the United States, South Africa, China, Singapore, and Cyprus all have their devotees. But only in Japan are experienced breeders able to capitalize on the long, hot summers and the unique mineral content of their mud ponds, essential to good growth and skin quality.

Even ordinary-grade Japanese fish compare favorably with the best koi from other countries and are a good choice for those who merely want a colorful display. As quality improves, the asking price rises, but balancing what you want against what you can afford is all part of the fascination of the hobby.

When to buy

The Japanese net their mud ponds in late October/early November, and that is when the finest fish become available. Coincidentally, fall temperatures best suit koi in transit, as cool water holds high levels of dissolved oxygen to sustain them through their flight. However, at other times of the year, sophisticated packing techniques and gradual temperature adjustment still ensure a safe journey in the aircraft's cargo hold.

It is common practice for dealers to travel out to hand-pick quality koi from the fall harvest on behalf of their customers, or acquire a whole pondful of fish at favorable rates. Hobbyists in search of something really special can accompany these koi professionals to Japan. The fish they choose are either shipped back home or, for a fee, remain with the breeders for a further year or more to grow. The risk is borne by the buyer, but the rewards can be great. Some dealers revisit Japan in the spring to buy the remainder of the koi from the fall harvest. These represent real bargains. If Japanese holding

Below: A dealer and his customers buying koi in Japan. Their preliminary selections are netted and bowled, but will be whittled down when the fish are inspected at closer quarters.

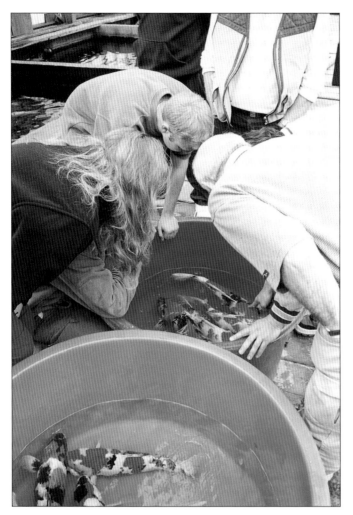

Above: It is important to view prospective purchases close-up, in a blue inspection bowl, and in good daylight. The customers may well like the fish, but not the price being asked by the koi farmer; in any event, this is not a procedure to be rushed.

Where to buy

Reputable koi dealers may not always tell you what you would like to hear or even sell you any fish until they are convinced your pond is suitable. Don't be put off by this. It means they care about their livestock and their responsibilities, and in the longer term they will be a valuable source of advice and assistance in return for your regular business.

If possible, buy koi only from special dealers – there are plenty to choose from. General aquatic outlets or pet stores are less likely to stock quality fish, or know much about keeping them. Long-established koi businesses pose the fewest risks, but new ones are being set up all the time. If you visit a new dealership, be guided by first impressions. Are the premises well laid out and tidy? Does the staff use separate nets for each pond or tank and disinfect them between use? Does the dealer stock all the necessary ancillary equipment as well as fish? The holding water should be well filtered and clear, as much for the well-being of the koi as for ease of viewing. If any fish appear obviously diseased, in discomfort, or unfit for sale – unless indicated as such and separately housed – go elsewhere.

Buying koi through the Web

Many koi retailers worldwide now have their own web site, or web page. This usually features a description of the company, along with a list of available koi and associated products for sale by mail order. Now that the

facilities are available, fish can be released in batches to satisfy demand throughout the summer.

Ordinary and middle-grade koi tend to be handled more by wholesalers and buying cooperatives who know the overseas market well. They will offer guaranteed prices to breeders who can consistently supply colorful, healthy stock. These koi are available all year round, especially in the smaller sizes.

Owners of heated ponds and quarantine tanks can safely buy koi at any time. For the rest, it is better to pay for selected fish and board them with the dealer until outside water temperatures stabilize above 10°C (50°F).

Below: The Internet can give some idea of fish available for sale, but however good the images, this is no substitute for seeing the koi firsthand.

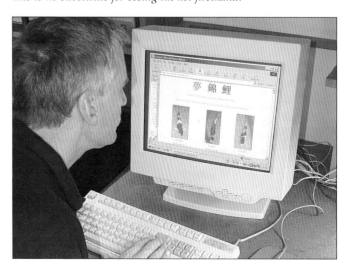

quality of photographs and graphics on computers has improved, they have become a very popular form of communication with many of the larger retailers. Koi are described in detail, along with a picture, so that prospective buyers can make an astute choice, even though they have not seen a fish "in the flesh." It enables a would-be buyer to view a classic koi without having to make a long trip, only to be disappointed on arrival at the retailer.

Left: These koi have recovered from the traumas of shipment and are now well acclimated to the dealer's pond. They have also been properly quarantined. This is the safest, if not the most exciting, way of buying koi.

Below: The less koi are handled, the better. Here a fish is simply being lifted in the net for a customer – if she wants a closer look, it can be transferred to a viewing bowl or basket.

If the retailer has a known and trusted outlet, buyers may even accept what they have seen or read on their computer and acquire the koi over the Web. The fish can then be dispatched via a courier service for immediate delivery. However, it is worth noting that even the best photographic images can give a misleading impression, so be cautious about buying koi without seeing them first.

With slightly more sophisticated computer technology, your trusted koi retailer can select a fish on your behalf while visiting Japan. Many dealers make seasonal buying trips to Japan and take close-up digital photographs of any exceptional koi they see while visiting a particular koi farm. The photographs are then downloaded onto a computer and e-mailed across the world to the retail outlet, or even directly to the customer to consider.

Choosing your koi

Until you gain experience, ask a seasoned koi keeper to accompany you on buying visits. Allow yourself plenty of time and never feel pressured to make a purchase unless you see fish you really want. Even after a period of dealer quarantine, newly imported koi sometimes show minor abrasions and splits in the fins. With correct care, these fish will mend and can be a real bargain, but beginners should stay with unblemished koi.

Many newcomers to the hobby imagine they will save money by buying small koi and growing them. However, although they cost more than babies, fish over

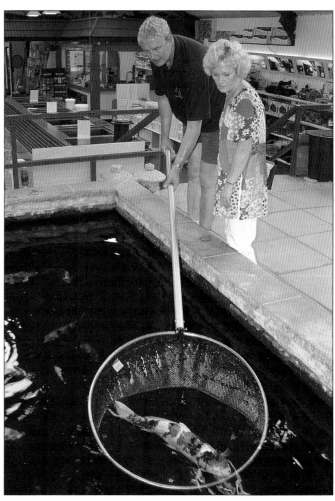

Buying koi checklist

Plus points
- Good body shape and skin quality
- Well-distributed pattern the full length of the body (in varieties such as Showa)
- Clear, well-shaped head
- Fins in proportion to the body
- Bilateral symmetry
- Straight spine
- Good, lively deportment.

Minus points
- Badly split fins; missing fins (usually one of the pelvic fins)
- Reddened vent or raised, angry scales (both signs of bacterial infection)
- Scars or missing scales below the lateral line (not visible when koi is viewed from above)
- Anchor worm (Argulus) parasites
- Fungus
- Broken dorsal and/or pectoral fin rays
- Clamped fins

- Gills not working at the same rate, or too-rapid respiration indicating gill damage
- Damaged/missing eye(s)
- Eroded or reddened barbels
- Listless behavior
- Erratic swimming
- Head-up/head-down position in the water
- Excessively thin body, especially just behind gills
- Rough feel to body (indicating lack of protective mucus)
- Part-missing or outcurled gill covers.

General
- Ask whether the fish is male or female (you do not want to pay for a female, only to find it is a male).
- Closely examine any fish, first in a bowl, then by holding up the bag to examine the underside and to check that all fins are present and correct.

---

30 cm (12 in) long are hardier and represent a better investment. On a limited budget, it is wiser to buy one sizeable koi rather than three or four youngsters, and build the collection slowly.

When you spot a likely purchase, watch it for a while to see how it behaves. It should swim with an easy, fluid motion in the company of the other koi and not hang near the surface or in the bubbles of a venturi or filter return pipe. Check for slow, regular respiratory movements of the gill covers, and ensure that they are both working at the same rate. Other things to look for at this stage are obvious wounds and blemishes, cloudy eyes, external parasites (such as anchor worm or fish lice), raised scales, or holes.

Next, ask the dealer to "bowl" the fish for your inspection. Larger koi are gently encouraged to swim into a shallow pan net, then transferred to a tilted, floating bowl or soft-meshed holding net. Smaller ones can be dipped from a tank and bowled using a "koi sock," an open-ended mesh sleeve.

At closer quarters (and preferably in good daylight), double-check for wounds and parasites. Ask the dealer to lift one of the koi's gill covers – the gills should be bright red, free of mucus, and uncongested. From above, look for any skeletal deformities resulting in kinks in the backbone or tail root, and ensure that the fish deports itself well, using both its pectoral fins.

Ask the dealer about pattern (where this applies) and skin quality; for novices this is a difficult attribute to appreciate. Also find out the name of the variety if you don't already know it – there is no stigma attached to this, and plenty of time to learn.

No koi is perfect. A fish will exhibit good points and bad, though in top-quality koi the merits will increasingly outweigh the faults. However, in the final analysis – and provided the koi is healthy – it's what you like that matters.

Transporting koi

Having made your selection, ask the dealer to bag the fish for you. Before the bag is sealed, lift it up to the light and make one final check on the koi, paying special attention to the belly region. Examine the eyes and barbels, and satisfy yourself that there are no deformities of the mouth and jawbone, a common fault in Showa.

The double or triple bag should contain just enough clean transit water to cover the koi's back, with the remaining space inflated from an oxygen cylinder. For long trips, the dealer will sometimes add a soothing, mildly antiseptic agent. The bag is then sealed with rubber bands.

Once you have paid for your koi, it becomes your responsibility to get it home safely. Fish travel best in the dark, so wrap the bag in a large black plastic bag and lay

Using a koi sock, an open-ended mesh sleeve, is a convenient way of moving koi.

Bagging your chosen koi

1 *This Kujaku has been singled out as a possible purchase. It is gently tipped from a catching net into a floating viewing basket and brought nearer to the prospective buyer for a closer inspection.*

2 *From above it looks good – blemish-free, good skin and pattern, and it deports well in the confines of the basket. Ask questions if you are unsure.*

The koi is upended by the dealer so that its underside can be checked, too.

3 *When you are satisfied, the dealer will bag the koi, but before the bag is sealed check the koi once again to make sure that all is well.*

4 *The koi is double-bagged with just enough water to cover its back, while the remainder of the space is taken up by oxygen from a cylinder. It will now go into a polybox for, ideally, a swift trip to its home pond.*

it on its side in a strong cardboard box or, better still, a large polystyrene container with a lid, as used to bring koi into the country. Your dealer may well give you one of these; it is a useful item to carry in the car at all times. The insulating properties of the polybox should maintain an even water temperature during the trip, but on very warm days, one or more icepacks from the freezer, wrapped in newspaper or a blanket in order not to make direct contact with the polybag, will provide added protection.

If the koi are large, lay the wrapped bags or boxes lengthways across the car trunk or in the space behind the front seats where they cannot shift around. That way, if the driver has to brake suddenly, the fish will not bang their noses. Do not carry the boxes in the front seat or on a passenger's lap, where they will get too warm and be vulnerable in the event of an accident. Avoid unnecessary stops on the trip and drive smoothly, cornering gently and taking the most direct route home.

On arrival, open the bag, or bags, roll down the tops to form a collar, and float them on the surface of the pond or quarantine facility. This is purely to equalize water temperatures and should take no more than 20 minutes. It is pointless to gradually add more water to the bag in the belief that this will acclimate the fish to any change in pH; to be of any benefit, this process would take weeks. Koi are far more likely to be damaged by being left too long in their transit water than by any small differences in water chemistry. Open the bag and carefully lift the fish out by hand or use a koi sock if it is too large to handle. Introduce the fish into the pond and discard the water in the bag.

If the fish go into a relatively low-volume quarantine tank, it is important to take an ammonia reading an hour or two later. Koi have a tendency to "dump" ammonia when they are moved from dirty into clean water, and you should perform a large partial water change through a purifier to dilute this toxin. Leave the new arrivals undisturbed, and on no account feed them for a couple of days. If possible, net over the pond or tank, as koi have a tendency to jump until they have become acclimated to their new surroundings.

The quarantine issue

Whether or not to quarantine new arrivals causes more debate among koi keepers than any other issue. In Japan, many dealers have their own holding facility, where fish are inspected, treated for parasites, and rested for some time before shipment. This is in addition to any treatment they may receive on arrival in their country of sale.

Dealer quarantine (withholding fish from sale for some weeks) allows koi time to recuperate from the stress of their trip. Run-down koi, like humans, are susceptible to ailments they would normally shrug off, but in a warm tank the more common protozoan parasites (especially white spot) will soon manifest themselves and can be successfully treated. However, other, more serious diseases have a longer incubation period, or can be triggered by environmental factors not yet fully understood. In other words, dealer quarantine alone is no guarantee that a fish is not carrying an infection that could easily wipe out a whole pond. A few dealers choose not to quarantine new arrivals. This is acceptable, provided they make it quite clear to their customers, and as long as obviously stressed fish are not offered for sale.

The main argument against quarantining at home is that it necessitates yet one more stressful change of environment for the koi, rather than a direct transfer from the dealer's tanks to your pond. Certainly, when you buy your first batch of fish, there is little point in quarantining them all together, as cross-infection can occur wherever they are housed.

Subsequent purchases are a different matter altogether. It does not matter where koi originate, or how expensive they are, they may be carrying serious bacterial infections or viral diseases. There is no known treatment against viruses and, increasingly, bacterial problems are becoming resistant to antibiotics. So it is best to segregate new arrivals to give any latent pathogens time to show themselves. The quarantine period is up to the hobbyist, and there is no cast-iron

guarantee that a problem will not emerge even months after purchase. Some koi keepers hold fish back from their ponds for up to a year to minimize the risk, while others quarantine for just a few weeks. However, it is not just the length of quarantine that is important; the quality of the accommodations and other factors, such as water temperature, all play a part.

A quarantine facility

The quarantine facility should provide an impeccable pond environment on a small scale. You can buy a ready-made system, but most hobbyists prefer to build their own in a garage or shed. The more swimming space the better, but aim for a minimum of 2,250 L (500 gal). A popular choice is a floor-level blockwork shell, either rendered and fiberglassed or with a crease-free box-welded liner dropped in. Although they are inadequate for koi ponds, "black box" filters come into their own for quarantining fish, as they can cope well with small volumes of water and are easy to service. As with all filters, make sure that they are fully matured before introducing any koi. When you first fill the quarantine tank, run the water through a purifier and record the capacity with a flowmeter. This ensures that in the future you can administer accurate doses of any necessary medication.

The tank should be heated. If your pond is heated by gas, you can run a loop from the system; otherwise use an inline electric heater. The temperature should be kept at 16°C (61°F) or above, for several reasons. First, warmth speeds up the life cycle of parasites, so that any latent infestation will show itself quickly. At the same time, the immune system of the koi will be fully geared up. Tissue healing, biological filter efficiency, and the viability of some medications are all dependent on higher temperatures, and finally, the appetite of healthy fish kept warm will be good.

The quarantine tank should also be well aerated and free from any projections on which koi might injure themselves. To save on electricity, insulate the walls with thick sheets of polystyrene and install a ventilated cover that will conserve heat and prevent the fish from jumping out.

Left: You can float the sealed bag with your newly purchased koi for a short while to equalize temperatures. Avoid doing this in warm weather, or the fish will overheat.

Feeding koi

In the summer months, when the pond water temperature is at its peak, there can be few greater pleasures for koi keepers than to see their koi swarming toward them in their eagerness to feed. Koi begin to feed actively once water temperatures start to exceed 15°C (59°F). Watching the koi while they are feeding is an important part of routine management, observing them but not interfering with them, which might alter their behavior. As they feed, there is time to glance over the body and fins of each fish to ensure that there are no lesions, wounds, ulcers, or large parasites, such as anchor worm and fish lice (see pages 88 and 89).

One of the early warning signs that a koi may be sick is a poor appetite at temperatures when others in the pond are hungry and feeding well. It is also important to

Right: Koi are natural bottom-feeders, but giving them floating foods makes them easier to observe. The pectoral fins guide the fish into position. The upper and lower jaws of koi are protrusible and extend to enclose the food particle, which is seen as a sucking action.

check that all the koi are feeding. Sometimes one fish may miss a feeding, but eats with a voracious appetite the next time it is fed.

A common reason why some koi do not eat is because the food is too large for them. Always make sure the food is of a size that the smallest koi in the pond can easily swallow. While the rate at which koi grow is dependent on feeding, other factors, such as temperature, water quality, and stocking levels in the pond, can also have an influence. Under optimum temperatures and water conditions, koi in a lightly stocked pond will grow very rapidly.

The koi diet

Koi are omnivorous, which means they will feed on both animal and plant material, although they prefer aquatic insects and larvae. However, few koi ponds contain any planting, as the koi are the main focus of the feature and nothing should detract from them. This absence of plant life, combined with the numbers of koi, means that you must supply a manufactured food to provide adequate food for all the fish.

The main component of any manufactured food is protein. Good-quality foods contain a large amount of protein derived from fish, but the problems of overfishing the seas have impacted on the availability and price of fish meal. It is therefore common to find protein from other sources, including plants such as soya, as well as animal products, incorporated into fish food. Although the protein content of the diet is very important for tissue maintenance, repair, and growth, proteins cannot

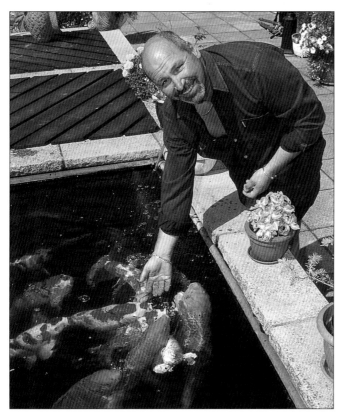

Above: The koi in this pond are greedily taking the food offered to them and this is the perfect opportunity to check each one for wounds, lesions, or larger parasites, such as fish lice or anchor worm.

Pellet foods

These large pellets are ideal for feeding to large adult koi.

Medium-sized pellets suit ponds with a range of koi of different sizes.

The smallest pellets are usually given to one- or two-year-old koi.

Pellets containing spirulina algae are high in protein and rich in vitamins, minerals, and iodine.

quantities as to be ineffectual or cannot be synthesized from raw ingredients. Interestingly, some of the vitamins essential for the welfare of koi are produced by bacteria that naturally live in the gut. This is a very good reason to avoid using antibiotic and antimicrobial drugs unless absolutely necessary, as these will also affect the natural, beneficial microbial populations. Although only small amounts of vitamins are required, their absence in the diet – termed "avitaminosis" – leads to a range of diseases and even mortalities.

Many vitamins are rather unstable and furthermore, the processing required to produce koi pellets and sticks affects the natural vitamin content of the raw ingredients. To overcome this problem, manufacturers add vitamin supplements to the mixture to ensure that there is more than an adequate amount in the food (see page 105).

Koi food also contains minerals, including calcium and phosphorus, that are important components of bone, and elements such as magnesium, which is needed for metabolism. Sodium and potassium are essential for the normal functioning of nerves and, taken together with

be stored by koi and any excess is excreted, mainly as ammonia, plus a small amount as urine. This is one of the principal reasons why you should feed sparingly. If the pond water is polluted with ammonia, the koi will be stressed by the poor water conditions.

Fatty acids, known more familiarly as "fats," are the second important component of fish food. Generally speaking, fats form an important energy source for koi, as well as helping them to absorb fat-soluble vitamins. Certain fats included in the feed are regarded as essential, which means that if they were omitted the koi would suffer and show evidence of stunted growth, fin erosion, and liver and heart disorders.

Carbohydrates are also incorporated into the diet. Some may be used for energy, but koi can use the basic components to produce nonessential fatty acids.

Vitamins are essential to life, although they vary greatly in composition. They must be incorporated into the diet, as they are either produced in such small

Floating sticks

Wheat germ sticks are ideal for feeding at cooler times of the year, such as in the fall and spring.

Variety sticks contain a mixture of color-enhancing food, with wheat germ and staple food. Ideal for summer.

These floating sticks are a staple summer food, with protein levels suitable for growth and reproduction.

Fresh and treat foods

Orange is a good source of vitamin C, which helps to reduce stress and improves the immune system.

Garlic is a real treat for koi, which are attracted to any food coated in it. It can be used to entice them to feed by hand.

Some koi keepers feed whole lettuce to their koi, which readily shred and eat this treat. It is a rich source of vitamin C and other nutrients.

Bloodworms are available live (the koi prefer these) or frozen (thaw before feeding). Offer bloodworms in summer.

Koi thoroughly enjoy prawns, a good source of protein. Feed these to koi in the summer, when the water temperatures are higher.

Brown bread is a good source of wheat germ and vitamins, but feed it sparingly, as it is rich in carbohydrate.

chlorine, for osmoregulation (see page 78). Finally, there is an assortment of trace elements, required only in minute quantities but nevertheless essential. They include substances such as iron, copper, manganese, zinc, and iodine. Although freshwater fish can absorb minerals directly from the water via the gills, the low concentrations of many minerals and trace elements in solution means they must be added to the diet.

You can choose from a range of brand name koi foods, but when changing from one type of diet to another, always begin by mixing a little of the new food with the original one. Over a period of seven to ten days, gradually increase the proportion of new food, while reducing the original food. Changing suddenly to a new brand or a different type of food often results in the koi refusing to feed.

Additives

Koi are prized for their beautiful color, and dietary additives can enhance the fishes' natural coloration. In summer, it is usual to mix color-enhancing foods with the diet. These contain shrimp meal and extracts of the algae

Spirulina platensis, which are considered by the Japanese to enhance the red coloration of koi. Bear in mind, however, that the red color patterns of koi are determined genetically and may not be stable. Although color-enhancing foods will provide the raw ingredients for the red color, if the red fades, these additives will not have any effect.

Treats and supplements

Koi will relish many extremely beneficial treat foods that provide a source of fresh vitamins and minerals. Lettuce is a great treat for many koi. When you first offer it, shred the leaves and float them in the pond. It takes only a few minutes for the koi to start feeding. Within a few weeks, you can float a whole lettuce on the water and the koi will enjoy tearing pieces off it, leaving just a stub of stalk!

Oranges are another great favorite. Cut them into segments and put these into the pond with the rind left intact. The koi will busily tear away the flesh, leaving the rind. Both lettuce and orange are a valuable source of vitamin C, which is important for growth, tissue repair, and reproduction. Once the fish have eaten the lettuce or orange, remove the stalk or rind. Bear in mind that feeding these foods can cause the water clarity to deteriorate for a few days.

Curiously, koi love garlic and a great treat is to coat their food in a little minced garlic! Other treats can include prawns, brown bread, and, when available, live foods such as glassworms (insect larvae) and bloodworms. Avoid offering peas and sweet corn, which are not easily digested by koi, and are very rich in carbohydrates, which makes the fish fat.

In recent years, there has been a great deal of interest in certain natural supplements that can be added to koi foods. These are designed to boost the immune system and general health of koi. Some of these supplements are already incorporated into manufactured foods, but new and more effective products are appearing in powdered form that you can mix with existing foods. It will not be long before these, too, are incorporated into manufactured foods.

Seasonal feeding

The amount of food that koi consume varies according to the season. In summer, when they are most active, they feed hungrily and will eat several times each day. With optimum temperatures and food availability, koi grow rapidly in summer, compared with the winter months, when they consume little and growth is very slow. This pattern of rapid growth in the summer

Below: These young koi are enjoying a segment of orange, eagerly tearing away the flesh to leave just the peel. Remove the remains of the peel from the pond when all the flesh has been eaten.

Medicated foods and supplements

Medicated pellets contain natural ingredients to promote koi health and improve colors.

Health-boosting snacks contain yeast derivatives to improve the immune system.

Some products designed to improve the immune system and reduce the bacterial load on koi are available in powder form to be mixed with food.

and slower growth in the winter is reflected in the rings found on the scales of koi. Rather like growth rings on a tree, these can be used to assess the age of a koi.

Feeding in the summer

The food consumed during the summer is used for energy, tissue maintenance and repair growth, storage to help the fish through the winter, and, in the case of adult koi, to produce eggs or sperm for spawning the following year. When water temperatures are between 18° and 20°C (64°-68°F), koi are often fed on high-protein diets designed to promote growth. The efficiency with which koi utilize protein is dependent on temperature. At 15°C (59°F), they digest about 87 percent of the protein content of the diet, but at 20°-25°C (68°-77°F), they digest 89 percent. The digestibility of protein decreases rapidly under low dissolved oxygen concentrations.

Feeding in the fall and spring

As the water temperature drops in the fall, koi appetites gradually decline. At this time, reduce the amount of food offered to koi and gradually change from a high-protein food to a wheat germ-based diet. Koi digest wheat germ foods more easily in the fall and spring, when the water temperatures are lower. At temperatures of less than 8°-10°C (46°-50°F), koi cease to feed altogether. Thus, during the coldest periods of the year, koi in an unheated pond will not feed at all. Depending on the water temperature in heated ponds, it is possible for koi to feed all year round.

Once the water temperature creeps up toward 10°C (50°F) with the onset of spring, koi will again begin looking for food. Offer them wheat germ feed, gradually mixed with the summer food as the water warms up.

How much food is enough?

How much and how often to feed koi are common questions. Technically, baby koi (koi fry and fish up to one year old) will eat 5-10 percent of their body weight daily, when the water temperature is about 20°C (68°F). At these temperatures, juvenile koi consume about 5 percent, and sexually mature koi – as a guide fish that are three or more years old – will consume 2 percent of their body weight each day. This means that at 20°C (68°F), an adult koi weighing 1 kg (2.2 lb) should be consuming 20 gm (0.7 oz) of food on a daily basis.

At low temperatures – 10°-15°C (50°-59°F) – koi will usually require feeding only once each day. As the water temperature rises, increase the frequency of feeding to two or three times a day at 20°C (68°F). Generally speaking, offer koi as much as they will consume within two or three minutes at each feeding. When the feeding is given, there is an initial surge of activity among the koi, but as they each get enough to eat, they feed more lazily. The point at which they begin to feed more casually is the moment to stop adding more food, and this really takes just a few minutes. Excess food will not necessarily harm the koi, but it is not digested efficiently. It is simply voided as waste and places a burden on the filtration system. Remove uneaten food from the pond; otherwise this becomes a source of ammonia pollution.

Vacation times

Vacations may disrupt the feeding patterns of koi for a short period in the summer. Ideally, ask someone to

Estimating koi weight

Use this graph to estimate the weight of your koi. Females full of eggs may weigh more than indicated.

Measure body length, not including the tail.

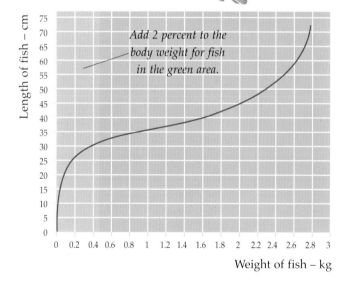

Add 2 percent to the body weight for fish in the green area.

Length of fish – cm

Weight of fish – kg

Below: These scales provide a quick way of working out how much your koi should be eating per day at 20°C (68°F). Simply compare the total koi weight with the feeding scale.

Conversion factors

cm to ins, multiply by .3937
kg to lbs, multiply by 2.205

gm to oz, multiply by .0353

Daily food consumption at 20°C (68°F)

Total weight of fish – kg

Weight of food per day – gm

Above: Sometimes it takes the introduction of a variety such as Chagoi (shown here), which have a particularly amiable nature and are less wary, to start feeding by hand and it does not take long before the others are encouraged to follow suit.

gradually reduce the amount of food offered until at three or four days before the event, the koi are not feeding on manufactured foods. However, they will continue to find insects, larvae, and even blanketweed in the pond.

Feeding by hand

Many koi keepers are very eager to encourage their koi to take food from their hand, but this requires patience and perseverance. Feed the koi from the same place each time and wait by the pond until they have finished feeding. Gradually approach them more closely until they associate you with feeding. Include a few treat foods, such as prawns or brown bread, and hold them very still in the water until the koi approach. On the first few occasions when they attempt to take the food from your hand, it is very likely that they will splash you in their eagerness to grab the treat. In time, the koi will associate you with feeding and become more relaxed about taking a treat or food from your hand. Certain varieties of koi, notably Chagoi and Ochiba Shigure, are renowned for being more friendly. It can certainly speed the process if one koi is willing to feed by hand, as this encourages the others to do the same.

Buying and storing feed

One of the most common mistakes made with koi food is to buy in bulk and use the same batch of food for several months. Although food manufacturers go to great lengths to ensure a more-than-adequate vitamin content, once the bag has been opened and exposed to both air and light, the vitamins are rapidly lost. A bag of feed will lose almost half its vitamin content within a month of being opened and from then on, the vitamins deteriorate even more rapidly. In terms of providing koi with a balanced diet containing an adequate vitamin content, it is more economical to buy smaller amounts of food and use them within three or four weeks than to buy a single, large bag of food to last all summer. Similarly, you should discard any leftover wheat germ feed at the end of fall or spring and buy a new supply when you recommence feeding with this diet.

Always store fish food in a dark, dry place and preferably in an airtight container, as this helps to reduce the vitamin loss. Damp food will encourage a range of molds to form, many of which are extremely poisonous to fish. Always discard any food that has come into contact with water.

check the pond on a daily basis to ensure that the pumps, filters, and aeration systems are running. At the same time, he or she can feed the koi sparingly. If the visitor is not a fishkeeper, prepare daily rations for him or her to feed to the fish. Clearly, it is sensible not to disrupt feeding too much in the summer, but if this is unavoidable, take the following steps. In the two weeks before your vacation, gradually offer the koi decreasing amounts of food until the day of departure, when you offer no food. The koi will survive for two weeks. On your return, feed them sparingly at first and gradually increase the amount of food offered until you return to normal feeding levels.

Many koi shows take place during the summer months and to prevent serious pollution problems in the show vat, it is a good idea to exhibit fish in a fasted state. Once again, in the fourteen days leading up to the show,

Showing koi

Whether or not to show your koi is a decision that only you can make. On the credit side, scooping an award at a major national event will confirm what you already suspected – that your fish can compete and win against the best in the country! Real satisfaction comes from knowing that your skills in choosing and then bringing koi into peak condition have been recognized by experienced judges. On the other hand, showing koi inevitably subjects the fish to the disruption of travel from home pond to show venue and back again. Furthermore, once the fish have been benched and introduced into their vats, responsibility for their welfare throughout the show is largely taken out of your hands. Problems do occasionally arise – with water quality, for example – and the mark of a well-run show is how quickly and effectively these are pinpointed and dealt with. Organizers understand that any question mark over

the fish health issue will keep exhibitors away and, as a result, show-running standards are probably higher today than at any time in the past.

This chapter starts with a guide to preparing fish for a show to give them the best chance of success, and also covers transport to and from the event. The various types of show are also described.

Preparing for a show

The natural attributes of a show-quality koi can be enhanced or ruined by the way it is cared for. Judges are not only looking for koi that represent excellent examples of their variety, but fish that literally shine with health. There is no point in submitting a koi with any suspicion of disease, major damage, deformity, or parasitic infestation; such faults will automatically disqualify it at the benching stage, and you will have had a wasted trip and gone down in the estimation of your fellow competitors.

Some koi never give their best at shows. In their home pond they look fine, but subject them to the stress of netting and unfamiliar surroundings and their white skin reddens up as tiny capillary blood vessels rupture. Only experience will tell you whether any of your koi fall into this category.

However careful you are, large koi in particular can suffer minor damage in transit. This may take the form of a rubbed nose or a slightly split fin. While the benching team will probably still allow the fish in, you should ask yourself whether that koi would be better off going right back home. Remember, you have the option at any time during a show of withdrawing a fish you suspect to be in trouble.

Seasoned koi exhibitors may attend many events during the year, but do not necessarily take the same fish

Below: The public always likes to match their wits with the judges, but although they can get a good view of the fish, only the judges are allowed behind the barrier. In this "English" or "Western" show format, each competitor's koi are housed together in the same vat(s) throughout the event.

Left: It doesn't matter how good a koi may be, if it reacts badly to showing, there is little point in taking it along. This Showa, for example, has reddening of the white skin caused by stress-rupture of capillary blood vessels. Other koi may not deport themselves well, or their colors may fade.

along to every one. It is better to have a "show pool" of likely candidates, so that while some are on the circuit, others are resting.

The size of a koi can boost or diminish its likelihood of success. For example, in UK shows run by the BKKS (British Koi Keepers Society), there are seven size categories: Size 1: up to 20 cm (8 in); Size 2: 20-30 cm (8-12 in); Size 3: 30-40 cm (12-16 in); Size 4: 40-50 cm (16-20 in); Size 5: 50-60 cm (20-24 in); Size 6: 60-70 cm (24-28 in); Size 7: 70 cm (28 in) and above. This means that a koi measuring 53.34 cm (21 in) entered in Size 5 could well be up against fish almost 7.5 cm (3 in) longer than itself. Koi keepers know to rest these "in-between" fish until they have grown enough to give themselves a

realistic chance. Koi kept in heated ponds grow quickly, which for show purposes is a definite plus. It means they will be eligible for entry into the larger size categories while they are only four or five years old and still retain the excellent skin quality of youth.

In the period preliminary to a show there are several things (besides the obvious attention to good diet and water quality) that you can do to give koi that extra sparkle. Adding montmorillionite clay to food or directly

When using montmorillionite clay, disperse it into a bucket of pond water before introducing it into the surface skimmer.

Below: Regular meals of color-enhancing pellets delivered through an auto-feeder are a good pre-show tactic. Follow this with a period of fasting (see page 107).

Above: Fresh treat foods, such as lettuce, may just give show koi that extra edge. In any event, it makes sense to offer them a varied diet, and something they have to work for.

to the pond replenishes essential minerals lost as water ages. Installing an automatic feeder to dispense regular small meals during the day optimizes growth and puts less strain on the filter than one or two large offerings heaped in morning and evening. Top-grade color food, supplementing the normal rations two or three weeks before showing, enhances hi (red) and sumi (black), and some koi keepers swear by natural food items, such as prawns, earthworms, lettuce, and fresh orange segments, to get their fish "buzzing." All this will stand the koi in good stead for the fasting period leading up the show. This is essential if the fish are not to pollute their transit water or the vats in which they will be held.

Taking koi to and from shows

When you buy a koi from a dealer it is double-bagged with oxygen and taken home without delay. The same procedure applies with fish taken to a show, except that now you have to provide all the necessary equipment for the outgoing and return trips. Luxury travel accommodations, sometimes offered by dealers (who will gain kudos if fish they supply win major awards), consists of a free-standing vat of soft opaque plastic with a zipped lid, and equipped with one or more shielded airstones fed from a regulated oxygen cylinder. The koi cannot damage themselves or jump out, and arrive

Nets and baskets

There are a number of points to consider when choosing a net. The pole and head combined should be at least 90 cm (36 in) deeper than the pond; otherwise it will be very difficult to maneuver in the water. The pole itself must be made from a strong but lightweight material, such as wood or aluminum. Plastic and carbon-fiber handles have a tendency to bend and can be difficult to handle at full stretch. Wooden handles are very easy to maneuver, as they are buoyant in the water. Although aluminum handles are heavier, they have the added advantage of being telescopic and will extend from 1.8-3.7 m (6-12 ft),

and the pole can be locked at any position in between.

The net heads are generally circular and available in 45, 50, 60, and 75 cm (18, 20, 24, and 30 in) diameters. The netting is made from nylon and should be reasonably fine so that a fish's fins do not get caught. Choose a shallow pan net, as deeper nets tend to create drag and are heavy in the water.

A floating koi basket is useful for transferring a fish, so you can examine it closely without it thrashing around in the net. The basket is supplied complete with a lid, which can be secured by a locking pin to prevent the fish from escaping and injuring itself.

Left: Having been selected to compete in a show, this large koi is gently netted. Some fish get used to the procedure and actually swim into the net. Others may resist; be patient.

Below: The koi is gently transferred from the net to a floating bowl for a final check before being bagged for transportation to the show. Damage to the fish, however minor, is the last thing you want at this crucial stage.

Right: Using a koi sock means that the fish is never directly handled. The koi is always released head first through the open end of the fine-mesh sleeve, in order not to damage its scales or fins.

unstressed at the show. Enthusiastic hobbyists can make their own version of this, but for most, the ubiquitous plastic bag is perfectly adequate.

When you are ready to catch your fish, put a floating basket or bowl in the water and switch off all pumps so that you can get a good view. Once you lower the net into the water, the fish become very nervous and descend to the bottom to avoid being caught. It is important to move the net very slowly and avoid chasing the fish around, as you may inadvertently catch an innocent fish with the rim, resulting in an ulcer at a later date. Slowly tease the intended catch into an area from which it cannot escape, such as a corner of the pond or a shallow area. Gently move closer to the fish as it swims away from you toward the pond wall and just as it makes a turn, try to catch it in the center of the net. With the fish in the net, begin to raise the net to the surface and try to keep the fish's nose facing into the net. If it looks toward the rim, it will see an opportunity to escape and jump out. If this does happen, do not try to stop it from escaping; let it go and try again, because all the thrashing around may cause an injury. Once the fish is near the surface, never lift it out of the water into the basket as it will flap around in the net and could lose scales or split its fins. Tip the floating basket or bowl with the rim of the net so that the edge is below the water level and coax the fish in. As you carefully remove the net, the basket will float up and the fish is safely landed.

Catch your koi as near to the time of departure as possible, so they spend the minimum time in confinement. Double or even triple bags are insurance against springing a leak. Unless the koi are very small, bag each one separately. Various chemicals can be added to

the transit water to calm the koi and neutralize ammonia excreted through their gills.

Add only enough clean pond water to cover the fish backs when the bags are laid on their side, then fill the rest of the space with oxygen. You will need to take your own cylinder along to the show, as you cannot rely on one being available there. Never blow into the bag to inflate it; instead of oxygen, the fish will have a suffocating layer of carbon dioxide above them.

Secure the bags with strong rubber bands, and make sure you have plenty of spares. Pack the koi securely in polystyrene fish boxes and make sure these will not slide around during the trip. Work out the shortest route to the show and make as few stops as possible on the way.

When the show is over and the debenching team has allowed you access to your koi, the bagging process is repeated. Take along your own koi sock to catch your fish from the net, rather than try to lift them bodily; both you and the fish will be tired by now, and accidents can happen when the ground underfoot is soaking wet.

On arrival back home, some koi keepers give their fish a short salt bath, while others put them right into the pond. Either way, watch the koi especially carefully for a few days after the show, notably for signs of white spot, which can be triggered by heating or cooling of vat water. Organizers try to maintain a steady temperature, but variations are bound to occur when water changes are made, or if vats (however well shaded) are exposed to the sun. You should also test your pond for ammonia an hour or two after the show fish have returned, as bagged fish have a tendency to dump this toxin on their release.

Types of shows

Interest in showing koi is usually kindled at club level, as it will indicate how well you are selecting and looking after your fish. Visiting other members' ponds will give

Left: A benching team at work. Koi are being transferred from their transit bags into the show vats and classified according to size and variety.

Below: Whenever a fish's eligibility for a particular size category is in question, the issue is settled by measuring it from nose to tail extremities against a scale marked on the side of the floating basket.

you some idea, but there is a big difference between competition and mere speculation on your part.

Club shows can either be closed, with entry restricted to members' fish alone, or open to outsiders. Depending on committee policy, or the association to which the club may be affiliated, the show can be Japanese or Western-style. The difference is described below. The organizers will decide which method to choose and advise entrants in advance. Size and variety classifications may also vary from show to show, taking into account the koi being put forward.

A typical Western-style show

The flagship koi show in the UK is the BKKS National, held annually in Western style. It is open to all koi keepers, whether or not they belong to the Society. Entries must be booked several weeks in advance, so that the organizers can allocate vats and collect competition fees. On arrival at the venue, ideally on the Friday afternoon prior to the show weekend or, failing that, early on Saturday before the public is admitted, koi keepers report to an official who checks their names off against the exhibitors' list and allocates a vat number. The fish are then carried in their unopened transit bags to the center ring and floated for up to 30 minutes in their vat until water temperatures have equalized. Then they are released.

On the first morning of the actual show, the benching team arrives to ensure that the fish are in sufficiently good health to compete, and then to categorize them

according to size and variety. These volunteers play no part in the judging. The koi are measured in a floating basket marked with a scale. The process takes only seconds, with an experienced member of the benching team holding the koi gently against the scale. If a fish is a borderline case between size categories, the owner has the right to ask for it to be remeasured. At the same time, the variety is noted down from a standard list of 13 possible show classes and the koi is cross-referenced to its vat number and photographed. These days, Polaroid cameras have been superseded by digital technology and the pictures are fed into a centralized computer that processes the results as they come through. The koi keeper signs the benching form and keeps a copy, which is proof of ownership of the fish.

With the benching completed, judging can begin. At a BKKS show, this is conducted by a team recruited and trained by the Judging and Standards Committee (JSC).

Normally, one full and one trainee judge work in pairs, the more experienced of the two controlling the decisions. In the event of any dispute relating to variety or eligibility of a fish for showing, the final word rests with the senior judge on the day.

Initially, judges select first and second places in each of the 7 sizes and 13 classifications, or as many as are possible from the entries – often there are gaps. From these are chosen first, second, and third in all sizes, regardless of variety. The next stage is to choose from this short list of up to 39 koi a Baby Champion (Sizes 1 and 2), Adult Champion (Sizes 3 and 4), and Mature Champion (Sizes 5, 6, and 7). These three are all possible contenders for the Grand Champion award, although in practice a baby koi almost never wins this, because it takes special skills to grow a koi and still retain good body shape, skin quality, and pattern. It is not "done" to talk to the officials while they are judging, but after the results are announced there is no harm in asking them how they arrived at their decisions.

As in Japan, the premier award tends to go to a Go Sanke (Kohaku, Sanke, or Showa), which is no reflection on the quality of fish in the other 10 classifications. In some UK shows, additional awards may be made for Best Tategoi (koi with the most potential to improve), Best Home-bred Koi, and Best Jumbo (the largest koi benched). The Jumbo award is the only one dependent on size alone.

Throughout the show, the vats should be continually tested for ammonia and falling pH, vacuumed to remove solids, and part water-changed. A watch is also kept on dissolved oxygen levels, and spectators are discouraged from dipping their fingers in the water, kicking the vats, or doing anything that might jeopardize the fish. Security vigils are mounted during the night, as many of the koi are extremely valuable.

On Sunday the results are known and posted and then the public can admire the winning koi. Prize presentations take place at the end of the day, after which competitors reclaim their fish, bag them up, and take them home without delay.

Left: *From the awards posted around the vat, this competitor's koi have fared rather well! Note the heavy aeration, which is only turned off briefly while the fish are being judged or for the benefit of photographers at the show.*

Above: *At a provincial English koi show, a senior judge works with a trainee so that the less experienced member of the team can be instructed and continuously assessed. Becoming a full judge can take three years or more.*

Left: Booking in koi at the All-Japan Show near Tokyo is carried out with production line efficiency. Dealers help out with this task.

Right: Same size, but different varieties – the Japanese show format is easiest on the judges.

Right: Koi are taken to their show vats in wheeled trolleys such as this, and rarely is a drop of water spilled on the way.

Japanese shows

In Japanese-style shows, at whatever level, koi of the same size and variety are grouped in the same vat, regardless of who owns them, and can be moved several times as judging progresses. This enables direct visual comparisons to be made between fish of very similar quality, which speeds the whole judging process and arguably makes for a fairer result.

The All-Japan Show

This premier indoor event in the koi calendar takes place in January on the outskirts of Tokyo. Organizers are the All-Japan Nishikigoi Dealers Association and the Zen Nippon Airinkai, who have affiliated chapters worldwide. The five-day show is open to all koi keepers, amateur and professional, but fish must be entered by the dealers, who also carry out benching duties and generally help out. Variety groupings are much the same as in the UK, except that the Japanese have separate categories for Doitsu koi and Goshiki. However, there are many more size groups and, in recognition of the physical differences

between male and female koi, from Size 10 (55.88-60 cm/22-24 in) upward the sexes are judged independently of one another.

The judges, including dealer guests from abroad, select first and second in all sizes and varieties, the top fish joining others in their size in a separate vat. From these are picked the winners of each size, regardless of variety. These koi are known as "Kokugyo." The penultimate stage is to award a Grand Prize in five size groupings – Baby Koi (Yogyo), Young Koi (Wakagoi), Adult Koi (Sogyu), Mature Koi (Seigyo), and Jumbo (Kyogoi). These then move to yet another vat, from which the Grand Champion is selected. To stand any chance at all, this fish must measure 80 cm (32 in) or more. Improving the growth rate and ultimate size of their koi is a primary aim of modern breeders, so more and more quality Jumbo-sized koi are in contention at the All-Japan Show.

Alternative show formats

The Japanese way does carry with it the risk, however slight, of cross-infection and parasite transfer, hence the Western-style show. Here, all koi belonging to one exhibitor are allocated their own vat, in which they stay for the duration. Logistically, a Western-style event is a headache for the organizers, with more vats and backup water required, while the judges need to carry around mental pictures of koi from different vats. However in the UK, at least, competitors are currently happiest with this format.

Following disease scares – first spring viremia of carp virus (SVC, see page 92) and, more recently, other viral bacterial infections – many more clubs are opting for the photographic show format. Here, fish never leave their home ponds. Instead, a team of judges visits each entrant in turn, bowls their koi, makes notes, and takes photographs. The evidence is collated and decisions are made; later, the club members are able to view the snapshots and voice their own opinions on the judges' skills.

Left: *A 40 cm (16 in) Doitsu Showa entered in the 2001 All-Japan show. Doitsu fish there have their own classes, which is probably fairer than expecting them to compete against fully scaled koi.*

Right: *Grand Champion of the 2001 All-Japan show, a 90 cm (36 in) Kohaku owned by a Taiwanese hobbyist. Such youthful skin and deep, clearly defined hi (red) are exceptional in such a large koi.*

Breeding koi

Breeding high-grade koi is a very complex subject that has intrigued breeders for centuries. In this chapter we enter the magical world of the famous Japanese breeders to find out how they perform miracles every season to produce bountiful selections of fantastic Nishikigoi. We then go on to see how we can put this knowledge into good practice to improve the breeding of the koi in our own ponds.

Left to their own devices and given the right conditions, koi will naturally spawn in late spring or early summer. The art of the professional fish farmer/breeder is to breed a particular variety of koi regularly and with consistent results. Hopefully, after successive spawnings over a number of seasons, a perfect specimen will have evolved. As in the case of many prized animals, such as cats, dogs, and horses, a pedigree line is developed. This entails a broodstock of near-perfect males and females, brought together simply for the process of procreating and producing the perfect offspring. The same principles relate to the breeding of high-grade Nishikigoi.

Below: A terraced mud pond in Japan. Similar ponds all over the Niigata region are infused with natural montmorillionite clay, allowing small fry and Tategoi to grow at amazing rates in summer. Producing high-grade koi is a lucrative industry.

Breeding Nishikigoi in Japan

Although koi are bred successfully in the Far East, Israel, South Africa, the United States, and Europe, Japan is still the home of Nishikigoi, so we will examine the success story of the breeders there.

Several areas in Japan are important for the high-grade koi they produce, notably Hiroshima, Shizuoka, Saitama, Toyama, and Kyushu, but the prefecture of Niigata remains by far the most distinguished. Here you will find many well-known resident Nishikigoi breeders and their fish. Kawasawa, Shinoda, Hosokai, and Dainichi read like names from a "Who's Who" of koi breeders.

Modern koi breeders, even those following in their father's footsteps, have probably studied fish farming and traveled the world, learning the complexities of fish genetics and breeding methods. Fish farming in Japan does not only mean the breeding, subsequent spawning, and raising of a breeder's own fry. Some farmers just buy koi fry or even the eggs and grow them in their own stock mud ponds. This is not cheating, but purely a practical answer to the lack of space for raising prized koi from the top breeders.

Although the mud ponds are vast and hold enormous stocks of koi, they are available only during the summer growing period. The ponds are emptied during the October harvest and do not contain any stock until the following May. All stock is brought down to the breeders' winter holding facilities, which are usually located near their homes. The koi are then over-wintered in specially built, greenhouse-style facilities that contain many huge ponds for raising their prized new-season Tategoi (certain fish chosen by the breeder for their prospective potential) and their broodstock.

Japan and koi breeding are synonymous with the famous "mud ponds" in

Left: *Yamabuki Ogons in a typical overwintering pond. The ponds are filled to capacity for the winter and many of the koi are sold off during the spring harvest. The Tategoi are retained before being returned to the mud ponds to improve in color and size.*

Above: *Thousands of Kohaku in an indoor holding pond. The koi literally climb over each other the moment they sense someone close by, hoping for a feeding. Note the paddle machine at the top of the picture; it agitates the water, forcing in much-needed oxygen.*

which young fry and Tategoi are raised. These man-made ponds are located on hillsides close to the paddy fields that they once served. These days, far more money is made selling Nishikigoi around the globe than from a kilo of rice! New ponds are dug with bulldozers; the clay is tamped down by machine to make them impregnable to water and smoothed off for the benefit of the koi and the ease of netting them later. The ponds vary in size, but range from 60 m² (646 ft²) to many acres, while the depth usually depends on the size of fish being grown: up to 1m (39 in) for fry to over 3 m (10 ft) for the larger fish. Stocking levels for these ponds range from 8,000 to 15,000 fry per 100 kl (22,000 gal) of pond water. This level of stocking allows for up to four culls throughout the summer growing season.

The summers in Japan are extremely warm (above 30°C/86°F), which means that the ponds need heavy aeration. This is achieved using large compressors or paddle-type machines that agitate the water surface. Both methods force air, or dissolved oxygen – the best aeration possible – into the water.

There is only one predator of koi (other than man) that causes problems for the breeder. The indomitable heron is a problem in Japan, just as it is in the rest of the world. Both the tried and tested nylon line and elevated moving scarecrows are used to deter herons from the moment the mud ponds are stocked.

Preparing the mud ponds

In early spring the mud ponds are drained off and allowed to dry out. The ponds are then rototilled and pure lime is added to the mud. The lime not only kills off any parasites that may be lurking in the mud, but also helps to increase the pH of the very acid, natural spring water from the mountains that is used to refill the pond. The breeder then adds phosphates and minerals to the

The koi harvest

Left: A very large natural mud pond being filled with water before the new season's koi are added. The mud allows the koi to root around on the bottom in search of food. This is a natural tendency in the entire carp family.

Right: When it is time to harvest the large koi, the mud pond is netted and the koi are drawn toward the bankside. Helpers enter the water in giant waders to help catch the prize fish by hand. The fish are then placed into floating baskets to await transport.

Above: Having been removed from the floating baskets, the large koi are transferred into containers that are lifted onto trucks. The koi are then transported to nearby indoor holding ponds for sale or overwintering.

pond base before it is tamped down again ready for refilling. As well as being very acid, the spring water also has a high mineral content, so the water in the pond tends to turn green very quickly.

A few days before spawning, chicken manure is added to the mud ponds and this produces millions of natural infusoria (a class of protozoa – a minute, waterborne life form), an essential food for young fry. The newly hatched fry require vast amounts of infusoria to sustain their growth rate from day one. Tategoi also enjoy this diet when they are returned to the new season's refreshed mud ponds, having been overwintered in the indoor ponds.

Meanwhile, the indoor spawning pools are also made ready. They are drained and cleaned thoroughly and the filters replenished with new oyster shells that help to raise the pH of the water. The pools are then refilled with exactly the same fresh spring water as the mud ponds. The broodstock, known as Oyagoi, are selected and placed in separate pools, one for males, the other for females.

Preparing for spawning

During May, the pools are prepared for the actual spawning. A large rectangular spawning net about 1 m (39 in) deep is suspended within the pool to prevent the mating koi from damaging themselves on the sides of the pool. Soft, artificial spawning grass (kin-ran) is then attached to the bottom of the net to induce spawning. In June, the brood koi are introduced to the spawning pool. Mature females (over five years old) and males (over four years old) are normally used for breeding. Experience has shown that younger females do not produce sufficient eggs, while males do not produce sufficient milt (sperm) to fertilize all the eggs, making a spawning commercially uneconomical.

For a natural spawning, one female is introduced to three males. In general, spawning takes place within two days of the fish being placed in the pool. With the help of the net and artificial grass to improve the breeding environment, the female drops her eggs, which are immediately fertilized by the male. The ambient water temperature should be about 17°C (62°F). Spawning nearly always occurs very early in the morning and takes between five and nine hours to complete. A mature female can shed up to 400,000 eggs at one spawning. A member of the breeding team is always available during the mating process to oversee "fair play" and check on the female's condition. The parents are quickly removed from the pool to an outside mud pond to recuperate and to prevent them from devouring their offspring.

The pool with the newly hatched eggs is then treated with a mild solution of malachite green to prevent fungal infection (*Saprolegnia*) from affecting the eggs. After spawning, the water quality of the pool is constantly checked for ammonia, nitrite, and oxygen levels, and where necessary, spring water is continuously trickled into the pool, creating a gentle but constant water change. Heavy aeration is maintained at all times to produce the high dissolved oxygen levels required. Depending on the water temperature, the eggs hatch in three to five days.

The fry

After hatching, the fry resemble tiny transparent slivers with eyes and a yolk sac. At first, they live off the yolk sac, and their swimbladder gradually inflates, but within a day they become horizontal in the water and free-swimming. Now the fry are about 7 mm (0.28 in) long and appear pale yellow. They are soon darting around in short bursts, hunting for food. At this stage, they are carefully transported to the enriched waters of the mud ponds to grow during the summer season.

The first cull takes place a few weeks later. The mud pond is carefully harvested, using huge, fine nets to avoid damaging the stock. About 80 percent of the stock – fish with deformities, or specimens showing poor color, size, and shape – are culled. The rest – those already showing signs of

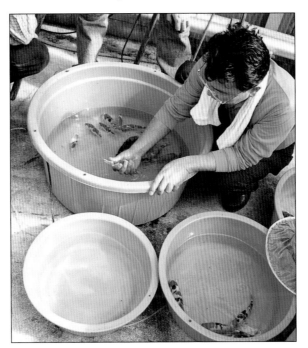

Above: Hand-selecting Tosai (less than one-year-old) koi for a prospective customer. Each transaction involves a certain amount of bartering, adding or removing a certain Tategoi from a consignment to achieve the right price.

good color or pattern – are retained. By this time, they are about 1.25 cm (0.5 in) long.

In late July, when the fry are about 2.5 cm (1 in) long, a further cull takes place. This time, about 50 percent of the fry are retained and their food is supplemented with powdered fry food, suspended in baskets in and around the ponds. The third cull takes place toward the end of August, when about 60 percent of the fry are retained for raising and the rest are destroyed. The baby koi, now approximately 5 cm (2 in) long, are fed mainly on pelleted food. During late October, when the fish reach about 10 cm (4 in), the mud ponds are completely harvested. Now only the best Tosai koi (less than one year old) are finally selected for raising in the indoor winter ponds, some of which are heated. A further 30 percent are destroyed and the rest are sold off very cheaply, mainly at auction. These are the koi that are sometimes raised in countries such as Thailand and Taiwan and sold cheaply around the world as Japanese-bred koi. You can now appreciate why the quality of koi to come out of Japan is so high; every fish will have survived as many as four separate culls, purely on merit.

Artificial spawning methods

Some countries outside Japan spawn koi to order, using hormone injections of gonadotropin (removed from the pituitary gland of donor wild carp) to induce an almost instant spawning. The method is widely used throughout the world for the mass production of fish destined for the food market, such as trout and salmon. However, Japanese Nishikigoi breeders frown on this process, which they consider poses a risk to their valuable broodstock, and because the natural method still produces more fry than they can economically handle.

Other spawning methods employed in modern koi breeding include "chipping." Here, the parent male and female are tagged with a microchip placed just beneath their scales. The fish can then be readily identified within a breeding program to ensure it "throws true" when attempting to breed a specific variety. This is a term used in breeding programs to describe the offspring from a particular spawning. If the subsequent progeny are identical to the parent (even in the case of cross-breeding – a planned new variety) and have not produced any "throwbacks" (fish varieties of unknown origin and parentage), then the offspring are said to have "thrown true." The information is collated and used for subsequent spawning to achieve the perfect progeny.

Breeding your own koi

Breeding your own koi can be the culmination of a dream. There is nothing quite like the achievement of bringing a living creature into the world and being involved in its development; in the case of koi, this means from the moment the egg hatches until it grows to full maturity. The following will enable you to tread in the steps of the revered Japanese breeders and perhaps even produce a winner in your local Open Koi Show. However, you should not take the breeding process too seriously. Expense dictates that you will not be able to match the "big boys" from Japan. Even on a very small scale, koi breeding is not cheap, either in terms of money or time, but it is still a very worthwhile experience.

Above: *Flock spawning in progress. The males coerce the female into a corner and encourage her to spawn in the blanketweed. Transfer the eggs from the algae (left) to a holding facility before the parents eat them.*

Natural spawning

Koi are oviparous breeders, which means they lay eggs. Once shed, the eggs fall to the bottom or surrounds of the pond and stick to any plant matter or other object in the pond, thanks to a sticky secretion on the outer surface. The survival of the fittest begins right away; remember, only the strongest, but not necessarily the best, will survive.

Koi will spawn naturally, given the ideal water conditions and a temperature of 17°C (62°F) or higher. As the water temperature rises in the spring, be prepared for the fish to spawn en masse. This is known as a flock spawning and can produce many koi, but their quality will leave much to be desired. The size, color, and patterns of these koi will be generally poor, although they may be perfectly healthy.

Sexing koi

Koi keepers often ask, "How do I tell the sex of my koi?" The answer is that even a professional breeder finds it very difficult to sex small koi. As a general rule, koi measuring less than 25 cm (10 in) are presumed to be sexually immature, but once past this stage, the sexual organs begin to develop. Mature females are generally plumper in the belly region, whereas mature males tend

Basic genetics

A koi will receive one gene from each parent for each characteristic. It cannot receive two genes from one and none from the other. If you mate a scaled koi with a scaleless (Doitsu) koi, you might expect to produce some of each type, but this is not always the case. One gene can mask the other completely – known as a *dominant* gene masking a *recessive* one. When breeding a particular variety of koi, you must first select suitable broodstock (parent fish). Like the breeders in Japan, select one suitable female to at least three males to ensure a successful spawning. The chosen parents, both male and female, need not be perfect in every respect (variety, color, shape, deportment, etc.). If you require good color, then select a koi for that feature alone; the fish's other attributes can be secondary. Over several seasons, you will be able to introduce all the prime features into the offspring.

to be more sylphlike and narrow-bodied when viewed from above. In male koi, the pectoral fins are usually longer, and the ventral fins are longer and more pointed than in females.

When males are ready to spawn, fine, white, raised spots called tubercles appear on the head, gill plates, and the leading edges of the pectoral fins. They resemble grains of salt and are often mistaken for – and treated as – white spot (*Ichthyophthirius*) disease by the inexperienced koi keeper, so it is vital to appreciate the difference. The tubercles are most prolific on the pectoral fins, where they occur in fairly regular rows and feel slightly rough. The male uses them during breeding, when he constantly nudges and chases the female to induce spawning.

Having sexed suitable koi, it is best to separate the males from the females in early spring, before any spawning activity takes place.

Planning for spawning

There is obviously an advantage to planning a spawning, so that you can control when your fish will mate. By having everything ready for a planned spawning you can start to develop your own strain of koi in your own breeding facility.

If you can divide your pond into sections using floating net cages, so much the better. If this is not feasible, you will need a separate breeding tank. Use either system before the actual spawning to keep the males and females totally separate.

You can make temporary net cages from very fine net curtain material draped over and tied to solid 40 mm (1.5 in) or 50 mm (2 in) pipework. Form the pipework into a large rectangular shape, using 90° bends so that the net can float in the pond, while the bottom is weighted to create a "pool within a pool." The breeding area will now be completely enclosed within the net, which protects the fish and retains all the eggs.

Now follow the professional breeders' regime and tie spawning ropes to the bottom of the netting to replicate the fishes' natural spawning grounds. This method is perfect, as the mating is really quite physical. Most fish, particularly the female, usually end up with scale damage after all the buffeting and bumping involved. Place the parent fish (one female to three males) within the breeding net a few days before the anticipated spawning.

Alternatively, use the excellent spawning ropes or floating spawning cages now available. Spawning ropes are made of fine nylon bristles twisted around a central wire, similar to the brushes used for filtration purposes, but much longer. They are suspended within the pool and imitate underwater plant fronds. When spawning is complete and the ropes are covered in eggs, remove them to a separate facility for hatching.

Floating cages resemble breeding nets, but are much smaller and generally round. The eggs adhere to the soft nylon fronds on the outside of the netting. When spawning has occurred, turn the cage inside out, which protects the eggs and subsequent fry from their parents, although both can remain in the same environment. This method is good for both fry and broodstock and causes them the least amount of stress.

You can make a breeding tank from any large container with an adequate surface area that can sustain some form of filtration and aeration. Always check

A floating spawning cage

Drape fine net over the pipe and tie it to the framework.

Use 90° bends to make up the frame.

Solid plastic pipe

Use weights to shape the netting.

Spawning ropes with nylon bristles.

Lay spawning material on the bottom.

A spawning rope

Green spawning ropes represent pond vegetation.

Remove the ropes with the eggs to a safe haven for hatching and growing.

Dried foods for newborn and small fry

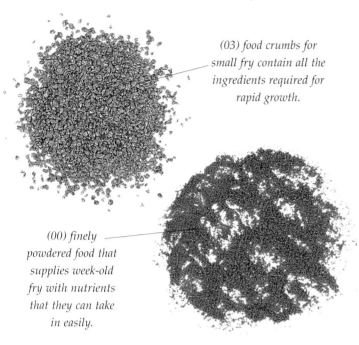

(03) food crumbs for small fry contain all the ingredients required for rapid growth.

(00) finely powdered food that supplies week-old fry with nutrients that they can take in easily.

where containers have come from and what may have been in them; certain materials or liquids could prove highly toxic to fish. A specially built quarantine tank can double up satisfactorily as a breeding unit. When required, top off the secondary tank with identical pond water so that there is no difference in water quality. This will ease the stress on the broodstock when they are moved.

The spawning

Now you can apply the same principles to breeding as the professional fish farmer. Clean the breeding tank (if you are using one) and make sure that the water quality and aeration are perfect. Use the same ratio of parent fish for breeding, namely one mature female to at least two or three mature males. This should result in a near-perfect spawning, with all eggs fertilized. Put the brood koi together and if they are ready to mate, the males will soon be chasing the female vigorously, nudging into her rear end, trying to induce her to release her eggs. This mating ritual is known as the "spawning dance."

This magical moment usually happens in the early hours of the morning after a warm night. If you wish to play the expectant parent, it really is an amazing sight. The early morning quiet is broken by the sound of violent thrashing in the water and the surface of the pond becomes a bubbling mass. The mating procedure

will last most of the morning and then the pond becomes motionless; in fact, an eerie stillness descends. When everything has settled down, the first thing is to remove the parents from the breeding area. This entails lifting your koi from the floating breeding net or separate breeding tank and returning them to the pond or, if you are using a floating spawning cage, turning it inside out. This is to save the eggs from the predatory instincts of the parent fish, which look upon their newly laid spawn as first-class beluga caviar!

The eggs can be either left in place or taken to another hatchery tank containing similar water. In both cases, treat the spawning media containing the eggs with a mild solution of malachite green (3 parts per million) to sterilize the eggs for 10-15 minutes. It is true that some breeders do not do this; they believe that the eggs absorb the chemical, which has a toxic effect and causes congenital defects.

Caring for the fry

Depending on water temperature, the eggs take four to seven days to hatch, although they do not all hatch together. Once hatched, the fry live off their yolk sac for two or three days and then require a constant supply of liquid or powdered fry food. Provide a high-protein diet, but take care not to pollute the water. The best advice is to feed little and often and test the water constantly for ammonia, nitrite, and oxygen content. Aerate the water well, but not so severely that it damages the small fry. Strong water currents built up by the airstones can easily lead to the fry being buffeted against the sides of the pond. If the young are held in a separate tank, keep the filtration at a low flow rate so they are not dragged into the filter media. To avoid a buildup of toxic levels of ammonia and nitrite within the hatchery tank, consider installing a constant water change facility, whereby a trickle flow of fresh water is in constant operation, thus avoiding major water changes later on.

Liquid or dry fry food is readily available from koi dealers and aquatic outlets. Choose a liquid fry food specifically for egglayers. It contains extracts that help form instant infusoria on which the minute fry can survive. Add the liquid to the water via a droplet bottle two to four times each day. The dried alternative is supplied in a dustlike powder, but performs in exactly the same way as liquid food.

After a few weeks under ideal conditions, the fry will readily accept broken-up flaked fish food or good-quality, powdered koi pellets. You can even add montmorillionite clay to the water on a regular basis to supply valuable trace elements in readily absorbed quantities, thus providing the fry with a really healthy start. Because koi do not have a stomach, continue feeding little, but often. Good-quality, dried tropical fish food is a useful addition to the diet of small koi as it contains many trace elements, plus animal as well as vegetable extracts. Your local aquarist center may also stock frozen fry food, such as daphnia and bloodworm, which will all be readily accepted. This is a much safer method of feeding "whole" food than catching or breeding your own; there is always the risk that you might introduce a waterborne parasite from a natural pond.

From an early stage, check for larger than average fry; these may well be eating the smaller fry. Remove the young "predators" to a separate holding facility or cull them if they show any deformity. Once the fry reach 5 cm (2 in), they should be feeding on good-quality dry food, either flake or mini-pellets. From then on, maintain your regular feeding program.

Pay regular attention to the water conditions to avoid any problems resulting from poor water quality. One of the problems of breeding koi outside Japan is that countries with a temperate climate do not enjoy the same long and very hot summers. Those extra few weeks feeding enable the fry to grow stronger before the onset of winter. In early fall, consider heating the breeding facility to extend the summer or bring the young fish in from the cold. A large aquarium in a shed, garage, or greenhouse is the most successful location for overwintering them. When spring comes, you can return them to the garden pond, healthy and well fed.

Above: This Taisho Sanke was chosen for its potential at one year old and is described as Tategoi. Koi breeders make these choices all the time.

Right: The same koi some years later. Note how the black has come out in just the right proportions over an excellent Kohaku pattern. The breeder probably had a good idea of what to expect, but the exact quality is the mystery and well worth the wait.

Recordkeeping

Remember to keep a record of your successes and failures. The log should show all the details of your brood koi, both male and female. A diary of the breeding program and relevant information, such as the prevailing weather conditions, etc., will help you when you start breeding your own fish and may even contribute to improving the quality of future generations. Record all deaths due to illness or damage. The accumulated information will help you in future breeding seasons.

Culling

In common with all the professional breeders, you will have to face the fact that culling is necessary. From your initial hatching, many fish will inevitably die of natural causes. Some will suffer from strange deformities or be a poor size, color, or shape, and they will all have to be culled. A fish anesthetic obtained from your koi dealer is the most humane method of disposal. Make up a stronger-than-usual dose and leave your culled fry in the anesthetic to pass away without stress. Further culling may become necessary as the fish grow up.

Part Two

Introduction

Beginners will frequently ask of a particular koi: "What species is that?" The question merits only one valid reply – Cyprinus carpio *– because that is the scientific name carried by all koi, however diverse they appear to be.*

So, is the word "breed" more appropriate? It works for pedigreed dogs, in the sense that if you cross a Corgi with another Corgi, more Corgis result. But, with koi, the outcome is nowhere near as certain. Put a male and a female Sanke together and the resulting fry will certainly contain a percentage of Sanke – plus Bekko, Kohaku, and many nondescripts.

The terms used to describe koi are "class" and "variety." These are purely arbitrary, as the fish have all been developed by man, but they do at least give us a yardstick by which koi can be bought and judged. Each class may contain one or many varieties. For example, Kohaku, Sanke, and Showa are single-variety classes, whereas the Kawarimono class is home to dozens of nonmetallic koi that do not readily fit elsewhere into the hierarchy. To confuse the issue further, there are subvarieties, with a Japanese terminology that distinguishes them from other, broadly similar, fish. To take the example of Kohaku, there are terms for two- , three- , and four-step pattern koi; words to describe their scalation; and others that relate to markings. So a Doitsu Sandan Maruten Kuchibeni Kohaku would be a white and red nonmetallic koi (Kohaku) with mirror scales (Doitsu), three-step pattern (Sandan), including a separate patch of red on the head (Maruten), and red lips (Kuchibeni).

Recognizing all the varieties takes time, and there will always be some koi that spark disputes, even among so-called "experts." More important is to recognize a healthy, well-shaped koi with good skin – the rest will come with practice.

Kohaku

The modern Kohaku reflects rapid cultural changes in the homeland of koi. As Japan broke from its inward-looking feudal traditions to become a living metaphor for the twentieth-century technological revolution, the Japanese began to revise their appreciation of this, their "flagship" koi variety. The result is that fish no longer need to conform rigidly to laid-down pattern guidelines to compete at the top level in shows. Today's Kohaku break the rules to challenge once-fixed ideals of beauty. This relaxation in attitude to pattern, but not overall quality, has fed through to the rest of the world, to the extent that koi keeping can never again "end with Kohaku"; this deceptively simplistic red and white fish presents breeders and hobbyists with endless opportunities still waiting to be explored. However, pattern is only one element of a good Kohaku; body shape, intensity of hi, and good skin are of equal importance, and the bloodlines favoring these qualities can be traced back more than a century.

The history of Kohaku

Red and white mutations of the ancestral black carp (Magoi) first appeared in the early 1800s among fish bred for food by rice farmers in Niigata prefecture. For curiosity's sake, rather than with any thoughts of commercial gain, the farmers kept these back as pets and spawned them together. "Kohaku-like" characteristics emerged in some of these offspring – red heads, gill covers, and lips, or small patches of hi on the back and belly, though nothing worthy of being called a pattern. That changed in 1888, when Kunizo Hiroi ran a red-

Hi in the dorsal fin of Kohaku is still regarded as a fault, but in this fish there is none to be seen.

There is plenty of movement in the forward area of hi, with a pleasing white "cut" into the shoulder.

Near-classic head hi avoids the eyes, leaving the pure white nose in prominent contrast.

KOI DEFINITIONS

Hi ~ Red

Kohaku ~ White koi with red markings

Kuchibeni ~ Red lips – literally "lipstick"

Magoi ~ Ancestral black carp

Maruten ~ A self-contained head marking, plus red elsewhere on the body

Tancho ~ Circular red spot on head. No other red on the body

Yondan ~ Four-step pattern

PERFECTLY BALANCED PATTERN
Balance is not the same as symmetry. The pattern on the Kohaku above does not favor one side of the fish at the expense of the other, and overall, the rather plain hi to the rear of the body is complemented by the interesting zigzag conformation forward of the dorsal fin.

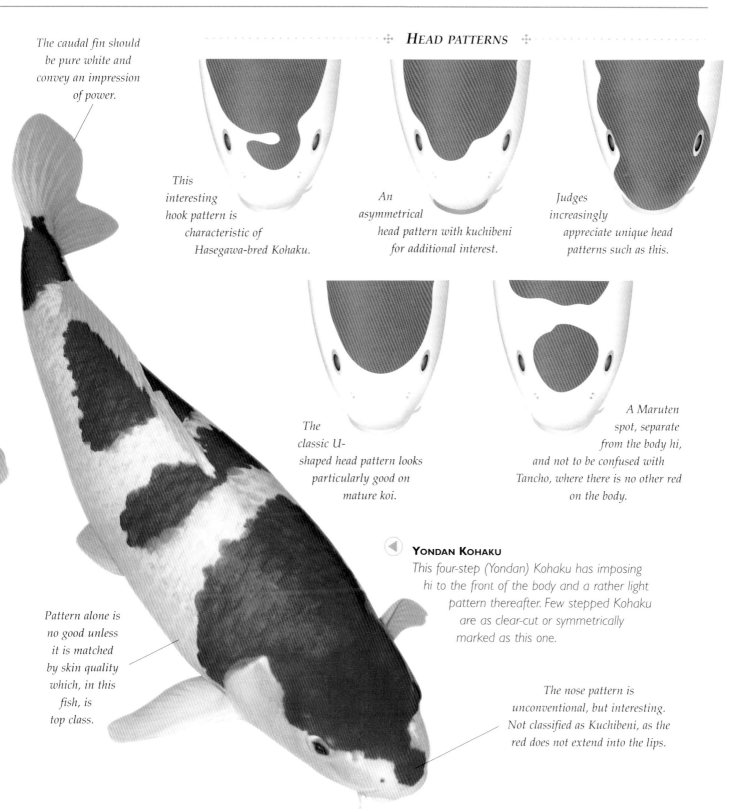

The caudal fin should be pure white and convey an impression of power.

❖ **HEAD PATTERNS** ❖

This interesting hook pattern is characteristic of Hasegawa-bred Kohaku.

An asymmetrical head pattern with kuchibeni for additional interest.

Judges increasingly appreciate unique head patterns such as this.

The classic U-shaped head pattern looks particularly good on mature koi.

A Maruten spot, separate from the body hi, and not to be confused with Tancho, where there is no other red on the body.

YONDAN KOHAKU
This four-step (Yondan) Kohaku has imposing hi to the front of the body and a rather light pattern thereafter. Few stepped Kohaku are as clear-cut or symmetrically marked as this one.

Pattern alone is no good unless it is matched by skin quality which, in this fish, is top class.

The nose pattern is unconventional, but interesting. Not classified as Kuchibeni, as the red does not extend into the lips.

headed female koi with one of his own male fish, whose markings resembled cherry blossoms. The resulting fry were used by other breeders to establish the now extinct Gosuke bloodline. All subsequent Kohaku bloodlines (Tomoin, Sensuke, Yagozen, Manzo) arose from fish of Gosuke lineage outcrossed to unrelated fish showing promise. They were named after the breeders who refined their koi over many generations of careful selection. Tomoin and Yagozen are the two major bloodlines today.

This tradition continues. We speak of a Matsunosuke bloodline, although the koi of Toshio Sakai and his protégé, Shintaro, draw heavily on their ancestry, even while they forge the future of Nishikigoi. The same can be said of probably the most famous Kohaku breeder of all, Dainichi (Minoru Mano), whose Kohaku have Tomoin blood.

The Kohaku of almost 100 years ago were recorded by the artist Hikosaburo Hirasawa, who painted the 28 fancy carp sent by the villagers of Niigata prefecture to the 1914 Taisho Exhibition in Tokyo. Looking back at images of these pioneering koi is a revelation – they show just how far Kohaku have progressed in the intervening years.

What makes a good Kohaku?

Kohaku are white koi with hi markings that should be of an even depth. Brownish red hi is preferred to the purplish type, and can be improved and stabilized over the years by color feeding and constant attention to water quality. The ground color should be snow white, with no yellowing or "shimis," and should exhibit a fine luster. The kiwa must be sharp. However, in young, unfinished Kohaku the scales are still kokesuke (semitransparent), which means the pattern definition will not be as good as in mature fish.

Although koi appreciation is no longer laid down in tablets of stone, some of the old terminology remains. Head hi is essential. On "classic" Kohaku, this forms a U-shape ending level with the eyes, but hanatsuki or kuchibeni are now just as acceptable. Hi extending over one or both eyes is not a demerit, but pure white finnage is still preferred. Kohaku whose hi is confined to the head alone are judged in the separate

IMPOSING SIMPLICITY

This Nidan (two-step) Kohaku is a very imposing fish. The pattern, with excellent kiwa and sashi, is far from complex but in a koi with such presence it is entirely appropriate. A white caudal peduncle would improve the appearance, but no matter—koi don't get much better than this in the larger sizes.

Left: *Sashi (where white scales overlay hi) is never as clearly defined as kiwa (where red scales overlay white).*

A CLASSIC SANDAN KOHAKU
This three-step Kohaku is a fish of the old school, with very clearly delineated blocks of hi. Note how the red on the head is a much deeper color than on the body; this is because there are no scales on the head to tone it down.

The contrast is good between the snow-white dorsal fin and the hi that straddles it.

FLOWERY BUT GOOD
Kohaku with patterns like this are said to be flowery. This is not a criticism, because in this koi the smaller configurations of hi are well balanced by the main blocks of color. The overall impression is of light frivolity, helped along by the intriguing head pattern.

Well-shaped, white pectoral fins counterbalance the imposing forward hi.

KOI DEFINITIONS

Hanatsuki ~ A hi pattern that reaches the mouth

Hi ~ Red

Kiwa ~ Border of red and white at the rear edge of hi patterns

Kokesuke ~ Semitranslucent

Kuchibeni ~ Red lips – literally "lipstick"

Nidan ~ Two-step pattern

Sandan ~ Three-step pattern

Sanke ~ White koi with red and black markings

Sashi ~ Overlap of red and white scales at the forward edge of hi patterns

Shimi ~ Undesirable individual dark brown or black scales on areas of ground color

Nidan Kohaku need a good flow to the pattern. This one has the desirable white caudal peduncle.

Yondan Kohaku can look fussy, unless all the steps are bold and well placed.

KOI DEFINITIONS

Inazuma ~
Lightning strike pattern

Maruten Kohaku ~
Kohaku with self-contained head marking, plus red elsewhere on the body

Nibani ~
Unstable secondary red

Nidan ~
Two-step pattern

Sandan ~
Three-step pattern

Sashi ~ Overlap of red and white scales at the forward edge of hi patterns

Tancho ~ Circular red spot on head. No other red on body

Yondan ~
Four-step pattern

Inazuma, or lightning strike pattern, is formed by sinuous hi running from head to tail.

This is a Sandan Kohaku – the head hi counts as one of the three pattern steps.

Tancho class, where the ideal marking is a perfect circle mirroring the sun on the Japanese flag and reminiscent of the head of their national bird, the Tancho crane. If a self-contained head marking is accompanied by hi elsewhere on the body of the koi, the term is "Maruten Kohaku."

Japanese names for the so-called "stepped" patterns of body and head hi (nidan, sandan, and yondan) are used more today for general descriptive purposes than as a measure of how good (or otherwise) a Kohaku is. Modern Kohaku can also exhibit smaller, complementary patches of hi, not to be confused with nibani.

For continuous head-to-tail hi patterns to be acceptable, they must be interesting. The best example is still the classic inazuma. Today's trend is for Kohaku patterns to be imposing, and this should be taken into account when buying young fish. As the skin stretches, areas of hi move apart from one another, so avoid young koi that appear to be small replicas of finished

LIGHTNING STRIKES

This is an Inazuma Maruten Nidan Kohaku. In the naming of koi, all the elements are run together to build up a picture of the fish, but no two individuals are the same.

Not Tancho, but Maruten; Tancho must be stand-alone hi.

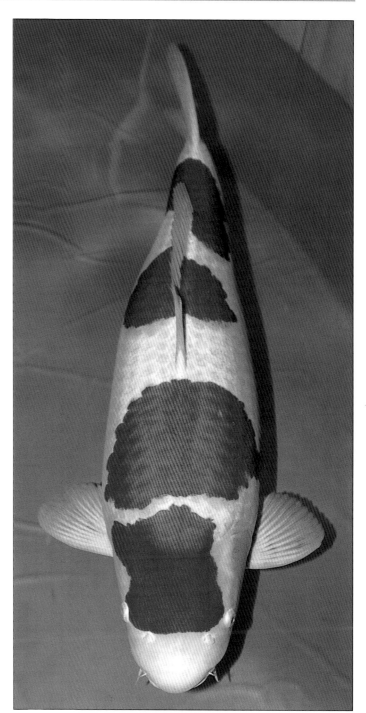

FOUR STEPS TO HEAVEN

A Yondan Maruten Kohaku — the hi here is reminiscent of cloud shadows over a snowfield. Kiwa is particularly good on this mature koi, and the skin quality is what one would expect to see on a much younger fish.

adults. Conversely, large, apparently dull blocks of hi can "break" later in life to form intriguing patterns. Body hi need not be symmetrical, or even conventionally balanced, as long as it is pleasing to the eye. But hi confined to one side of the koi when viewed from above, or making the fish head-heavy or tail-heavy, is a fault. The Japanese still prefer a break in hi at the base of the tail, although many top-grade Kohaku do not have a white caudal peduncle.

Doitsu, Gin-Rin, and metallic Kohaku

Doitsu Kohaku, which lack overall scaling, appear very clean-cut, with razor-sharp kiwa, but are considered rather two-dimensional by the Japanese. In shows without a separate Doitsu judging class, these fish will always lose out to fully scaled fish.

Gin-Rin Kohaku – fish with too many reflective scales to count individually – are judged along with Gin-Rin Sanke and Showa in their own class. The mutant scales, originally known as "dia," appear gold over hi and silver over white areas of skin. Gin-Rin scales are sometimes described as "fukurin," a term that should properly be reserved for the lustrous skin around the scales of metallic koi.

Metallic Kohaku used to be known as Platinum Kohaku but are now termed Sakura Ogon, and are judged in Hikarimoyo. The Doitsu version is called a Kikusui. All stem from Kohaku x Ogon crosses.

⁂ GIVE IT A BREAK ⁂

Some white on the caudal peduncle is desirable, particularly when hi is heavy.

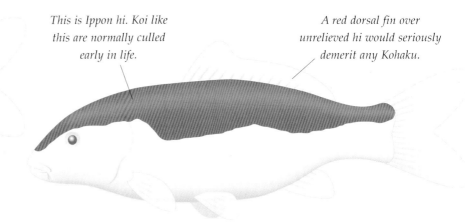

This is Ippon hi. Koi like this are normally culled early in life.

A red dorsal fin over unrelieved hi would seriously demerit any Kohaku.

132

KOI DEFINITIONS

Doitsu ~ Koi with no scales other than enlarged scales along the lateral line and two lines running either side of the dorsal fin

Fukurin ~ Net effect of lustrous skin around the scales of (usually) metallic koi

Gin-Rin ~ Koi with reflective silver scales

Hi ~ Red

Hikarimoyo ~ Class for all multicolored metallic koi except Utsuri and Showa

Ippon hi ~ Where solid red runs from nose to tail without a break

Kikusui ~ Doitsu platinum koi with metallic orange markings

Kiwa ~ Border of red and white at the rear edge of hi patterns

Ogon ~ Single-colored metallic koi

Sakura Ogon ~ Metallic Kohaku

Sanke ~ White koi with red and black markings

Sashi ~ Overlap of red and white scales at the forward edge of hi patterns

Showa ~ Black koi with red and white markings

SHOW-WINNING KOHAKU

This Kohaku has it all – superb full body shape, an interesting, though unfussy, pattern, and the all-important contrasting snow-white skin. Rarely do all these elements come together so well. When they do, you have a show winner.

THE SPARKLE OF GIN-RIN

A high-quality Gin-Rin Kohaku. The reflective scales shine silver over white skin and gold over hi. This would still be an impressive koi without the added embellishment, but inferior Gin-Rin fish can make a good first impression that is not borne out by closer scrutiny – "flashy" does not necessarily mean a quality koi. This one passes the test on all counts, however.

Sanke

Kohaku may be the purists' favorite koi, but the tricolored Sanke is almost as subtle. Its sumi markings set off hi and white skin in almost limitless permutations. The two varieties are closely linked and are the only ones with traceable bloodlines, although exactly when Sanke as we know them first appeared is open to debate. They used to be known as Taisho Sanke, or Taisho Sanshuko (after the era when they were allegedly developed, 1912-1926), but plain Sanke is now the accepted term.

The history of Sanke

A mature Sanke was brought by Gonzo Hiroi to the Tokyo Exhibition in 1914. This suggests that the variety, or at least its forebears, may have been in existence at the end of the nineteenth century (which would place it in the Meiji era). Whether there were conscious attempts to linebreed these fish is not known.

In the same year – 1914 – white koi with red and black markings appeared spontaneously in a brood of Kohaku belonging to Niigata rice farmer Heitaro Sato. Attempts to replicate the event were disappointing, and the three parent fish were passed to another breeder before being acquired by Eizaburo Hoshino of Takezawa – the village known as the birthplace of Nishikigoi. In 1917, Mr. Hoshino crossed one of these female Kohaku from Sato with a Shiro Bekko. The resulting fry showed the three characteristic Sanke colors in more or

less equal proportions, with added sumi stripes on their pectoral fins.

However, the breeder who "fixed" the strain was Torakichi Kawikame. He spawned a female Hoshino Sanke with a Yagozen Kohaku and the bloodline became known as Torazo, the name of Kawikame's father and the family business. All modern Sanke are the product of Torazo and the unrelated Sanba strain, which has since died out. The most famous current bloodlines are Matsunosuke, Jinbei, Sadazo, and Kichinai.

Matsunosuke Sanke are the joint triumph of Toshio Sakai, who runs the Isawa Nishikigoi center, and his elder brother Toshiyuki, based in Niigata. The bloodline has been reinvigorated with Magoi genes to maximize growth, while retaining quality hi and sumi pigmentation. These koi, slimly built when young, are increasingly showing Fukurin scalation, which imparts a unique sheen.

Sanke colors

A Sanke is essentially a Kohaku with Bekko-type sumi, which should not extend below the lateral line. As with Kohaku, the ideal skin is snow-white

This scarlet hi is accented by small areas of sumi. Where black overlays red, it is known as Kasane sumi.

◀ WHEN LESS IS MORE
A good Sanke is a Kohaku with added sumi, which may or may not extend into the fins. Today's fashion is for less sumi than ever before, and some Tategoi Sanke are easily confused with Kohaku until the black comes fully through.

GONE BUT NOT FORGOTTEN
Doris, arguably the finest Sanke ever to enter the UK, but sadly now no longer with us. She was bred by Sakai Matsunosuke, the best breeder of this variety in the world, and was still improving at the time of her death in summer 2001. She won two consecutive BKKS Nationals.

Most of Doris's hi stood alone, with sumi confined to the white ground. This is called Tsubo sumi.

A charming, if unconventional, head pattern.

HOW SUMI DEVELOPS
The way sumi develops on Sanke is very much down to bloodline. This fish displays areas of finished sumi toward the tail, and emergent sumi forward of the dorsal fin. This will eventually deepen to jet black, but the process could take years before the pattern is completely stabilized and the koi is said to be "finished."

This is emerging sumi and not a shimi, or blemish.

Beautiful white skin and a regular head pattern make this Sanke very special.

KOI DEFINITIONS

Bekko ~ Black Sanke-type markings on red, white, or yellow base

Fukurin ~ Net effect of lustrous skin around the scales of (usually) metallic koi

Kohaku ~ White koi with red markings

Magoi ~ Ancestral black carp

Shimi ~ Undesirable individual dark brown or black scales on areas of ground color

Shiro Bekko ~ White koi with black Sanke-type markings

Sumi ~ Black

Tategoi ~ "Unfinished" koi of any age that should continue to improve and lustrous and the overlaying hi deep and even, with no "windows" (a solid area of red with areas of white inside the pigment) – an early sign that the pattern may be breaking up and disappearing.

Young high-grade Sanke are easily confused with Kohaku, as in some bloodlines no sumi is discernible until the age of two. Nor is there a guarantee that once the sumi is there it will be stable; it may fade again, only to reemerge later.

Young Matsunosuke Sanke show faint blue-gray sumi that gradually deepens; however, Sanke of the Kichinai bloodline exhibit stable sumi at a very early age, and the only real change in their pattern results from the skin stretching as the koi grow. Early sumi that stays is known as moto sumi, while black markings that appear later are termed ato sumi.

Sumi is also named for where it appears on the koi. If it overlays the hi, it is kasane sumi, whereas if it is on white skin it is known as tsubo sumi. The latter is highly prized, but most examples of Sanke combine the two. Ultimately it is the overall effect that matters.

Sanke patterns

Changing fashions have influenced Sanke patterns, so that fish with heavy sumi are no longer as popular as those with small, accent areas of black – now very much the supporting color. Large areas of red unrelieved by cuts in the pattern are equally frowned upon – fish showing these are known as Aka Sanke.

❖ HEAD PATTERNS ❖

Sanke very rarely display any sumi on the head, only hi.

Head sumi points to Showa – but it is not a foolproof way to tell the varieties apart.

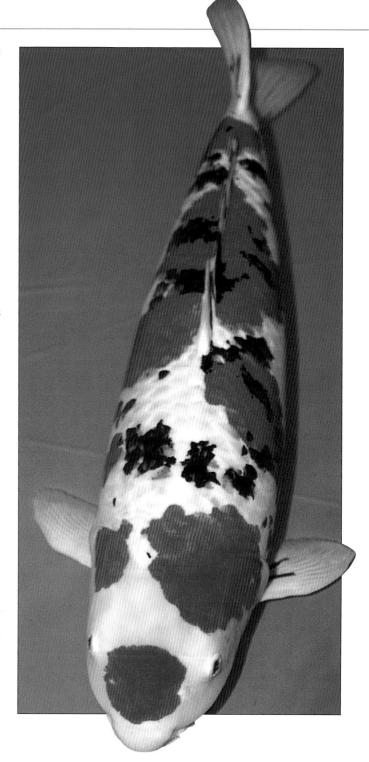

▲ **A FLOWERY SANKE**

This rather flowery Sanke has a fascinating triple hi marking on the face and shoulders. It shows well the difference between Tsubo and Kasane sumi, and how the black is configured Bekko-style, above the lateral line. Note the pectoral fin stripes.

❖ **BODY MARKINGS** ❖

Viewed sideways, the hi on Sanke does not usually extend far below the lateral line.

Sumi, too, tends to be confined to the upper part of the body.

Kasane sumi (black on red).

Tsubo sumi (black on white).

▷ **BEST OF BOTH WORLDS**
The secret with champion koi is to achieve size and volume in a fish retaining all the youthful plus points relating to skin quality and pattern. This 70 cm (28 in) Sanke shows it can be done.

This hi is already fragmenting.

"Windows" in blocks of hi, or dappled hi, suggest that the koi may later lose its red patterning entirely.

KOI DEFINITIONS

Aka Bekko ~ Red koi with black Sanke-type markings

Aka Sanke ~ Koi with large areas of red, unrelieved by cuts in the pattern

Ato sumi ~ Black markings that appear later in a koi's life

Bekko ~ Black Sanke-type markings on a white, red, or yellow base

Hi ~ Red

Kasane sumi ~ Black that overlays red

Kohaku ~ White koi with red markings

Moto sumi ~ Early sumi that remains on the body

Sanke ~ White koi with red and black markings

Sumi ~ Black

Tsubo sumi ~ Black on white skin

Sanke are not supposed to have any sumi on the head, just hi on white. When sumi does appear forward of the shoulders, depending on its position, it can look charming or else detract from the dignity of the fish. The same is true of kuchibeni; neither will make a dull koi more interesting, but if the rest of the pattern is good, it is not seen as a fault.

Hi on any of the fins is less well tolerated, but sumi on the pectoral, dorsal, or caudal fins is a desirable characteristic. The way this black is configured is one sure way of identifying Sanke – stripes on the pectoral fins are quite distinct from the motoguro found in the balljoint of Showa pectorals. Some Sanke, however, have pure white fins becoming translucent toward the leading edges. These are quite acceptable.

Symmetry of markings is never achieved on Sanke, nor should too much store be placed on balance. It is the total impact of the tricolored pattern that matters, though if all the sumi or hi runs down one flank of the koi this will not be pleasing to the eye. Similarly, not enough hi or too much sumi toward the caudal peduncle (where the body tapers) will make the fish appear head- or tail-heavy.

Sanke with a separate head hi marking and more on the body are known as Maruten Sanke; if the only hi is on the head, the fish is a Tancho Sanke and judged in that class. The term Menkaburi Sanke is

❖ FIN MARKINGS ❖

Sanke pectoral fins can be clear, or striped, as here. Sometimes the striping is confined to just one fin.

A block of sumi in the pectoral fin joint – motoguro– points to Showa or Utsurimono.

▲ A PROMISING YOUNGSTER

This young Sanke could do with more volume, which will come with age. Its large, symmetrically striped pectoral fins are a strong point, as is the cluster of shoulder sumi. Separate head hi makes the fish a Maruten Sanke.

A CLEAR-CUT DOITSU SANKE
This Doitsu Sanke has many apparently Showa traits – but is still 100 percent Sanke, despite the small patches of sumi on the head and the heavy black body markings. Note the single sumi stripe, too, in the left pectoral fin.

A very striking, though by no means classic, head pattern sets one color off against another.

KOI DEFINITIONS

Doitsu ~ Koi with no scales other than enlarged scales along the lateral line and two lines running either side of the dorsal fin

Hi ~ Red

Hikarimoyo ~ Class for all multicolored metallic koi except Utsuri and Showa

Kawarimono ~ Class for all nonmetallic koi not included in any other group

Kindai ~ White skin predominates

Kuchibeni ~ Red lips – literally "lipstick"

Maruten Sanke ~ Sanke with self-contained head marking, plus red elsewhere on the body

Menkaburi ~ Red head

Motoguro ~ Solid black coloration in the base of pectoral fins on Showa and related varieties

Sanke ~ White koi with red and black markings

Showa ~ Black koi with red and white markings

Sumi ~ Black

Tancho ~ Circular red spot on head. No other red on body

Yamatonishiki ~ Metallic Sanke

reserved for fish whose head hi extends down the nose and over the jaws in a hoodlike pattern. In Budo Sanke all the sumi overlays the hi. There is no sumi on the white skin and the fish is benched in Kawarimono or Koromo (see also page 166).

Doitsu and other Sanke

Doitsu Sanke look clean-cut, as there is no blurring of the hi and sumi fore and aft. Good examples appear almost synthetic, as though the colors had been applied with a brush.

Although the Japanese do not rate these fish as highly as other Sanke, they do at least give them a separate Doitsu judging class, but in most other countries all Sanke are entered together – when the fully scaled fish almost always tend to win.

All hybrids between Sanke and other, non-metallic, varieties are judged in the Kawarimono class, while Yamatonishiki are grouped in Hikarimoyo, meaning metallic koi of more than one color.

Showa

The Showa is the last of the Big Three varieties collectively known as Go Sanke, and historically by far the youngest. It was developed in 1927, in Niigata, by Jukichi Hoshino, who crossed a Ki Utsuri with a Kohaku. These early fish displayed very poor, yellowish hi and indifferent sumi, and it was not until 1965 that Tomiji Kobayashi improved the strain by crossing female Showa with male Sanke and Yagozen Kohaku (see page 128), resulting in the deep scarlet hi, glossy black, and snow-white skin we appreciate today.

Outcrosses with Sanke and Kohaku continue to be made, not only to maintain brilliant color, but also to produce fish that satisfy the modern taste. As we shall see, while some Showa closely resemble their forebears, others could be mistaken, at first glance, for Sanke. This is a common error for beginners to make, and not surprising, as both varieties are red, black, and white koi. However, Showa are black fish with red and white markings and the distribution and positioning of the sumi is (or at least used to be) very distinctive. Sanke sumi is a subsidiary color, appearing only above the lateral line and rarely on the head, in typical Bekko tortoiseshell configuration, while the glossy black of Showa is better described as "wrapping"; in some examples it appears to extend from the belly up around the body. Large areas of sumi can blend together to produce a pattern like a lightning bolt (inazuma). This is especially noticeable on the head, where the black cutting across an area of hi can generate bold and striking effects.

The traditional Showa usually has red as the dominant color, with sumi and white in roughly equal proportions. If more than half the body is red, viewed from above, the fish is referred to as a Hi Showa.

SANKE OR SHOWA?

Sanke

Sumi stripes in the pectoral fins are a Sanke characteristic.

In most Sanke, sumi is confined to above the lateral line and the hi pattern is Kohaku-like.

Showa

Motoguro in the pectorals is typical of Showa and Utsurimono.

Showa sumi can extend up from the belly in bold wrappings.

KOI DEFINITIONS

Bekko ~ Black Sanke-type markings on a white, red, or yellow base

Go Sanke ~ Koi from the Kohaku, Sanke, and Showa classes

Hi Showa ~ More than half the body viewed from above is red

Ki Utsuri ~ Black koi with yellow markings

Kohaku ~ White koi with red markings

Motoguro ~ Solid black coloration in the base of pectoral fins on Showa and related varieties

Sanke ~ Three-color. White koi with red and black markings

Shimi ~ Undesirable individual dark brown or black scales on areas of ground color

Utsurimono ~ Black koi with white, red, or yellow markings

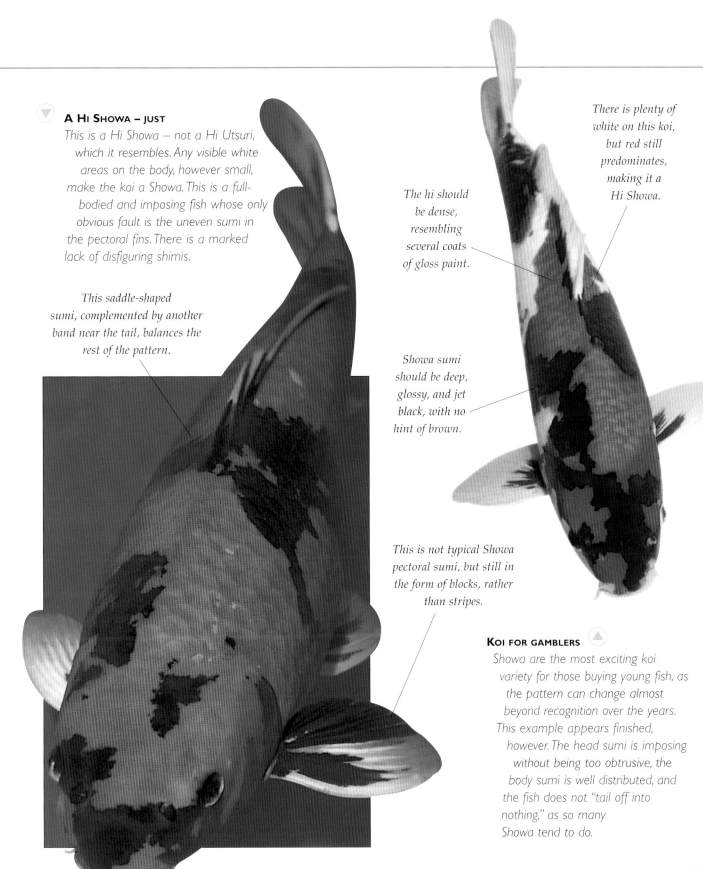

A HI SHOWA – JUST

This is a Hi Showa – not a Hi Utsuri, which it resembles. Any visible white areas on the body, however small, make the koi a Showa. This is a full-bodied and imposing fish whose only obvious fault is the uneven sumi in the pectoral fins. There is a marked lack of disfiguring shimis.

This saddle-shaped sumi, complemented by another band near the tail, balances the rest of the pattern.

There is plenty of white on this koi, but red still predominates, making it a Hi Showa.

The hi should be dense, resembling several coats of gloss paint.

Showa sumi should be deep, glossy, and jet black, with no hint of brown.

This is not typical Showa pectoral sumi, but still in the form of blocks, rather than stripes.

KOI FOR GAMBLERS

Showa are the most exciting koi variety for those buying young fish, as the pattern can change almost beyond recognition over the years. This example appears finished, however. The head sumi is imposing without being too obtrusive, the body sumi is well distributed, and the fish does not "tail off into nothing," as so many Showa tend to do.

This is a lovely Kindai Showa – until you look at the tail region, where the pattern is not as strong.

White is the dominant color, making this a Kindai Showa.

A traditional Showa pattern, red and black in equal measure, with relatively little white.

A MODERN SHOWA ▲

This is a bright, modern Showa, with plenty of sumi still to come through. The black nose, though unusual, imparts charm to an accomplished fish.

When no white is visible from above, this "Showa" becomes a Hi Utsuri.

KOI DEFINITIONS

Aka Sanke ~ Koi with large red areas unrelieved by cuts in the pattern

Hi ~ Red

Hi Utsuri ~ Black koi with red or orange markings

Kage ~ Shadowy black reticulated marking over white (or red on Hi Utsuri)

Kawarimono ~ Class for all nonmetallic koi not included in any other group

Kindai ~ Where white skin predominates

Kiwa ~ Border of red and white scales at the rear edge of hi patterns

Motoguro ~ Solid black coloration in the base of pectoral fins on Showa and related varieties

Sanke ~ Three-color. White koi with red and black markings

Sashi ~ Overlap of red and white scales at the forward edge of hi patterns

Sumi ~ Black

Tategoi ~ "Unfinished" koi of any age that should continue to improve

But whereas an Aka Sanke is not a very subtle fish, its Showa equivalent can look stunning. This is because the sumi takes a more active role in the pattern, which needs very little white to accent it. The effect is helped along by the pectoral fins and their motoguro though, again, perfectly acceptable modern Showa may have clear white fins.

Hi Showa are sometimes difficult to distinguish from Hi Utsuri, but if any white skin is visible when the koi is viewed from above it is a Showa – in name if not in spirit.

Kindai Showa are becoming more popular than ever, and very real classification difficulties present themselves in fish that lack two or more of the traditional Showa identification points, such as head sumi, motoguro, or wrap-around markings. At first glance, koi like these can easily be mistaken for Sanke, but experienced hobbyists can get the variety right by a process of elimination in virtually every case. The difficulty is compounded in young Showa because very often the nature and distribution of the sumi alters dramatically as the fish grow. Tategoi Showa represent not just a challenge, but a substantial gamble. Only by studying many other fish from the same breeder is it possible to make even an educated guess as to how the sumi will look when the koi matures. Areas of red, too, will come and go; it is a myth that hi is always stable and sumi transient, something you can confirm by keeping a photographic record of Showa as they grow.

Emerging Showa sumi can appear blue-gray or brownish-black, and rather than having clearly defined kiwa and sashi, it may cover an area of skin in a reticulated pattern that allows individual scales to show through. Koi that retain a predominance of this shadowy sumi into adulthood are known as Kage Showa, but for

Not Sanke sumi, although it can look similar when not fully developed.

Shadowy finished sumi should not be confused with sumi still to emerge fully.

▶ **OUT OF THE SHADOWS**
True Kage Showa are rare, but this is a good example. There are two distinct types of sumi here: the deep, glossy bands and the dappled, shadowy markings. Kage Showa are now benched Showa, rather than Kawarimono, because who is to say when a koi is finished?

MORE BLACK TO COME
This Tategoi modern Showa could easily be mistaken for a Sanke but for the shoulder sumi, which will probably extend into the head as the fish grows. There is certainly some Sanke influence at work here, though.

every true example there are many more in which the sumi will ultimately develop fully to a deep, lacquerlike gloss. To avoid any judging anomalies, Kage Showa in the West are automatically grouped in the main Showa variety, but in Japan they go into Kawarimono. "Boke Showa" is used today only as a descriptive term for fish that do not conform to the standard view of what a Showa ought to look like.

Pattern configuration in Showa is not set in stone; rather, each fish should be judged on the overall impression it makes. It is true to say that really good examples of mature Showa are harder to come by than their Sanke or Kohaku equivalents. A common defect is seen in fish that look wonderful from the head to a point along the dorsal fin, with well-proportioned hi, sumi, and white skin, but lack any bold areas of hi from that point back to the caudal fin. The initial impression may still be good, as Showa rely on color contrast for their impact, but for a koi to win shows it must display uniform excellence from nose to tail.

The pectoral fins can let down an otherwise good Showa. Motoguro can be present on one and not on

In the classic motoguro, the sumi in the pectorals forms an even block spreading up from the ball joint of the fin.

Motoguro plus radiating stripes is still the mark of a Showa, rather than a Sanke.

the other or, more commonly, both fins are a uniform black. Depending on the parentage, the sumi may or may not recede later. There are even cases of koi with one pectoral fin showing motoguro and the other the typical striping of a Sanke – the result of outcrossing to a Sanke parent.

Showa do not have bloodlines in the same sense as the other Go Sanke, and a relatively small percentage of any spawning will be true to type. The first culling retains only all-black fish, which may represent as little as 30 percent of the total, while subsequent thinnings need to be severe. Inbreeding in this variety leads to a higher than normal number of fish with congenital defects, which may be as obvious as a deformed mouth or spine, or as subtle as a slight misalignment of the tail when viewed from above.

The Showa variety lends itself to some interesting crosses, notably Koromo Showa

 HEADING FOR PERFECTION
A head study of a classy Hi Showa, showing the three primary colors – black, red, and white – setting one another off to perfection. The white element in the fins relieves any impression of pigment overkill.

KOI DEFINITIONS

Boke Showa ~ Showa with indistinct grayish black pattern

Chagoi ~ Nonmetallic brown koi

Doitsu ~ Koi with no scales other than enlarged scales along the lateral line and two lines running either side of the dorsal fin

Go Sanke ~ Koi from the Kohaku, Sanke, and Showa classes

Hi ~ Red

Hi Showa ~ More than half the body viewed from above is red

Kawarimono ~ Class for all nonmetallic koi not included in any other group

Kin-Gin-Rin/Gin-Rin ~ Koi with highly reflective gold and/or silver scales

Koromo Showa ~ Solid black joins black reticulation over the red

Motoguro ~ Solid black coloration in the base of pectoral fins on Showa and related varieties

Sanke ~ Three-color. White koi with red and black markings

Showa Shusui ~ A Doitsu koi with intermediate markings showing elements of both varieties

Sumi ~ Black

Tancho ~ Circular red spot on head. No other red on body

Shiro Utsuri ~ Black koi with white markings

(judged in Showa) and Showa Shusui (judged in Kawarimono). Tancho Showa are effectively Shiro Utsuri with a patch of hi confined to the head. This is usually struck through with sumi in the same way as the head marking of conventional Showa. A word of warning here: If a Shiro Utsuri displays any hi at all, even a tiny marking barely noticeable on the lip, it is technically a Showa.

Gin-Rin Showa, with the other two Go Sanke classifications, are the only ones judged in Kin-Gin-Rin in the West. In all other varieties, these reflective scales do not affect how it is benched, so a Gin-Rin Chagoi is still a Chagoi and grouped in Kawarimono.

Doitsu Showa, although regarded as unrefined by the Japanese, are striking koi that carry the interaction of the three colors on the head right along the body, with no scales to blur the pattern edges. Good examples must also have impeccable white skin and a high luster. Doitsu Go Sanke do have their own judging class in Japan, which would seem a fair and logical way of evaluating their clear-cut charms.

▲ CLEAN AND STRIKING PATTERN

This Doitsu Showa has an imposing and strong body shape, excellent skin, and clean finnage. Note the extent of the hi, which is consistent over most of the body length (in many Showa, hi pattern stops at the dorsal line). The white skin offers an ideal contrast to the bright, consistent hi and excellent sumi.

Utsurimono

Although a trio of koi reside in this variety, only one is truly popular – the Shiro Utsuri. Another is relatively rare, while a third is almost never seen. Despite their monochrome black and white patterning, Shiro Utsuri have achieved a status only a little below that of Kohaku, Sanke and Showa, to the point where they are sometimes referred to as "honorary Go Sanke."

The history of Utsurimono

The origin of Utsurimono is unclear. Some authorities claim that the fish are of Magoi lineage, first produced in 1925 by Kazuo Minemura. Others maintain that they are of much more recent Showa descent. Both theories are hard to disprove; all koi originate from Magoi, and a Shiro Utsuri could be viewed, unkindly, as a defective Showa without the hi, just as a Shiro Bekko is basically a Sanke lacking a third color. Nowadays, however, Shiro Utsuri parent koi are spawned together to produce this specific variety, and only a few arise unwanted from Showa spawnings.

Shiro Utsuri are most often confused with Bekko, but by applying the same criteria that differentiate Showa from Sanke, the difference becomes clear. A Shiro Utsuri is a black fish with white markings, a Shiro Bekko the reverse, and all Utsuri sumi is of the typical Showa wraparound type.

Hi Utsuri are best visualized as Showa without the white. Until recent years, the hi was rarely scarlet, but outcrossings with Kohaku have greatly improved it. Some breeders have also reintroduced Magoi genes into their strain of Hi Utsuri, which allows the koi to attain a greater size without any fall-off in pattern or skin quality. The pectorals rarely show true motoguro: more often they are candy-striped black and red, with a red leading edge.

Ki Utsuri is a very old variety traceable back to 1875, at the beginning of the Meiji Era. Eizaburo Hoshino, who was also responsible for improving

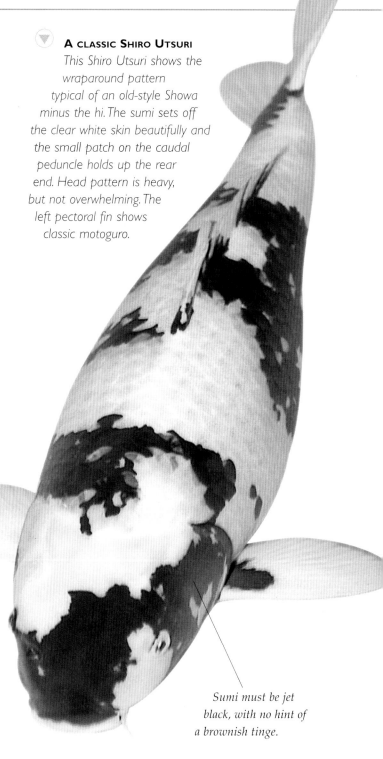

A CLASSIC SHIRO UTSURI
This Shiro Utsuri shows the wraparound pattern typical of an old-style Showa minus the hi. The sumi sets off the clear white skin beautifully and the small patch on the caudal peduncle holds up the rear end. Head pattern is heavy, but not overwhelming. The left pectoral fin shows classic motoguro.

Sumi must be jet black, with no hint of a brownish tinge.

HEAD PATTERNS

Lightning strike or Menware head pattern is a showstopper.

Here the head sumi is in two parts – clean and balanced.

This interesting, but rather heavy and fussy head sumi may fuse together later.

In modern-style Shiro Utsuri the head sumi is uncluttered to show off the white skin.

▶ **GOOD POTENTIAL**
This Tategoi Shiro Utsuri has more sumi still to come through, but already the pattern, though sparse, is pleasing. The skin quality is breathtaking and body shape potential is promising for what is presently a slim, young fish.

MOTOGURO

Motoguro may take the form of a solid patch of sumi at the pectoral fin ball joint or a radiating style, as here. Both are quite distinct from Sanke pectoral fin patterns.

KOI DEFINITIONS

Bekko ~ Black Sanke-type markings on a white, red, or yellow base

Go Sanke ~ Koi from the Kohaku, Sanke, and Showa classes

Hi ~ Red

Hi Utsuri ~ Black koi with red or orange markings

Kohaku ~ White koi with red markings

Magoi ~ Ancestral black carp

Menware ~ Showa head pattern

Motoguro ~ Solid black coloration in the base of pectoral fins on Showa and related varieties

Sanke ~ White koi with red and black markings

Shiro Bekko ~ White koi with black, Sanke-type markings

Showa ~ Black koi with red and white markings

Sumi ~ Black

Tategoi ~ "Unfinished" koi of any age that should continue to improve

Utsurimono ~ Black koi with white, red, or yellow markings

Sanke bloodlines in the early twentieth century, coined the term "Ki Utsuri" for the fish that were earlier known as Kuro-Ki-Han. The yellow of this variety tends to be pale and washed out, and both Hi Utsuri and Ki Utsuri are prone to developing shimis.

Curiously, Kin Ki Utsuri are quite common, while the nonmetallic equivalent has almost vanished from the hobby.

Shiro Utsuri share more than just body pattern with Showa; ideally, the pectoral fins display the classic motoguro, and the taste for fish with a preponderance of white is now common to both varieties.

Because a Shiro Utsuri, like a Kohaku, is a classically simple two-colored fish, great store is placed on the quality of the white skin. This should be the color of snow, with a subtle sheen, but the skin of young examples often gives few clues as to how the finished koi will look. The most common "fault" in yearling Shiro Utsuri is a yellowish head. This is variously interpreted as a sign that the fish is male, or that it will grow into a quality koi – and to confuse the issue further, some examples never quite lose this tinge. Similarly, the white on the body can appear rather dingy, as areas of sumi still to come out give the skin a bluish gray tinge. It is said that the best guide to how the finished koi will

SURPRISE, SURPRISE

A fine, mature modern Shiro Utsuri. The absence of more than a suggestion of sumi on the head is unusual, but compensated for by the eyebrow-shaped shoulder markings, which give this koi a somewhat surprised expression!

KOI DEFINITIONS

Gin-Rin ~
Koi with reflective silver scales

Hi ~ Red

Hikariutsuri ~ Class for metallic Utsuri and Showa

Hi Utsuri ~ Black koi with red or orange markings

Kage ~ Shadowy black reticulated marking over white (or red on Hi Utsuri)

Ki ~ Yellow

Kin Ki Utsuri ~ Metallic yellow koi with Showa-type sumi

Ki Utsuri ~ Black koi with yellow markings

Kohaku ~ White koi with red markings

Menware ~ Showa head pattern

Motoguro ~ Solid black coloration in the base of pectoral fins on Showa and related varieties

Sanke ~ White koi with red and black markings

Shimi ~ Undesirable individual dark brown or black scales on areas of ground color

Shiro Utsuri ~ Black koi with white markings

Showa ~ Black koi with red and white markings

❖ **GROWING UP** ❖

Modern-style Shiro Utsuri have less sumi than their predecessors.

The tail wrist is often the first area to show "finished" white.

Traditional sumi pattern, with Menware head markings.

Kage Shiro Utsuri blend shadowy, with clearly defined, sumi.

the pectorals, low-grade Shiro Utsuri exhibit solid sumi at the ball joint, which radiates outward. If this spread is excessive, the whole fin will appear black. Dorsal and caudal fins are allowed some sumi, but again, if there is too much, the koi will appear unbalanced. Ideally, the white on the finnage should set off the body sumi.

Head pattern on Shiro Utsuri can range from the classic lightning strike or V-shape shared with Showa to relatively small counterpoints on the white skin. These need not be symmetrical, but the edges should be clearly defined. Too much black on the head, especially if there are several small patches rather than a continuous pattern, makes for an inferior fish.

As Shiro Utsuri breed relatively true to color, body shape may suffer in shipments of mass-produced ordinary-grade fish, and this variety often enters the country of sale in an emaciated state. When choosing from a number of fish, go for those with thick shoulders and caudal peduncle, as early volume is an indication that the koi will grow large. Avoid examples that appear pinched in behind the gill covers, or with long, pointed heads.

The chemistry of the water in which these koi are kept can influence how they look. Sumi develops best in hard, alkaline water, but in softer, more acidic ponds it takes on a grayish tinge.

A Gin-Rin Shiro Utsuri can be an impressive fish. The reflective scales show silver over both white skin

look is to examine the white base of the tail, which clears sooner than the rest of the body.

When choosing young Shiro Utsuri, steer clear of fish that look like miniature versions of the ideal adult. More sumi will almost certainly come later, making the koi black heavy.

The sumi should ideally be jet black and glossy, as in Showa. The Japanese recognize several shades of black, and although this sounds strange to Western hobbyists, they have a point: on close inspection in good daylight, some Shiro Utsuri have very dark, chocolate-brown markings. Another fault is too much black in the finnage. Rather than neat motoguro on and sumi. Such koi will be benched Kin-Gin-Rin in Western-style shows, but they have to be good Shiro Utsuri first and good Gin-Rin second.

In Kage Shiro Utsuri and Kage Hi Utsuri, like Showa, the shadowy sumi may or may not stabilize.

Doitsu Shiro Utsuri are unlikely to be confused with any other variety except, perhaps, Kumonryu (see page 170). Both are black, German-scaled fish with white markings, but the overall impression of the latter is of cloudlike patterns on a black ground, rather than an asymmetrical checkerboard. The head of a Kumonryu also lacks the traditional Utsurimono markings, and its white skin often carries a bluish tinge – sea ice, rather than snow.

 BLACK, WHITE, AND BEAUTIFUL
For that 1960s look, this "designer" Doitsu Shiro Utsuri is hard to beat. More sumi may yet emerge, as the shoulder patch is not as clear-cut as it might be. The body could do with more volume, but that will come. Pectoral sumi is beautifully balanced.

❖ MAKE-OR-BREAK FINS ❖

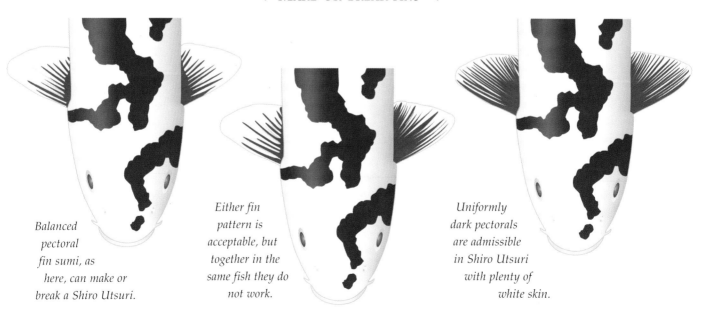

Balanced pectoral fin sumi, as here, can make or break a Shiro Utsuri.

Either fin pattern is acceptable, but together in the same fish they do not work.

Uniformly dark pectorals are admissible in Shiro Utsuri with plenty of white skin.

KOI DEFINITIONS

Doitsu ~ Koi with no scales other than enlarged scales along the lateral line and two lines running either side of the dorsal fin

Gin-Rin ~ Koi with reflective silver scales

Hi Showa ~ More than half the body viewed from above is red

Hi Utsuri ~ Black koi with red or orange markings

Kage ~ Shadowy black reticulated marking over white (or red on Hi Utsuri)

Kumonryu ~ Black doitsu koi with some white on head, fins, and body

Shimi ~ Undesirable individual dark brown or black scales on areas of ground color

Shiro Utsuri ~ Black koi with white markings

Showa ~ Black koi with red and white markings

Sumi ~ Black

Utsurimono ~ Black koi with white, red, or yellow markings

RED MEETS BLACK

Hi Utsuri are Utsurimono with red as the secondary color. Often confused with Hi Showa, the way to tell them apart is to look at them from an angle of 45°; if any white is evident, the fish is a Showa. This Hi Utsuri's pectoral fins spoil an otherwise nice, though rather slim, koi.

Skin on a Hi Utsuri should be bright red, contrasting with deep, lacquered sumi.

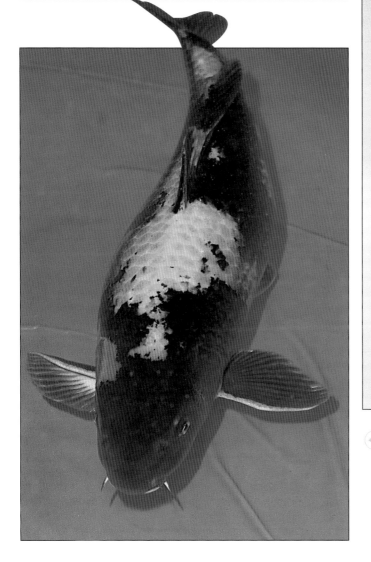

RARE, AND WELL DONE

You could spend a lifetime in koi and not see a Ki Utsuri, let alone one as accomplished as this. It is a nonmetallic black koi with yellow markings. Shimis often plague this variety, but this fish is free of any blemishes.

Bekko

Certain koi varieties are subject to the vagaries of fashion, first enjoying spells of popularity and then fading from favor. Bekko are a case in point. When koi keeping began to take off outside Japan about 30 years ago, these fish were very much in vogue; indeed, they were given (and still have) their own benching classification. However, Bekko today are underrepresented at most shows. This is a pity, as good specimens are as appealing as ever, in a chic and understated way.

Although three types of koi are recognized as Bekko, only one – the Shiro Bekko – is widely known. This is a Sanke derivative, but lacking any hi – in other words, a white koi with sumi markings. Although they are still produced from parent fish of this variety, they are just as likely to be thrown from spawnings of Sanke, especially Tancho Sanke. Bear in mind that any hi at all on a Shiro Bekko, even on the lips, technically makes it a Sanke, and a fish like this would be valueless for showing.

The sumi on Shiro Bekko has evolved in line with that of Sanke. Ten years ago, examples would have had a fairly heavy complement of tortoiseshell dappling, whereas today the sumi tends to be more sparsely distributed in smaller patches. It should be confined to the area above the lateral line, over the dorsal surface.

The judging standard now permits a little sumi on the head, as in Sanke, but the best examples have a clear white face, with the black markings beginning on the shoulder. A common fault is a yellowish head, which may or may not clear as the koi develops. The eyes are usually blue. The skin should be snow-white with a high luster. Sumi patterning need not be symmetrical, but should balance overall; if confined to one side of the fish, the effect is not pleasing. Avoid Bekko with too much sumi on the caudal peduncle. Ideally, as in Kohaku, there should be an area of white at the junction of body and tail fin.

Shiro Bekko finnage can either be white or striped with sumi, similar to that of Sanke. It is widely

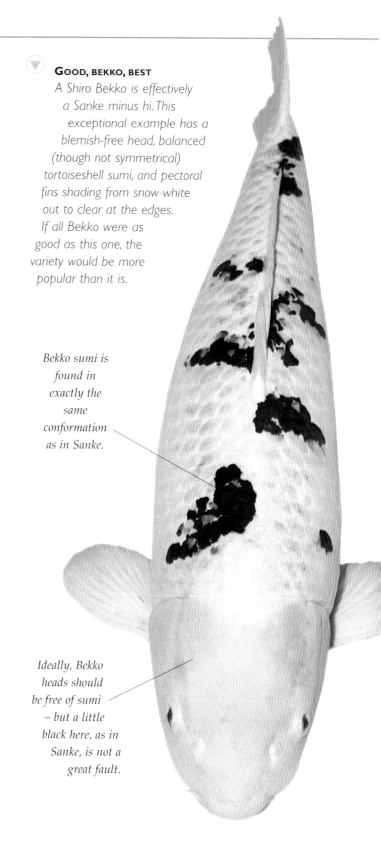

GOOD, BEKKO, BEST
A Shiro Bekko is effectively a Sanke minus hi. This exceptional example has a blemish-free head, balanced (though not symmetrical) tortoiseshell sumi, and pectoral fins shading from snow-white out to clear at the edges. If all Bekko were as good as this one, the variety would be more popular than it is.

Bekko sumi is found in exactly the same conformation as in Sanke.

Ideally, Bekko heads should be free of sumi – but a little black here, as in Sanke, is not a great fault.

❖ **BEKKO OR SANKE?** ❖

Aka Bekko sumi style prevents confusion with Hi Utsuri.

Not a Bekko, but an Aka Sanke – the giveaway is the presence of white.

An Aka Bekko – a red fish with black markings.

KOI DEFINITIONS

Aka Bekko ~ Red koi with black, Sanke-type markings

Aka Sanke ~ Koi with large areas of red unrelieved by cuts in the pattern

Bekko ~ Black Sanke-type markings on white, red, or yellow base

Hi ~ Red

Hi Utsuri ~ Black koi with red or orange markings

Kohaku ~ White koi with red markings

Sanke ~ White koi with red and black markings

Shiro Bekko ~ White koi with black markings

Sumi ~ Black

Tancho ~ A patch of red confined to the head

Sometimes head sumi is found on Aka Bekko, as it is on some Sanke.

Bekko sumi, seen from the side, does not extend below the lateral line.

Shoulder sumi contrasts with a clear, white head.

Bekko, like Kohaku and Sanke, often have blue eyes.

153

accepted that Japanese koi are visibly superior to those from anywhere else in the world, yet Shiro Bekko are a variety at which the Israeli fish farmers seem to excel. Their warm climate is conducive to good sumi development.

Aka Bekko (never Hi Bekko) are red koi with sumi markings. Pure red koi are usually thrown from Kohaku spawnings and not highly regarded unless the hi is a deep, even crimson, in which case they are called Benigoi (and benched Kawarimono). These fish are rather plain for most tastes, but when the hi is overlain with deep sumi, the effect is striking. The only fish likely to be confused with Aka Bekko are Aka Sanke, which show white areas when viewed from above. Aka Bekko are allowed some hi in the finnage, which tends to appear in blotches rather than stripes, although pure white pectoral fins set off the hi nicely.

Ki Bekko are the rarest koi in the group, and sport a lemon-yellow body overlain with sumi. They are not a variety deliberately spawned, but may arise from

 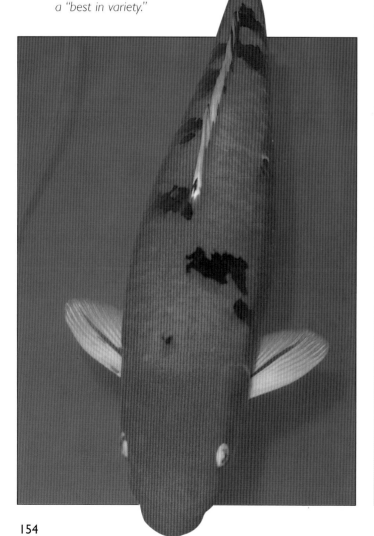

This Aka Bekko has pectoral fins typical of a Sanke, but with no visible white on the body, it has to be benched Bekko – where, incidentally, this particular example would stand the better chance of winning a "best in variety."

BETWEEN TWO STOOLS

This is a Doitsu Aka Sanke – just! Although a pleasing koi, its chances in a show would be remote, first because it is Doitsu, rather than fully scaled, and second because the small area of white means it must be judged in Sanke, rather than in the Bekko classification with which it has more affinity.

This fish does have some white on the body, but is very nearly an Aka Bekko. Note the tortoiseshell sumi.

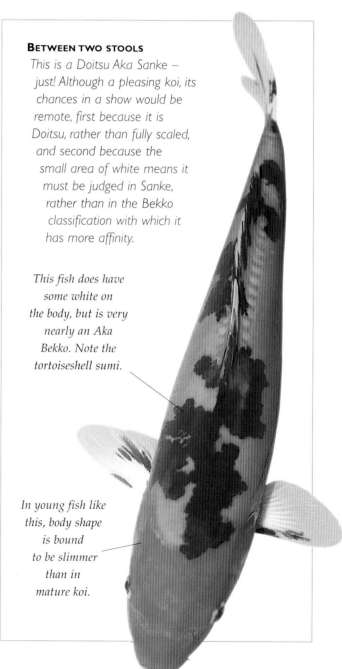

In young fish like this, body shape is bound to be slimmer than in mature koi.

Shiro Bekko x Kigoi or Sanke x Kigoi crosses. Curiously, the metallic equivalent of a Ki Bekko (known as a Tora, or Tiger, Ogon) is quite commonly seen.

Doitsu and Gin-Rin Shiro Bekko (both benched Bekko in the UK) make striking pond fish. The dorsal mirror scales of the former are silvery white, contrasting beautifully with any sumi they overlay.

 BEKKO THROUGH FROSTED GLASS
An accomplished Gin-Rin Shiro Bekko. It stands up well, first as a Bekko, second as a Gin-Rin koi. The sparkling scales over the jet black sumi give a frosted glass effect. A yellow head is a common fault in Shiro Bekko, but this one has beautifully clear skin.

Tortoiseshell sumi, typical of Bekko – and the closely allied variety, Sanke.

KOI DEFINITIONS

Aka Bekko ~ Red koi with black Sanke-type markings

Aka Sanke ~ Koi showing large areas of red unrelieved by cuts in the pattern

Bekko ~ Black Sanke-type markings on a white, red, or yellow base

Benigoi ~ Nonmetallic, deep crimson koi

Doitsu ~ Koi with no scales other than enlarged scales along the lateral line and two lines running either side of the dorsal fin

Gin-Rin ~ Koi with reflective silver scales

Kawarimono ~ Class for all nonmetallic koi not included in any other group

Ki Bekko ~ Lemon-yellow with black Sanke-type markings

Kigoi ~ Nonmetallic yellow koi

Kohaku ~ White koi with red markings

Sanke ~ White koi with red and black markings

Shiro Bekko ~ White koi with black Sanke-type markings

Sumi ~ Black

Tora, or Tiger, Ogon ~ Metallic equivalent of Ki Bekko

Asagi and Shusui

Asagi are fully scaled, nonmetallic fish with a long history, but because they closely resemble Magoi (the wild black carp), some hobbyists see them as unrefined, dull, and not proper koi at all. Certainly they are an acquired taste, far removed from the brilliantly tricolored modern Showa or the flashy koi grouped in Hikariutsuri. But their quiet elegance serves as a counterpoint to their more exotic pondmates and they also have the potential to grow very large.

The Japanese recognize three types of Magoi, one of which, the Asagi Magoi, is the forerunner of all modern koi. Its back is bluish, with a reticulated scale pattern, and some hi is present on the cheeks, flanks, and pectoral fins. About 160 years ago, two mutants arose from this proto-koi, namely the Konjo and the Narumi Asagi. Although instrumental in the development of Matsuba koi, the dark Konjo Asagi are valueless in their own right except as food fish. However, Narumi Asagi have gone on to become one half of a recognized judging variety – the other being their Doitsu counterparts, Shusui.

The history of Asagi

The prefix "Narumi" is derived from the town of the same name in Ichi Prefecture, where a locally made fabric was said to resemble the pattern on the backs of these koi. Asagi seem to have appeared all over Japan, not just in Niigata – this at a time when interest in mutant fish led to their being kept back from the food crop and bred together for curiosity's sake, long before koi were seen as a commercial proposition.

Modern Asagi

Because they breed relatively true, countless ordinary-grade Asagi are produced each year, and newcomers to koi can gain an unfavorable impression of the variety because really good examples are so seldom seen. Ideally, the back should be evenly covered in scales that are pale blue where they enter the skin,

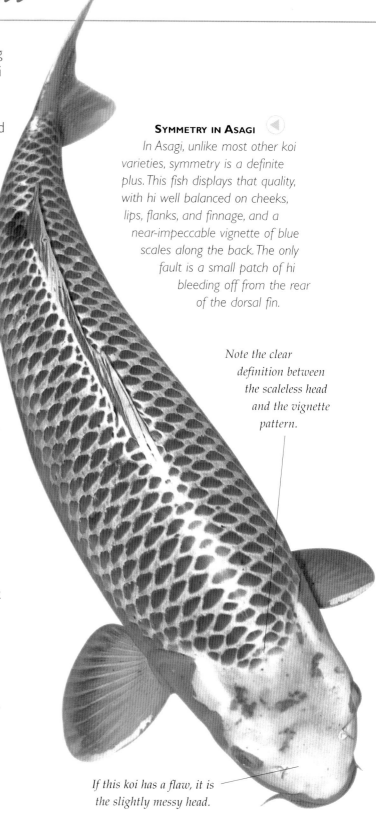

SYMMETRY IN ASAGI

In Asagi, unlike most other koi varieties, symmetry is a definite plus. This fish displays that quality, with hi well balanced on cheeks, lips, flanks, and finnage, and a near-impeccable vignette of blue scales along the back. The only fault is a small patch of hi bleeding off from the rear of the dorsal fin.

Note the clear definition between the scaleless head and the vignette pattern.

If this koi has a flaw, it is the slightly messy head.

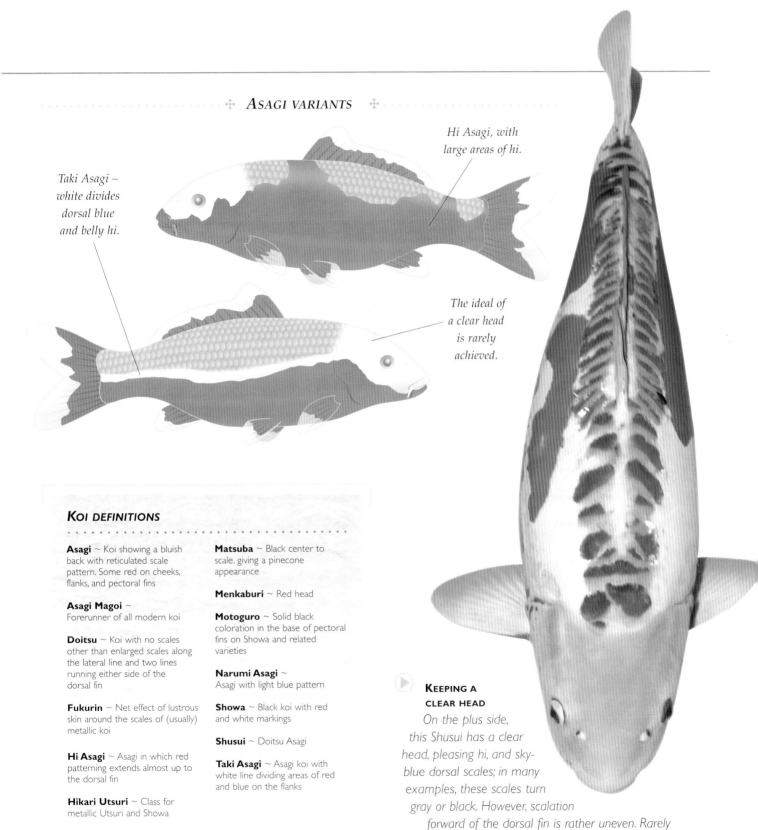

❖ ASAGI VARIANTS ❖

Hi Asagi, with large areas of hi.

Taki Asagi – white divides dorsal blue and belly hi.

The ideal of a clear head is rarely achieved.

KOI DEFINITIONS

Asagi ~ Koi showing a bluish back with reticulated scale pattern. Some red on cheeks, flanks, and pectoral fins

Asagi Magoi ~ Forerunner of all modern koi

Doitsu ~ Koi with no scales other than enlarged scales along the lateral line and two lines running either side of the dorsal fin

Fukurin ~ Net effect of lustrous skin around the scales of (usually) metallic koi

Hi Asagi ~ Asagi in which red patterning extends almost up to the dorsal fin

Hikari Utsuri ~ Class for metallic Utsuri and Showa

Matsuba ~ Black center to scale, giving a pinecone appearance

Menkaburi ~ Red head

Motoguro ~ Solid black coloration in the base of pectoral fins on Showa and related varieties

Narumi Asagi ~ Asagi with light blue pattern

Showa ~ Black koi with red and white markings

Shusui ~ Doitsu Asagi

Taki Asagi ~ Asagi koi with white line dividing areas of red and blue on the flanks

KEEPING A CLEAR HEAD

On the plus side, this Shusui has a clear head, pleasing hi, and sky-blue dorsal scales; in many examples, these scales turn gray or black. However, scalation forward of the dorsal fin is rather uneven. Rarely do all elements come together in this variety.

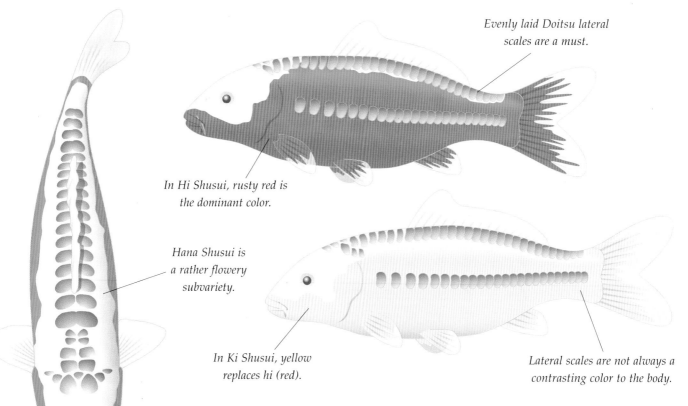

Evenly laid Doitsu lateral scales are a must.

In Hi Shusui, rusty red is the dominant color.

Hana Shusui is a rather flowery subvariety.

In Ki Shusui, yellow replaces hi (red).

Lateral scales are not always a contrasting color to the body.

but with a darker edging – not the other way around, as is sometimes stated. The sharper the definition between these two shades, the more impressive the koi will look. As the fish grow, the skin stretches and this reticulation becomes even more apparent – this is true Fukurin. Because they are so obvious in this variety, missing or damaged scales will seriously devalue an otherwise good koi. The head is often a disappointing feature in Asagi. Ideally, it should be a uniform clear white but more often takes on a blue or grayish tint. In young examples, the bones of the skull show through, but this effect disappears as the translucent skin thickens. If there is a lot of head hi forming a hood pattern, the fish is known as a Menkaburi Asagi.

Asagi hi is more of a rusty red than the bright scarlet associated with the Kohaku. Typically, it runs up from the belly to the lateral line or beyond, also covering the jaw, cheeks, and some or all of the fins. On the pectorals it can be configured like the motoguro of Showa, or else spread out over the

entire area of the fins. Wherever hi appears in this variety it should be symmetrical. Some Asagi have a greater than usual percentage of red patterning, which can extend almost up to the dorsal fin. These are known as Hi Asagi. Others – Taki Asagi – have a white line dividing the areas of red and blue on the flanks. Both these subvarieties are still grouped in Asagi.

Shusui

The second element of an odd variety partnership is the Shusui, which means "autumn water" in Japanese. At first sight, these mirror-scaled koi seem to have little in common with Asagi, but that variety was first crossed with a German table carp in 1910 by Yoshigoro Akiyama, resulting in the first Shusui.

The color distribution is essentially the same as in the Asagi, but because there are no normal scales to give an overall reticulated effect, the smooth, sky-blue back is instead highlighted by the Doitsu scalation. In good examples, these armored scales form a regular pattern on the shoulders of the koi and then run in two lines on either side of the dorsal fin, returning to a single line on the caudal peduncle. A further line is usually present along each flank, roughly following the lateral line.

The most common fault on Shusui is a messy shoulder scale pattern that lacks symmetry. Rogue scales can appear elsewhere on the body, further devaluing the fish. In hard water, the mirror scales can turn grayish or black, and once this happens they never revert back to blue. A clear head is essential on Shusui, as it is on Asagi. The skin is never snow-white, more of an ice blue, but should be blemish-free.

The distribution of the red and blue on a Shusui determines its

KOI DEFINITIONS

Ginsui ~ Metallic Shusui with a silver luster

Goshiki Shusui ~ Doitsu, nonmetallic blue Goshiki

Hana Shusui ~ Red in a wavy pattern to give a flowery effect

Hikarimoyo ~ Class for all multicolored metallic koi except Utsuri and Showa

Hikarimuji ~ Class for single-colored metallic koi

Hi Shusui ~ Red extends up over the back contrasting with the dark blue

Kawarimono ~ Class for all nonmetallic koi not included in any other group

Ki Matsuba ~ Metallic gold koi with pinecone scalation

Kinsui ~ Metallic Shusui with a gold luster

Ki Shusui ~ Shusui with yellow instead of red coloration

Midorigoi ~ Greenish yellow with mirror scales

Ogon ~ Single-colored metallic koi

Sanke Shusui ~ Doitsu Sanke whose pattern is underlaid with the blue back of the Shusui

Showa Shusui ~ Doitsu koi with intermediate markings showing elements of both varieties

Taki Asagi ~ Asagi koi with white line dividing areas of red and blue on the flanks

▲ THE FACE OF QUALITY

A lovely Hi Shusui with an unusual head pattern and impressive blue dorsal scales. The intrusion of hi into the fins merely adds to the interest of this beautiful fish.

subclassification. On Hi Shusui the hi extends up over the back, so that the two contrasting colors are red and dark blue. These are unsubtle, but quite striking, koi. Hana Shusui also have more red than normal, but here it is in the form of an extra band between the lateral line and dorsal fin, with a break in between. In the best examples, the hi is laid on in a wavy pattern to give a flowery effect.

In Ki Shusui, yellow replaces the red. This is a confusing subvariety, because if the blue dorsal scales turn black it is easy to confuse with a Doitsu Ki Matsuba. Another rare, Shusui-like koi is the Midorigoi, which is greenish yellow with mirror scales. This one is benched in Kawarimono.

Shusui have been crossed with several normally scaled koi varieties to produce interesting variations on a theme. The most common in the hobby are Showa Shusui, Sanke Shusui, and Goshiki Shusui. Crosses with the Ogons (in the Hikarimuji classification) resulted in Ginsui and Kinsui, which used to be quite popular, but have now been superseded by more refined Doitsu fish in the Hikarimoyo class.

Koromo

Koromo means "robed" in Japanese and describes a group of koi whose quiet elegance finds favor with connoisseurs, even though the fish did not become available until the early 1950s. Strictly speaking, Koromo are crossbred fish; the first example resulted from a spawning between a male Kohaku and a female Narumi Asagi.

Ai Goromo

The collective name "Koromo" covers several varieties, the best known being Ai Goromo. This is a white koi with the hi pattern of a Kohaku, but each red scale is reticulated in black or dark blue – an indication of Asagi ancestry. To obtain a good Ai Goromo you must first have a good Kohaku, with all the qualities expected of that variety: snow-white skin, deep crimson hi, and an interesting traditional or modern pattern. The dark edging to the scales appears only faintly to begin with and may take years to come out fully. Too much sumi early in life is an indication that this color will eventually overwhelm the koi. But in mature fish, the sumi should be evenly distributed over all patches of hi, with the exception of the head.

From a classification point of view, it is important that the black/dark blue color does not intrude into the white areas. If it does, the fish is no longer an Ai Goromo, but becomes a Goshiki. This extremely variable variety is now grouped in Koromo in the West, but still judged in Kawarimono in Japan. Many apparently good-quality baby Ai Goromo develop into Goshiki, which are in no way inferior koi; it was purely to avoid benching disputes in borderline cases that Goshiki went into Koromo.

Sumi Goromo

There is much confusion between Ai Goromo and Sumi Goromo. The latter are white koi with black patterns, the edge of each scale reticulated in red – a mirror image of what happens in Ai Goromo. An alternative definition of a Sumi Goromo is a red and white koi in which the areas of hi are lightly overlaid

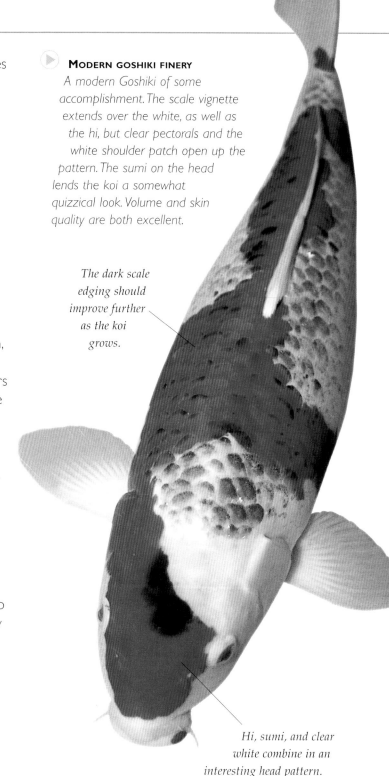

▶ **MODERN GOSHIKI FINERY**
A modern Goshiki of some accomplishment. The scale vignette extends over the white, as well as the hi, but clear pectorals and the white shoulder patch open up the pattern. The sumi on the head lends the koi a somewhat quizzical look. Volume and skin quality are both excellent.

The dark scale edging should improve further as the koi grows.

Hi, sumi, and clear white combine in an interesting head pattern.

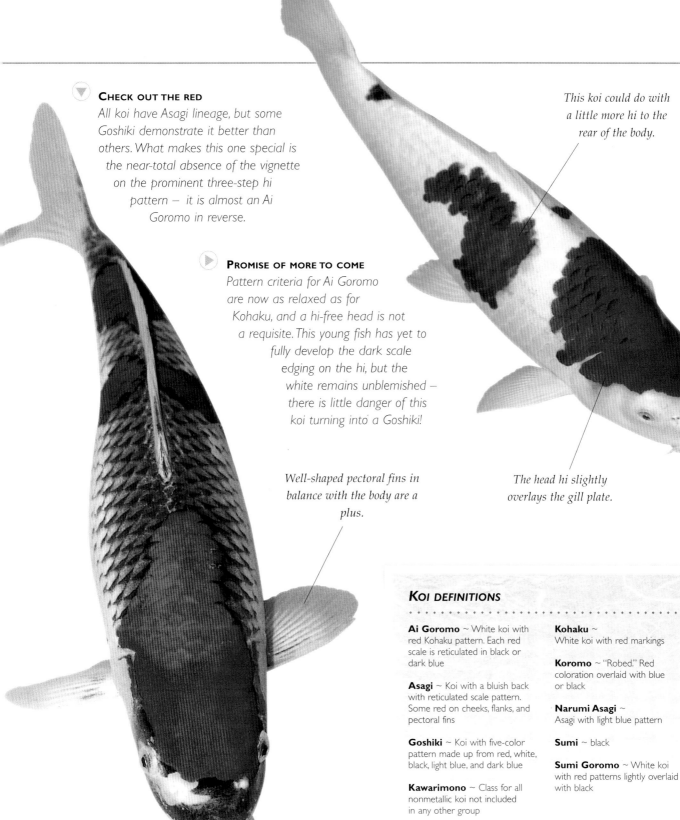

CHECK OUT THE RED
All koi have Asagi lineage, but some Goshiki demonstrate it better than others. What makes this one special is the near-total absence of the vignette on the prominent three-step hi pattern – it is almost an Ai Goromo in reverse.

PROMISE OF MORE TO COME
Pattern criteria for Ai Goromo are now as relaxed as for Kohaku, and a hi-free head is not a requisite. This young fish has yet to fully develop the dark scale edging on the hi, but the white remains unblemished – there is little danger of this koi turning into a Goshiki!

This koi could do with a little more hi to the rear of the body.

Well-shaped pectoral fins in balance with the body are a plus.

The head hi slightly overlays the gill plate.

KOI DEFINITIONS

Ai Goromo ~ White koi with red Kohaku pattern. Each red scale is reticulated in black or dark blue

Asagi ~ Koi with a bluish back with reticulated scale pattern. Some red on cheeks, flanks, and pectoral fins

Goshiki ~ Koi with five-color pattern made up from red, white, black, light blue, and dark blue

Kawarimono ~ Class for all nonmetallic koi not included in any other group

Kohaku ~ White koi with red markings

Koromo ~ "Robed." Red coloration overlaid with blue or black

Narumi Asagi ~ Asagi with light blue pattern

Sumi ~ black

Sumi Goromo ~ White koi with red patterns lightly overlaid with black

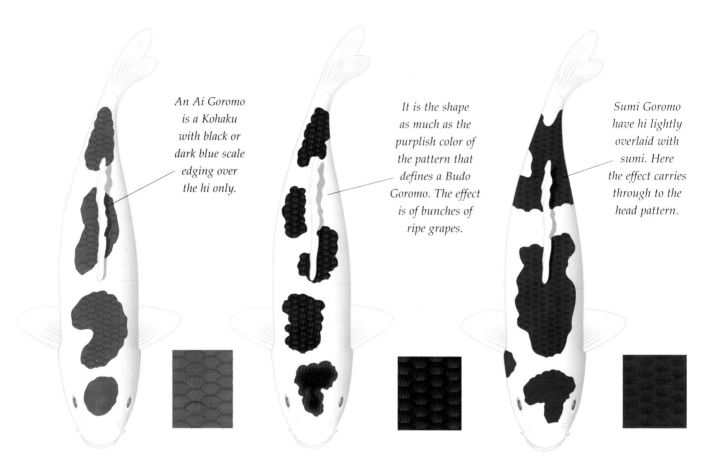

An Ai Goromo is a Kohaku with black or dark blue scale edging over the hi only.

It is the shape as much as the purplish color of the pattern that defines a Budo Goromo. The effect is of bunches of ripe grapes.

Sumi Goromo have hi lightly overlaid with sumi. Here the effect carries through to the head pattern.

with black. This ties in with the dusky red head of these fish, but does not explain the distinct scale reticulation still apparent. The truth is, dark Ai Goromo and light Sumi Goromo can look very similar. However, once again, if sumi migrates on to the white areas of skin, a Sumi Goromo becomes a Goshiki.

Budo Goromo

Budo Goromo is a variant of the Sumi Goromo, the overall effect being of a white fish with purplish patches of overlaid hi. The leading edges (kiwa) show individual scales picked out against white, reminiscent in both shape and color of bunches of grapes.

Budo Sanke

This fish is simply a Budo Goromo with additional Hon sumi. For judging purposes, it goes in Kawarimono, although obviously of Koromo lineage.

Koromo Sanke

This is a Taisho Sanke x Ai Goromo cross, similar to the above but with more distinct reticulation. It is essentially an Ai Goromo with Sanke Hon sumi, in addition to the black edging to each red scale.

Koromo Showa

This Showa x Koromo cross can be a very striking koi, even though the hi tends to be more rusty red than crimson. The Hon sumi here is a dominant color, extending over the head in typical Showa fashion.

Doitsu Ai Goromo

This very rare and prized koi is easily confused with a Doitsu Sanke, as both are tricolored German-scaled koi. However, in the Doitsu Ai Goromo the only blue/black scales are the enlarged ones along the back. In all other respects the fish is a Doitsu Kohaku, with no

▼ **CLEARLY A BUNCH OF GRAPES**
A very light Budo Goromo, proving that clear white skin is essential to set off any pattern. This fish shows the "bunch of grapes" markings characteristic of the variety.

further intrusion of a third color into the body hi. As all recognized Doitsu koi, with the exception of Go Sanke, are benched under their own variety, the correct classification of this type of fish is Koromo.

Goshiki

This is probably the most diverse koi variety known. Goshiki are said to be five-colored koi, although you need to be very creative to pick out the alleged red, black, white, light blue, and dark blue elements. Confusingly, a sixth color – purple – is formed when black and blue overlay one another.

Goshiki have strong Asagi lineage, which lends a reticulation to some or all of the scales. The traditional Goshiki is a rather dark fish, with messy, indistinct patterning, sometimes relieved by clear patches of hi, especially on the face and back. Others look like straight Kohaku x Asagi crosses, with a black, netlike reticulation covering the whole body. However, the best modern Goshiki are simply amazing.

KOI DEFINITIONS

Ai Goromo ~ White koi with red Kohaku pattern. Each red scale is reticulated in black or dark blue

Asagi ~ Koi showing a bluish back with reticulated scale pattern. Some red on cheeks, flanks, and pectoral fins

Budo Goromo ~ White koi with purplish patches of black overlaying red in a pattern resembling bunches of grapes

Budo Sanke ~ Budo Goromo with additional solid black markings

Doitsu ~ Koi with no scales other than enlarged scales along the lateral line and two lines running either side of the dorsal fin

Doitsu Ai Goromo ~ Only the enlarged scales running along the back are blue/black.

Go Sanke ~ Koi from the Kohaku, Sanke, and Showa classes

Goshiki ~ Koi with five-color pattern made up from red, white, black, light blue, and dark blue

Hon sumi ~ Solid Sanke-type black markings

Kawarimono ~ Class for all nonmetallic koi not included in any other group

Kiwa ~ Border of red and white at the rear edge of hi patterns.

Kohaku ~ White koi with red markings

Sanke ~ White koi with red and black markings

Showa ~ Black koi with red and white markings

Sumi Goromo ~ White koi with red patterns lightly overlaid with black

Taisho Sanke/Taisho Sanshoku ~ Full names for Sanke

In 1993, a UK koi company based in the Midlands imported a fish called Polo, whose distinguishing feature is a black-bordered window of white on the large, otherwise clear forward hi marking. The fish has snow-white skin and nose sumi that would do credit to any Showa. The rear hi pattern is classic Ai Goromo. In fact, this fish was close to being a Koromo Showa; only a little reticulation over the white tipped it over into Goshiki. An even better Goshiki arrived at the same company four years later, a female from the breeder Maru. This one has a classic stepped Kohaku pattern touched with gray and black, perfect skin, and a fetching nose spot set off by bright blue eyes.

Gin-Rin Goshiki and Doitsu Goshiki add further to the complexity of an already fathomless variety. Because the appearance of the reflective scales is influenced by the skin colors beneath, they can appear gold, silver, or bluish gray in a good Gin-Rin Goshiki. Often these combine in a single fish and the effect is almost unreal.

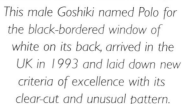

A TOTALLY EXCEPTIONAL KOI

This male Goshiki named Polo for the black-bordered window of white on its back, arrived in the UK in 1993 and laid down new criteria of excellence with its clear-cut and unusual pattern.

GOSHIKI, WHAT A BEAUTY

Arguably the best Goshiki currently in the West. The clear white saddle, deep vignetting on the hi, and charming nose spot are teamed with a voluminous body to make this koi a winner all down the line.

▶ **GIN-RIN PLUS POINTS**

This is a Gin-Rin Goshiki. This variety needs clearly delineated patterning for the sparkling scales to work to the koi's advantage, and this is a good example, with uncluttered hi. The body could do with a little more volume, however.

▼ **THE FACE OF THE FUTURE**

This is a modern Goshiki – almost an Ai Goromo – in which white predominates. The head hi is particularly interesting, and note the blocks of hi in the joints of the pectoral fins – a nice finishing touch.

KOI DEFINITIONS

• •

Ai Goromo ~ White koi with red Kohaku pattern. Each red scale is reticulated in black or dark blue

Asagi ~ Koi showing a bluish back with reticulated scale pattern. Some red on cheeks, flanks, and pectoral fins

Doitsu ~ Koi with no scales other than enlarged scales along the lateral line and two lines running either side of the dorsal fin

Gin-Rin ~ Koi with reflective silver scales

Goshiki ~ Koi with five-color pattern made up from red, white, black, light blue, and dark blue

Kohaku ~ White koi with red markings

Koromo ~ "Robed." Red coloration overlaid with blue or black

Showa ~ Black koi with red and white markings

Kawarimono

Kawarimono is the catch-all classification for nonmetallic koi not benched elsewhere. Some are varieties in their own right, while some are crosses that display characteristics of both parents. Others are truly "one-of-a-kind," whose origins would be hard to pin down. Finally, there are a few koi that deviate so much from the judging criteria applied to their variety that they are placed in Kawarimono to give them a realistic chance against the opposition. One example is the Kanoko Kohaku, with dappled hi, where individual scales show against the white ground like the markings of a young deer. It could never compete against conventionally marked Kohaku.

However, Kawarimono is by no means a dumping ground for the oddities of the koi world. There is no place in this classification (or anywhere else) for sub-standard fish whose only claim to fame is their uniqueness, because no two koi of any variety are ever exactly alike. The usual criteria of good body shape and skin quality and, where applicable, an interesting pattern, still hold. Crossbred koi should display the best, rather than the worst, features of the union, combined in a pleasing manner. That, after all, is how several accepted varieties were developed in the first place.

For convenience, varieties in Kawarimono can be grouped into single-colored koi, black koi (of Karasu lineage), and others. Some are readily available, but others are not bred intentionally — they arise as "sports" from other spawnings.

Single-colored koi
Benigoi, or Aka Muji, are all-red Kohaku derivatives resembling giant goldfish. Their fins can be either red or tipped with white. Koi with the latter feature are sometimes known as Aka Hajiro. For the fish to be of any value, the hi must be uniformly deep crimson, and the body shape voluminous without being fat. The plainer the koi, the more obvious any minor blemishes.

Shiro Muji are also thrown from Kohaku spawnings, but this time the hi is absent. These all-white fish are normally culled out, but occasionally one with exceptional skin quality is kept back and raised. Albinos, with red eyes, are sought-after rarities, as are those with Gin-Rin scalation.

Kigoi are koi of a uniform lemon yellow, and quite an old variety. When the metallic Ogons first appeared, these koi lost popularity, but are now staging a comeback. Two types are available: leucistic (with black eyes) and true, red-eyed albinos, known as Akame Kigoi. These fish – particularly the males – can grow to 1 m (39 in) or more. Good examples are free from red blemishes or silvery patches above the lateral line. Black-eyed Kigoi are sometimes confused with saffron-colored Chagoi, as the latter vary greatly in color.

KOI NOT GOLDFISH
All-red koi are known as Benigoi, but when the fish has white-tipped fins – as here – it is known as an Aka Hajiro. The overall impression is similar to that of the Hajiro (hence the name), but the latter is an all-black koi with white on its fins.

A clear, crimson head is an essential attribute of Benigoi.

❖ **PLAIN AND DAPPLED** ❖

To be of value, Benigoi must be flawless in shape and color.

The dappled Kanoko Kohaku is benched Kawarimono.

KOI DEFINITIONS

Aka Hajiro ~
Red koi with white-tipped fins

Aka Muji ~
Nonmetallic all-red koi

Akame Kigoi ~
Red-eyed albino koi

Benigoi ~
Nonmetallic, deep crimson koi

Chagoi ~
Nonmetallic brown koi

Hajiro ~ Black koi with white
nose and white-tipped fins

Kanoko Kohaku ~
Kohaku with dappled red pattern

Kawarimono ~ Class for all
nonmetallic koi not included
in any other group

Kigoi ~
Nonmetallic lemon-yellow koi

Kohaku ~
White koi with red markings

Ogon ~
Single-colored metallic koi

Shiro Muji ~
All-white, nonmetallic koi

▶ **LEMON FIZZ**
Not a Gin-Rin Ogon, which would be a metallic fish, but a Gin-Rin Kigoi. The clear, lemon-yellow skin is overlaid with even, sparkling scales.

❖ **THE EYES HAVE IT** ❖

Red-eyed Kigoi (Akame Kigoi) are sought-after fish, now rarely bred.

Black-eyed (leucistic) Kigoi are not true albinos, but still eye-catchers.

In Magoi, the scales are actually deep bronze, but the fish appear black when viewed from above. Magoi are not recognized as true koi by some show organizers, but that does not stop them from being kept. Free of the stunting effects that can arise from selective breeding for color or pattern, these fish can become huge. For that reason, Magoi blood is being reintroduced into some Go Sanke bloodlines to speed and maximize growth.

Chagoi are uniform brown koi. The word "Cha" derives from the Chinese/Japanese for tea, which describes their color. They are noted for two qualities: their capacity to grow very large and their extreme friendliness. Introducing a Chagoi to a pondful of nervous koi has a calming effect, and soon they will all be feeding from the hand of their owner. The color of Chagoi can vary from saffron through reddish brown to almost black, the paler fish being

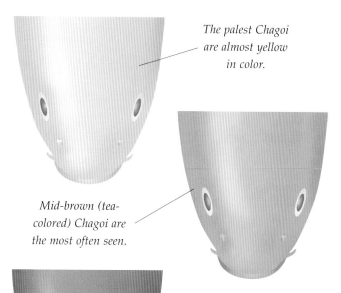

The palest Chagoi are almost yellow in color.

Mid-brown (tea-colored) Chagoi are the most often seen.

Occasionally an almost brick-red Chagoi is produced.

the most highly valued. Good, blemish-free scale reticulation is a requirement. Some Japanese breeders are introducing metallic blood into this variety to produce fish with matt scalation but Ogon-like pectoral fins. Gin-Rin Chagoi are also finding favor.

Soragoi are plain blue-gray koi. They are not a popular variety in their own right, but crossed with Chagoi they become Ochiba Shigure. Here, the gray base color of the Soragoi is patterned with the brown of the Chagoi. The best examples show Kohaku-like markings, but more often the brown is confined to the head or to small patches on the body. Doitsu and Gin-Rin Ochiba are available.

BIG AND FRIENDLY

With mature Chagoi, one could be forgiven for thinking koi were sold by weight and volume. But "battleships" like this big female need to display more than just bulk to be acceptable koi.

KOI DEFINITIONS

Chagoi ~
Nonmetallic brown koi

Doitsu ~ Koi with no scales other than enlarged scales along the lateral line and two lines running either side of the dorsal fin

Gin-Rin ~
Koi with reflective silver scales

Go Sanke ~ Koi from the Kohaku, Sanke, and Showa classes

Kohaku ~
White koi with red markings

Magoi ~ Ancestral black carp

Ogon ~
Single-colored metallic koi

Ochiba/Ochiba Shigure ~
Blue-gray koi with a brown pattern

Soragoi ~ Plain blue-gray koi

TEUTONIC ELEGANCE

This Doitsu Ochiba Shigure clearly lacks reticulated scalation, but this clear-headed and evenly German-scaled example would look well in anyone's pond.

LEAVES ON THE WATER

The gray fish marked with brown, known as Ochiba Shigure (meaning "leaves on the water"), is probably a Chagoi/Soragoi cross. This variety has become very popular, but really good examples are still hard to find.

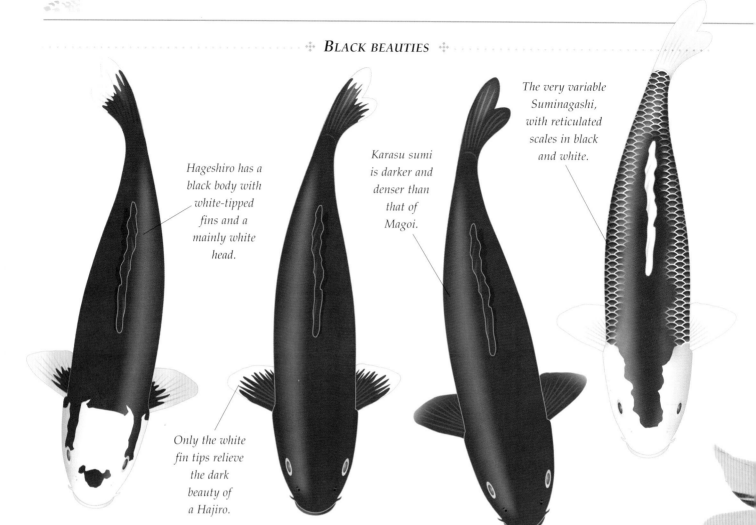

Hageshiro has a black body with white-tipped fins and a mainly white head.

Only the white fin tips relieve the dark beauty of a Hajiro.

Karasu sumi is darker and denser than that of Magoi.

The very variable Suminagashi, with reticulated scales in black and white.

Black koi and their derivatives

The Karasu, or Crow, is a very old variety, with matt black fins and body and a white or orange belly. The very similar Hajiro is a black koi with a white nose and white-tipped pectoral fins, which make it more visible in the water. The Hageshiro adds a white head to this color combination, while the Yotsujiro's fins are completely white. All four koi should display deep and even sumi, darker than that of the Magoi.

Suminagashi are fully scaled koi with black scales picked out in white. In this highly variable variety, the reticulated scales can cover all or part of the body. The similar-looking Matsukawabake is an oddity, in that the distribution of black and white areas changes according to the seasons and the temperature of the water in which it is kept. However, this does not amount to a complete reversal of pattern. Fish can turn completely black or completely white under

some circumstances, but display interesting shadowy sumi in the transition period.

Kumonryu, which first appeared in the 1980s, is the most popular of all black koi derivatives in Kawarimono. The name means "dragon fish" and is applied to these koi because their markings are reminiscent of the coiled bodies of these mythical beasts as depicted in Oriental paintings. Kumonryu are always Doitsu, which means the delineation between areas of white and sumi is sharp. Patterning is highly variable; the best examples show large, wavy-edged blocks of white along the flanks and dorsal surface. However, these fish are effectively Doitsu Matsukawabake, so their patterning can change dramatically for better or worse after you have bought them. In extreme cases, the hobbyist ends up with an all-white Doitsugoi, which is valueless.

KOI DEFINITIONS

Doitsu ~ Koi with no scales other than enlarged scales along the lateral line and two lines running either side of the dorsal fin

Hageshiro ~ Black koi with white on the head and white-tipped pectoral fins

Hajiro ~ Black koi with white tail tip and white-tipped pectoral fins

Karasu ~ Koi with matt black fins and body and a white or orange belly

Kawarimono ~ Class for all nonmetallic koi not included in any other group

Kumonryu ~ Black doitsu koi with some white on head, fins, and body

Magoi ~ Ancestral black carp

Matsukawabake ~ Nonmetallic black and white koi, whose pattern changes significantly with season/water temperature

Sumi ~ Black

Suminagashi ~ Koi with black scales picked out in white

Yotsujiro ~ Black koi with white head, pectoral, dorsal, and caudal fins

▶ KING OF KAWARIMONO

This lovely Kumonryu shows why the Japanese revere the variety. Always Doitsu, note how the sumi runs from head to tail, rather than in patches from flank to flank and over the dorsal surface. The effect is of ink calligraphy.

▶ QUICK CHANGE ARTIST

The distribution of sumi and white on Matsukawabake can change from season to season and according to water temperature and chemistry. Some of these fish will end up all white, and the black may or may not then return.

Nose sumi sets off an otherwise clear white head.

Other Kawarimono

Matsuba, or Matsubagoi, are most commonly bred as metallic fish, and benched in Hikarimuji. The reticulated scalation is counted as only one color by the Japanese. However, matt-scaled Matsubagoi go into Kawarimono. These are understated koi and quite rare, although Aka Matsuba are sometimes seen entered in the Jumbo class; being a very early variety, they grow large. Aka Matsuba are red koi with dark scale reticulation, and of Asagi lineage. However, the head should be red, rather than white. Any patches of blue and the fish is classed as an Asagi.

Ki Matsuba are most often seen in their Doitsu form, and resemble a Shusui in which the red and blue skin is replaced by yellow. The white equivalent is the rare Shiro Matsuba.

Midorigoi are green Doitsu koi, the only variety to show this color. The actual shade is more of a translucent greenish yellow, while the mirror scales can be black or silver. These fish originally resulted from a cross between a Shusui and a Yamabuki Ogon. The only variety likely to be confused with them is the Doitsu Ki Matsuba. Crossings between Shusui and Midorigoi occasionally throw up the rare Enyu, a purplish koi with hi markings.

Hybrids

Several koi in Kawarimono have Shusui lineage, but first-generation crosses between these and Sanke or Showa can result in particularly striking Doitsu Kawarimono.

Kage Utsuri and Showa

These koi are benched Kawarimono in Japanese shows, but under their own variety elsewhere. For example, a Kage Hi Utsuri would go into Utsurimono. The shadowy Kage sumi overlays the base red, white, or yellow skin in a reticulated pattern, alongside solid black patterning, but may not stay throughout the lifetime of the koi. Likewise, Goshiki in Japan are benched Kawarimono, but in the West they are classed as Koromo.

UP-AND-COMING VARIETIES

Gin-Rin scalation adds an extra dimension to otherwise rather plain koi grouped in Kawarimono. Quick to pick up the trend, Japanese breeders are now producing many Gin-Rin Chagoi, Soragoi, and Ochiba Shigure. In single-colored koi, there is nothing to distract the eye from the beauty of even, sparkling scales, while in varieties such as Ochiba Shigure, the Gin-Rin takes on a quality of its own, depending on which skin color the scales overlay.

Left: *Gin-Rin Soragoi. Reflective silver scales add a new dimension to a great blue-gray fish.*

Right: *This Gin-Rin Ochiba is a large and imposing koi with real presence.*

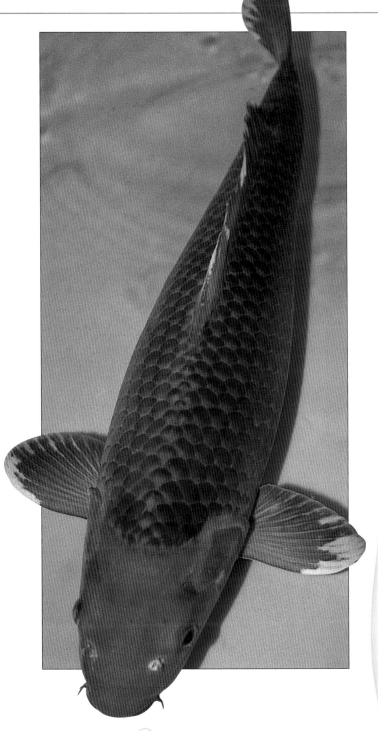

KOI DEFINITIONS

Aka Matsuba ~ Red koi with dark scale reticulation

Asagi ~ Koi with a bluish back with reticulated scale pattern. Some red on cheeks, flanks, and pectoral fins

Chagoi ~ Nonmetallic brown koi

Doitsu ~ Koi with no scales other than enlarged scales along the lateral line and two lines running either side of the dorsal fin

Enyu ~ Purplish koi with red markings

Gin ~ Silver

Gin-Rin ~ Koi with reflective silver scales

Goshiki ~ Koi with five-color pattern made up from red, white, black, light blue, and dark blue

Hi ~ Red

Hikarimuji ~ Class for single-colored metallic koi

Hi Utsuri ~ Black koi with red or orange markings

Kage ~ Shadowy black reticulated marking over white (or red on Hi Utsuri)

Kawarimono ~ Class for all nonmetallic koi not included in any other group

Ki Matsuba ~ Nonmetallic yellow koi with pinecone scalation

Kin ~ Gold

Koromo ~ "Robed." Red coloration overlaid with blue or black

Matsuba/Matsubagoi ~ Black center to scale, giving a pinecone appearance

Midorigoi ~ Greenish yellow koi with mirror scales

Ochiba/Ochiba Shigure ~ Blue-gray koi with a brown pattern

Ogon ~ Single-colored metallic koi

Sanke ~ White koi with red and black markings

Shiro Matsuba ~ White koi with black pinecone reticulation

Showa ~ Black koi with red and white markings

Shusui ~ Doitsu Asagi

Soragoi ~ Plain blue-gray koi

Sumi ~ Black

Utsuri ~ Reflections

Utsurimono ~ Black koi with white, red, or yellow markings

Yamabuki Ogon ~ Yellow-gold Ogon

RARITY VALUE

Aka Matsuba, unlike Gin and Kin Matsuba, are nonmetallic koi and grouped in Kawarimono. It is rarely seen nowadays, but good examples have crimson scales with the typical "pinecone" dark reticulation. This variety can grow to a huge size.

Midorigoi are greenish yellow Doitsu koi with rather translucent skin. Good examples, with even dorsal scalation, are rare, and the yellow color tends to fade with age.

173

Hikarimuji

The Japanese word Hikari means shining, and Hikarimuji are single-colored koi with an overall dull, metallic luster. The fish most commonly associated with this group are Ogon (formerly spelled Ohgon), but the classification also takes in metallic Matsuba, even though to Western eyes the scale reticulation of these involves an extra color, namely black.

The history of Ogon

In 1921, a Magoi with a gold-striped back was caught from a river in Takezawa, Yamakoshi prefecture, by Sawata Aoki. Fascinated by this unusual carp, he and his son Hideyoshi embarked on a process of selective breeding, keeping back only those fish that showed some golden scalation. After four or five generations, Aoki succeeded in producing the forerunners of the Ogon – Ginbo and Kinbo, and Kin Kabuto and Gin Kabuto. The latter had silver edges to their dark scales and a characteristic helmet-shaped head marking, rather like that found on today's ghost koi. All four types are still thrown in spawnings today, but are considered valueless.

Aoki spawned the first true Ogon in 1946, the result of a union between a female Shiro Muji and eight males from his 25-year breeding program.

Modern Ogon

Ogon have an immediate appeal to newcomers to the hobby. These koi grow large, are easily visible in the pond and are lively and intelligent. Later, as koi keepers become more discerning, Ogon tend to be abandoned in favor of the Go Sanke, but few ponds are without at least one of these imposing, shining fish as a reminder of early days in the hobby.

Modern Ogon are produced in huge numbers all around the world, and their overall quality is not good. To succeed in shows they must be exceptional specimens, with fine skin, even, blemish-free scalation and a clear, broad, lustrous head. The metallic sheen should extend into the finnage,

KOI DEFINITIONS

Ginbo ~ Dark koi with an overall silver sheen

Gin Kabuto ~ Black-helmeted koi with silver edges to scales

Go Sanke ~ Koi from the Kohaku, Sanke, and Showa classes

Hikarimuji ~ Class for single-colored metallic koi

Kigoi ~ Nonmetallic lemon-yellow koi

Kinbo ~ Dark metallic koi with an overall golden sheen

Kin Kabuto ~ Black-helmeted koi with gold edges to scales

Magoi ~ Ancestral black carp

Matsuba ~ Black center to scale giving a pinecone appearance

Ogon ~ Single-colored metallic koi

Shiro Muji ~ White, nonmetallic koi

Yamabuki Ogon ~ Yellow-gold Ogon

WHAT'S MATSUBA ABOUT THIS?
This type of koi can cause huge identification problems. It's a Doitsu Kin Matsuba – although, with enlarged scales confined to the flank and dorsal surface, the pinecone effect is mainly absent. Because there is no true "pattern," the koi is classed as single colored.

A good metallic shine should be present on the fins, as well as on the body.

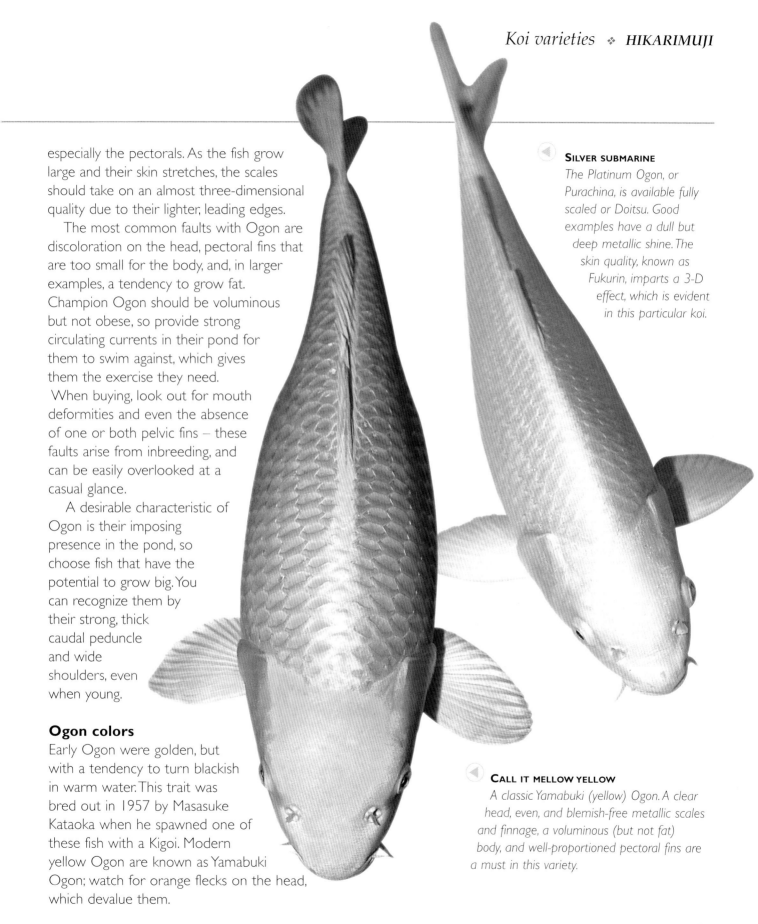

especially the pectorals. As the fish grow large and their skin stretches, the scales should take on an almost three-dimensional quality due to their lighter, leading edges.

The most common faults with Ogon are discoloration on the head, pectoral fins that are too small for the body, and, in larger examples, a tendency to grow fat. Champion Ogon should be voluminous but not obese, so provide strong circulating currents in their pond for them to swim against, which gives them the exercise they need. When buying, look out for mouth deformities and even the absence of one or both pelvic fins – these faults arise from inbreeding, and can be easily overlooked at a casual glance.

A desirable characteristic of Ogon is their imposing presence in the pond, so choose fish that have the potential to grow big. You can recognize them by their strong, thick caudal peduncle and wide shoulders, even when young.

Ogon colors

Early Ogon were golden, but with a tendency to turn blackish in warm water. This trait was bred out in 1957 by Masasuke Kataoka when he spawned one of these fish with a Kigoi. Modern yellow Ogon are known as Yamabuki Ogon; watch for orange flecks on the head, which devalue them.

SILVER SUBMARINE
The Platinum Ogon, or Purachina, is available fully scaled or Doitsu. Good examples have a dull but deep metallic shine. The skin quality, known as Fukurin, imparts a 3-D effect, which is evident in this particular koi.

CALL IT MELLOW YELLOW
A classic Yamabuki (yellow) Ogon. A clear head, even, and blemish-free metallic scales and finnage, a voluminous (but not fat) body, and well-proportioned pectoral fins are a must in this variety.

Platinum Ogon, or Purachina, are white koi whose body shines with the same luster as the precious metal. These first appeared in 1963, probably from outcrossing Kigoi with the grayish silver Nezu ("Mouse") Ogon – which remains a variety in its own right. At about the same time, the Cream Ogon became popular. This is an understated metallic koi, midway between a Purachina and a Yamabuki Ogon. Examples are still obtainable from one or two breeders, but rare.

Orenji Ogon resulted from crossing Higoi with the original yellow metallics, and later with Yamabuki Ogon. These are startlingly bright koi, but rather prone to shimis.

Kin-Gin-Rin Ogon

When the overall sheen of an Ogon is overlaid by sparkling Kin-Rin or Gin-Rin scales, the effect can be stunning. A good, clear head with Fuji (where the skin appears to have been sprayed with metallic car paint that has then developed tiny bubbles) is the hallmark of a fine Kin-Rin or Gin-Rin Ogon. This koi will still be benched Hikarimuji in Western shows.

Doitsu Ogon

Doitsu Ogon are grouped with their normally scaled counterparts for judging purposes. The Doitsu scalation should be neat and symmetrical and the same color as the body of the koi. These scales counterpoint what should be a deep luster on the areas of naked skin. There is also a "leather" version of the Doitsu Purachina, which is completely scaleless and very striking.

Matsuba Ogon

Matt-scaled Matsuba are grouped in Kawarimono, but their metallic equivalents are benched Hikarimuji. The most commonly available are Kin Matsuba (metallic gold, first produced in 1960) and the Gin Matsuba, its silver equivalent. Orenji Matsuba and Aka Matsuba Ogon are not often seen. The pinecone scalation must be pronounced; if the black is more of a gray, these koi look washed out. Beginners are often confused by the Doitsu Matsuba Ogon, as the scale reticulation is

not present. Instead, the black, German scales are aligned in the usual position, where they contrast sharply with the metallic body. Orange Doitsu Ogon, though rare, are particularly striking. They are also known as Mizuho ("Rice Ear") Ogon.

Ogon are important fish in their own right, but have also been instrumental in the development of many other metallic koi varieties in Hikari Utsuri and Hikarimoyo.

▽ **CREAM OF THE CROP**
This Cream Ogon, the forerunner of the Yamabuki, is a very subtle fish still being bred by a few Japanese enthusiasts. The color is that of rich cream.

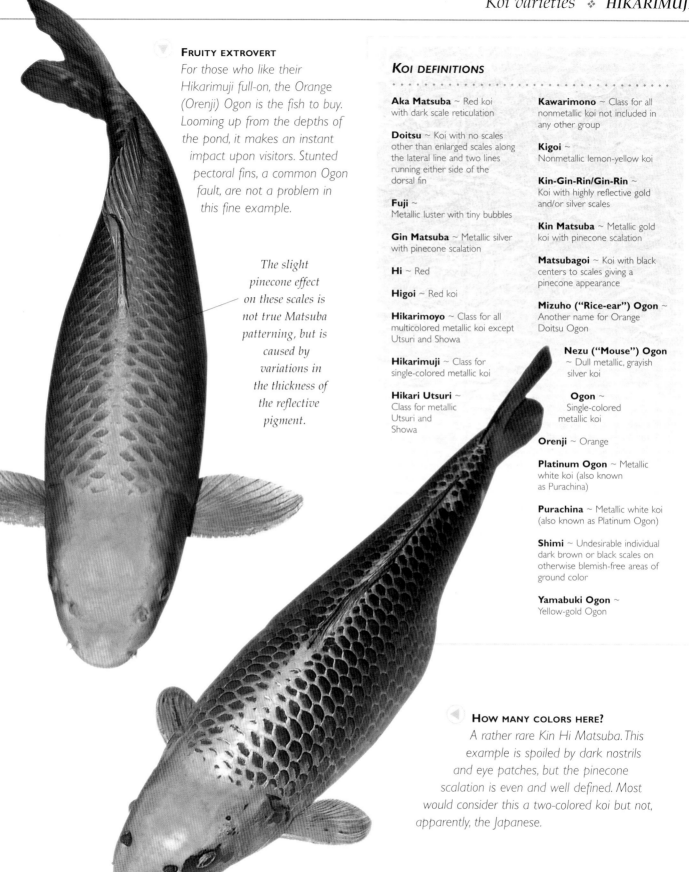

FRUITY EXTROVERT

For those who like their Hikarimuji full-on, the Orange (Orenji) Ogon is the fish to buy. Looming up from the depths of the pond, it makes an instant impact upon visitors. Stunted pectoral fins, a common Ogon fault, are not a problem in this fine example.

The slight pinecone effect on these scales is not true Matsuba patterning, but is caused by variations in the thickness of the reflective pigment.

KOI DEFINITIONS

Aka Matsuba ~ Red koi with dark scale reticulation

Doitsu ~ Koi with no scales other than enlarged scales along the lateral line and two lines running either side of the dorsal fin

Fuji ~ Metallic luster with tiny bubbles

Gin Matsuba ~ Metallic silver with pinecone scalation

Hi ~ Red

Higoi ~ Red koi

Hikarimoyo ~ Class for all multicolored metallic koi except Utsuri and Showa

Hikarimuji ~ Class for single-colored metallic koi

Hikari Utsuri ~ Class for metallic Utsuri and Showa

Kawarimono ~ Class for all nonmetallic koi not included in any other group

Kigoi ~ Nonmetallic lemon-yellow koi

Kin-Gin-Rin/Gin-Rin ~ Koi with highly reflective gold and/or silver scales

Kin Matsuba ~ Metallic gold koi with pinecone scalation

Matsubagoi ~ Koi with black centers to scales giving a pinecone appearance

Mizuho ("Rice-ear") Ogon ~ Another name for Orange Doitsu Ogon

Nezu ("Mouse") Ogon ~ Dull metallic, grayish silver koi

Ogon ~ Single-colored metallic koi

Orenji ~ Orange

Platinum Ogon ~ Metallic white koi (also known as Purachina)

Purachina ~ Metallic white koi (also known as Platinum Ogon)

Shimi ~ Undesirable individual dark brown or black scales on otherwise blemish-free areas of ground color

Yamabuki Ogon ~ Yellow-gold Ogon

HOW MANY COLORS HERE?

A rather rare Kin Hi Matsuba. This example is spoiled by dark nostrils and eye patches, but the pinecone scalation is even and well defined. Most would consider this a two-colored koi but not, apparently, the Japanese.

Hikarimoyo

Ogon, Kin and Gin Matsuba fall into the Hikarimuji classification. But these fish have all been crossed with other varieties to produce metallic koi of more than one color, known as Hikarimoyo (abbreviated from Hikarimoyo-Mono). The only exceptions are Hikari Utsuri, which are essentially metallic Utsuri or Showa and judged in a separate class.

Hikarimoyo are immediate eye-catchers that appeal both to beginners and more experienced hobbyists. The color permutations are almost limitless and this quality, enhanced by a high luster, makes a strong impact. Even low-grade examples can look stunning when young, but as they grow any defects become more apparent. Chief among these are dark lines running from the eyes down to the nose – a throwback to the Gin and Kin Kabuto forerunners of the Ogon – and discoloration on what should be a clear head.

Hikarimoyo are subdivided, somewhat arbitrarily, into Hariwake and the rest. Hariwake are two-colored koi with a platinum base color overlaid with yellow, and are available in fully scaled or Doitsu form. Hariwake Matsuba have the same coloration but the scales have Matsuba markings.

The aristocrat of Hikarimoyo is the metallic Sanke known as Yamatonishiki. This variety came on to the market in the 1960s from two distinct sources, the first breeder being Seikichi Hoshino, who took 15 years to develop it. The complex process involved an initial cross between an Asagi and a Kin Kabuto and subsequent introductions of Sakura Ogon blood. A similar fish – Koshi-nishiki – was bred in Yamakoshi by crossing a Yamabuki Doitsu with a Gin Showa. Both are now grouped together as Yamatonishiki.

Metallic skin in koi of Hikarimoyo can dull the underlying colors because the light is diffused through them. This results in sumi appearing dark gray rather than black, and red becoming more orange. However, in Yamatonishiki this is compensated for by the platinum skin and finnage, which may or may not

THE PEOPLE'S CHOICE
Doitsu Hariwake is a perennially popular pondfish. The difference between this and the very similar Kikusui lies in the color, not the configuration, of the pattern – yellow in Hariwake, orange in Kikusui. Some koi fall neatly between the two.

Note that the dorsal scales take on the color of the skin they overlay – here, silver and yellow.

carry Sanke-style sumi stripes. The head of this variety is preferably adorned with hi markings in the manner of a normal Sanke.

Kujaku

Kujaku, or Kujaku Ogon as they are still sometimes known, are highly regarded by the Japanese, as the patterning on a good specimen can rival that of Go Sanke. Like Goshiki, they are said to be five-colored koi, but this sometimes stretches credulity – not all modern examples display white, black, red, brown, and yellow markings. The first ones were bred in Ojiya in 1960 by Toshio Hirasawa

PERFECT PECS
Fully scaled Hariwake are more subtle than their Doitsu equivalent. This one has a Kohaku-like pattern, and the white area on the face lends it balance. There are no head blemishes, and the pectoral fins are imposing.

Dark "spectacles" are a common fault in metallic koi.

BANDED BEAUTY
Clear-cut color contrasts make this Doitsu Yamatonishiki (metallic Sanke) a showstopper. The large, lustrous pectoral fins line up with the silver band behind the head, with striking effectiveness.

The head of all metallic koi should have a deep luster.

KOI DEFINITIONS

Asagi ~ Koi showing a bluish back with reticulated scale pattern. Some red on cheeks, flanks, and pectoral fins

Doitsu ~ Koi with no scales other than enlarged scales along the lateral line and two lines running either side of the dorsal fin

Gin Kabuto ~ Black koi with silver edges to scales

Gin Matsuba ~ Metallic silver with pinecone scalation

Gin Showa ~ Metallic Showa with a silver luster

Go Sanke ~ Koi from the Kohaku, Sanke, and Showa classes

Goshiki ~ Koi with five-color pattern made up from red, white, black, light blue, and dark blue

Hikarimoyo ~ Class for all multicolored metallic koi except Utsuri and Showa

Hikarimuji ~ Class for single-colored metallic koi

Hikari Utsuri ~ Class for metallic Utsuri and Showa

Kin Kabuto ~ Black koi with gold edges to scales

Kin Matsuba ~ Metallic gold koi with pinecone scalation

Koshi-nishiki ~ Cross between Yamabuki Doitsu and Gin Showa

Kujaku (Ogon) ~ Metallic koi with red pattern on a white base and Matsuba scalation

Matsuba ~ Black center to scale, giving a pinecone appearance

Ogon ~ Single-colored metallic koi

Sakura Ogon ~ Metallic Kohaku

Sanke ~ White koi with red and black markings

from a female Shusui and a male Kin Matsuba and Hariwake. (Koi are normally spawned in trios, with one female and two males. It is therefore impossible to establish the exact parentage of the first Kujaku.) The result was a metallic platinum fish with black Matsuba scalation overlaying a hi pattern, a clear red head, and some blue derived from the original female parent koi. Many of these first Kujaku (the word literally means "peacock") were Doitsu, again the result of the Shusui influence.

Doitsu Kujaku are sometimes mistaken for Ginsui and Kinsui (these days not popular varieties). However, in the German-scaled Kujaku, the hi overlaid with black forms a distinct pattern along the dorsal surface and lateral lines, while in Ginsui, if much hi appears at all, it is in typical Shusui configuration – on the cheeks and flanks – and the platinum skin tends to have a bluish tint. Judging standards for modern Kujaku have become quite

flexible. For instance, "interesting" head patterning (provided there is no black intruding) is just as acceptable as plain red or platinum. A subvariety, the Beni Kujaku, is predominantly red.

Sakura Ogon

Kohaku of the Hikarimoyo are known either as Platinum Kohaku or Sakura Ogon. The distinction between them used to be drawn on the basis that in the latter, the hi patterning resembled that of a Kanoko Kohaku (namely dappled), while Platinum Kohaku displayed more traditional hi. A more accurate assessment would be that Sakura Ogon show a more flowery pattern – small (but cohesive and stable) patches of red scales. In both varieties, the hi overlaying platinum skin is actually more of an orange color.

▶ **PROUD AS A PEACOCK**
This koi shows you why Kujaku are held in high esteem by the Japanese. The more you look at it, the better it gets – the head marking resembles an island, while the body has a strong Matsuba scalation over a subtle color combination.

 PROMISING YOUNGSTER
A young Doitsu Kujaku. The German scales are not very even, but the overall coloration is stunning. This koi should eventually grow into its presently rather oversized pectoral fins.

The Doitsu version of the Sakura Ogon is known as a Kikusui ("water chrysanthemum"), a platinum fish with orange overlay running in wavy lines on either side of the dorsal fin or else placed in traditional Kohaku manner. Orenji Hariwake Doitsu is an old-fashioned term for this koi, but describes exactly what it is.

A Shochikubai is a metallic Ai Goromo, a variety not often seen. The higher the metallic luster, the more likely the reticulated hi is to appear brown, but this only lends a dignified appearance to this rare fish.

 ORANGE EQUALS KIKUSUI
Kikusui are always Doitsu. This one has a rather flowery Kohaku-style pattern, with a charming nose spot, but it is orange (as opposed to yellow) markings that make it Kikusui and not Doitsu Hariwake.

KOI DEFINITIONS

Ai Goromo ~ White koi with red Kohaku pattern. Each red scale is reticulated in black or dark blue

Beni Kujaku ~ Predominantly red subvariety of Kujaku

Doitsu ~ Koi with no scales other than enlarged scales along the lateral line and two lines running either side of the dorsal fin

Ginsui ~ Metallic Shusui with a silver luster

Hariwake ~ Two-colored koi with platinum base overlaid with orange or gold

Hikarimoyo ~ Class for all multicolored metallic koi except Utsuri and Showa

Kanoko Kohaku ~ Kohaku with dappled red pattern

Kikusui ~ Platinum koi with metallic orange markings and always Doitsu

Kinsui ~ Metallic Shusui with a gold luster

Kohaku ~ White koi with red markings

Matsuba ~ Black center to scale, giving a pinecone appearance

Orenji ~ Orange

Sakura Ogon ~ Metallic Kohaku

Shochikubai ~ Metallic Ai Goromo

Shusui ~ Doitsu Asagi

Sumi ~ Black

Tora, or Tiger Ogon ~ Metallic equivalent of Ki Bekko

Yamabuki ~ Yellow-gold

Yamatonishiki ~ Metallic Sanke

Gin Bekko (not to be confused with Gin-Rin Bekko) is simply a cross between a Shiro Bekko and a Platinum Ogon. The sumi markings tend to be subdued by the bright skin. Kin Showa are benched in another class, namely Hikari Utsuri.

Hariwake

Hariwake are derived from Ogon or Ogon/Matsuba lineage and display two metallic colors – a platinum base overlaid with either yellow-gold (Yamabuki) or orange (Orenji) markings. These immensely bright and showy koi, much loved by beginners, are relatively easy to produce. The Doitsu versions are particularly popular. A Doitsu Orenji Hariwake is properly known as a Kikusui.

Ideally, fully scaled Yamabuki and Orenji Hariwake should have clear platinum heads, although if the second color intrudes it is not a disaster. The nicest examples show a lot of metallic white on the body, but others have only small areas of this platinum skin. As in Hikarimuji, the scales should convey a three-dimensional impression.

Doitsu Hariwake often fall down on the positioning of the mirror scales, which, as in all other Doitsu koi, should be bilaterally symmetrical and evenly spaced. Many examples show coarse scalation all over the

▲ RARE AND SUBTLE

A very subtly marked Shochikubai (metallic Ai Goromo). Hikarimoyo need not be brash to be good, and the pattern and skin quality of this fish put it right in among the best Go Sanke. The robing over the hi will develop further with age.

KOI DEFINITIONS

• •

Bekko ~ Black Sanke-type markings on a white, red, or yellow base

Beni ~ Red

Gin Bekko ~ Cross between a Shiro Bekko and a Platinum Ogon

Gin-Rin ~ Koi with reflective silver scales

Hariwake ~ Two-colored koi with platinum base overlaid with orange or gold

Heisei-Nishiki ~ Doitsu Yamatonishiki-type koi, but with Showa-style sumi

Hikarimuji ~ Class for single-colored metallic koi

Hikari Utsuri ~ Class for metallic Utsuri and Showa

Ki Bekko ~ Lemon-yellow with black Sanke-type markings

Kikokuryu ~ Metallic Kumonryu

Kin ~ Gold

Kin Showa ~ Metallic Showa with gold luster

Kujaku (Ogon) ~ Metallic koi with red pattern on a white base and matsuba scalation

Kumonryu ~ Black Doitsu koi with some white on head, fins, and body

Shiro Bekko ~ White koi with black Sanke-type markings

caudal peduncle, while in others, the scales are overly large, with an armored appearance. Look beyond the overt appeal of these fish to be sure of acquiring a good specimen.

Fully scaled Hariwake Matsuba are virtually indistinguishable from Kujaku. The dark pinecone insertion point to each scale is toned down because of the metallic overlay. Hariwake Matsuba Doitsu are another matter, because the dark scales are only those along the back and flanks. No other sumi appears on the platinum/yellow body. These fish give a very clear-cut impression.

The Hariwake Tora Ogon is a Yamabuki Hariwake with Bekko sumi, a straight cross between these two varieties. The plain Tora Ogon is a Shiro Bekko x Yamabuki Ogon cross and not, as has been suggested, a metallic Ki Bekko.

New koi varieties are being developed all the time, and a recent recruit to Hikarimoyo is the Kikokuryu. Always Doitsu, and metallic, these fish display a head pattern not unlike that of a ghost koi or the helmet of those proto-Ogons, Kin Kabuto. The pattern distribution on some examples is reminiscent of Kumonryu, although these fish can be almost any color. To set off the rather plain body, good metallic luster on the finnage is an asset.

Another new variety yet to establish itself is the Heisei Nishiki, bred by Hiroi of Iwamagi. Heisei is the era of the Emperor Akahito, following on from the Showa era. The fish resembles a Yamatonishiki, except that the sumi markings are more Showa than Sanke type. However, it is not a full Kin Showa; otherwise the fish would have to be benched Hikari Utsuri.

▶ **SHADES OF GHOST KOI**
A more typical Kikokuryu, with a head pattern reminiscent of that of a ghost koi. The dull, metallic luster over the body is pleasing, and the dorsal scales are neatly aligned, but this variety is still at an early stage of development and will improve further.

◀ **IDENTITY CRISIS**
A real puzzler, this one. It is actually a Kin Kikokuryu, though at first sight it could be seen as a Kin Showa or a Doitsu Kujaku. To add to the confusion, if there were no white skin, it would be a metallic Beni Kumonryu!

Hikari Utsuri

Koi classified in Hikari Utsuri are basically metallic Showa and Utsurimono, the result of crossing Showa and Utsurimono with Ogon. Fish in this classification are nowhere near as popular as they once were and are underrepresented at shows. The reason is probably twofold. First, subtle appreciation of the finer points of koi is spreading from Japan to other parts of the world, and serious hobbyists are moving away from the flashier varieties. Second, while the metallic luster of Hikari Utsuri is a plus, it can tone down hi and sumi, so although these koi sparkle in the pond, their patterning is not always clear-cut. This makes koi that overcome this potential drawback very valuable, and efforts have indeed been made to improve the overall quality of Hikari Utsuri by back-crossing to the original, nonmetallic half of the partnership.

All metallic Showa are known as Kin Showa. Kin and Gin Matsuba are recognized varieties in Hikarimuji, as they are either gold or silver, but there is no such thing as a Gin Showa, whatever the prevailing skin color may be.

The first point to appreciate is that under the metallic luster there should be a good Showa in its own right. All the key elements should be there, such as wraparound sumi, motoguro in the pectoral fins, and the classic intrusion of an interesting black pattern into the head and face. Hi and sumi should be as strong and well placed toward the rear of the body as in the area ahead of the dorsal fin, and there must be no congenital deformities.

Ideally, the hi should be crimson, but is typically more brownish, reminiscent of that on nonmetallic Showa when they were first developed. However, Showa sumi is particularly strong and can usually hold its own against the toning down effect of the metallic

▶ **A GIANT ACHIEVEMENT**
An imposing 85 cm (33 in) Kin Ki Utsuri that won "best in variety" in the 2001 All-Japan Show. What makes it a winner are the imposing full body, even metallic luster, dark sumi in a pleasing arrangement, and the indefinable quality known as "presence." To grow this variety to its present size is an achievement in itself.

Sumi in metallic koi is always toned down – less so here than in most Kin Ki Utsuri.

▼ SHOWA WITH METTLE

A fine Kin Showa. Hi and sumi are not as dark as in the nonmetallic equivalent, but this is still a bright koi with an uncluttered pattern that holds up well toward the tail. There is little head sumi, but on modern Showa this is not a fault. Body conformation is especially good.

◄ KINETIC ENERGY

This Kin Showa shows scalation on the forward patch of hi more typical of a Kujaku, but the other Showa characteristics place it firmly in Hikari Utsuri. The patch of white behind the shoulders relieves otherwise rather heavy hi. Compare it to the fish on the left – this is a highly variable variety.

Motoguro is not confined to nonmetallic Showa.

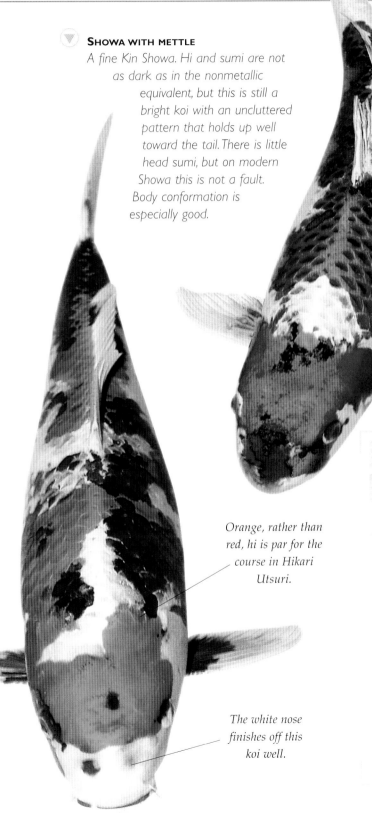

Orange, rather than red, hi is par for the course in Hikari Utsuri.

The white nose finishes off this koi well.

KOI DEFINITIONS

Doitsu ~ Koi with no scales other than enlarged scales along the lateral line and two lines running either side of the dorsal fin

Gin Matsuba ~ Metallic silver with pinecone scalation

Hikarimuji ~ Class for single-colored metallic koi

Hikari Utsuri ~ Class for metallic Showa and Utsurimono

Kindai Showa ~ Where white skin predominates

Kin Ki Utsuri ~ Metallic yellow koi with Showa-type sumi

Kin Matsuba ~ Metallic gold with pinecone scalation

Kin Showa ~ Metallic Showa with gold luster

Kujaku ~ Metallic koi with red pattern on a white base and matsuba scalation

Motoguro ~ Solid black coloration in the base of the pectoral fins on Showa and related varieties

Ogon ~ Single-colored metallic koi

Showa ~ Black koi with red and white markings

Utsurimono ~ Black koi with white, red, or yellow markings

Gin Bekko ~ Cross between a Shiro Bekko and a Platinum Ogon

Gin Shiro ~ Metallic Shiro Utsuri

Hikarimoyo ~ Class for all multicolored metallic koi except Utsuri and Showa

Hi ~ Red

Hi Utsuri ~ Black koi with red or orange markings

Kage ~ Shadowy black reticulated marking over white (or red on Hi Utsuri)

Kindai Showa ~ White skin predominates

Kin-Gin-Rin/Gin-Rin ~ Koi with highly reflective gold and/or silver scales

Kin Hi Utsuri ~ Metallic black koi with red or orange markings

Kin Ki Utsuri ~ Metallic yellow koi with Showa-type sumi

Ki Utsuri ~ Black koi with yellow markings

Shimi ~ Undesirable individual dark brown or black scales on areas of ground color

Shiro Utsuri ~ Black koi with white markings

Yamabuki ~ Yellow-gold

Yamatonishiki ~ Metallic Sanke

▲ **QUALITY SHOWA SUMI**
There is not much sumi on this Kin Ki Utsuri, but what there is, is pleasingly dark. However, the head could be said to be a little "untidy."

skin, as shown on the fish on page 184. Metallic Kindai Showa (those with much white on the body) are particularly striking.

A metallic Shiro Utsuri is known as a Gin Shiro (Gin Bekko are benched Hikarimoyo). The sharp contrast between the black and white areas of the parent Shiro Utsuri is not present, but the subtle sheen on these koi makes up for this. They look best if bred to the modern taste for limited areas of sumi. All-white pectoral fins, or those with neat motoguro, set off the rest of the fish better than dark fins, which do not contrast so effectively with the metallic luster.

Kin Hi Utsuri are arguably the most successful Hikari Utsuri. The red in good specimens is bright crimson, and while the sumi may be toned down, this does mean that any shimis – normally the plague of Hi Utsuri – are less obvious. The pectoral fins – candy-striped black and white with a golden overlay – can practically glow. Head sumi is not generally as well defined as in Shiro Utsuri, and dark nostrils on an otherwise all-red head are a common fault.

The final fish in this classification is the Kin Ki Utsuri – a metallic yellow koi with wraparound sumi. Whether this is a cross between Ki Utsuri and Ogon

Kin Showa can be Kindai (as here) or the traditional type.

Yamatonishiki (metallic Sanke) such as this can be confused with Kindai Kin Showa.

When in doubt, check sumi placement and type.

Head sumi on Kin Ki Utsuri is highly variable.

Three metallic colors complement one another on a scaleless head.

is doubtful – a more likely parentage would be Yamabuki Ogon/Shiro Utsuri, since matt-scaled Ki Utsuri, although a very old variety, are hardly ever seen in the hobby nowadays. The yellow on these koi is a bright gold, and body sumi on good specimens gives each scale an almost tricolored appearance – dark where it enters the skin, blackish gold in the center, and dark again at the rim.

Subvarieties of this classification can be Doitsu or Kin-Gin-Rin; the latter look as though they are wearing a rich coat of mail with the double reflective qualities of metallic and sparkling scales. Kage patterning is also recognized, but does not affect how they are benched.

◀ **JET BLACK ON SILVER**
Metallic Shiro Utsuri are known simply as Gin Shiro. This is another koi with remarkably dark sumi, and this time the head pattern is as good as that on the body.

Kin-Gin-Rin

In 1929, Japanese koi enthusiast Eizaburo Hoshino first discovered individual sparkling scales on koi he had bred and named them Gingoke. These mutant scales were later termed Dia, but today the accepted word outside Japan is Kin-Gin-Rin – often shortened to plain Gin-Rin.

Gin-Rin scales are quite different from those on the three groupings of metallic koi. Instead of an overall flat gleam, caused by the reflective pigment guanine, Kin-Gin-Rin scales have a sparkling deposit over all or part of their surface and, depending on the type, may be flat or raised. The color they appear is determined by the pigment they overlay – silver (Gin) in the case of sumi or white, and golden (Kin) over hi (red).

Subvarieties of Kin-Gin-Rin

Gin-Rin can be divided into four subvarieties. In Beta-Gin the whole surface of the scale is reflective, while Kado-Gin describes scales where only the leading edge carries this pigment. The latest type to appear – Diamond, or Hiroshima, Gin-Rin – originated in 1969 on the Konishi koi farm in southern Japan. Here, the reflective element radiates out from the insertion point of the scales in a fan shape. The Japanese like this type of Gin-Rin least of all, as it makes the koi appear flashy and unrefined and can blur the edges of hi and sumi

▶ SPARKLING CHAGOI

This rather plain Gin-Rin Chagoi is "lifted" by the sparkling coat of scales that overlay the entire body. But it is also a fine Chagoi in its own right, with a well-filled-out body, pectoral fins in proportion, and the requisite clear head. It is more difficult to justify Gin-Rin scalation on Go Sanke, which some would argue do not require any further embellishment. And Gin-Rin can lend a misleading impression of quality to otherwise mediocre koi.

✦ STYLES OF REFLECTION ✦

Beta-Gin, or fully reflective, scales.

Diamond Gin-Rin, the most recent form to appear.

Kado-Gin, where only the scale edges are reflective.

Pearl Gin-Rin, with a slightly raised central area to each scale.

In Japan, this fish would be shown in the Gin-Rin B class (koi other than Go Sanke).

patterns. Additionally, the leading edge of these scales is often ragged, coming to a series of small points, rather than being pleasantly rounded.

Where the sparkling deposit is heavy, the surface of the scales becomes slightly raised; this is Pearl Gin-Rin, also known as Tsubu- or Tama-Gin. More than one type of Gin-Rin scale can appear on the same fish. Beta-Gin is usually found on the abdomen, along the lateral line or in individual rows toward the dorsal surface. Diamond and Kado-Gin tend to cover the back of the koi. Most hobbyists today do not differentiate between the types of Gin-Rin, but accept them as enhancing already beautiful koi.

Already a fine two-step Kohaku, the Gin-Rin scales serve to make this fish still more impressive.

Metallic Kin-Gin-Rin

Even metallic fish are now being bred with this scalation and a good Gin-Rin Ogon is an unforgettable sight. To qualify as Gin-Rin, a koi should have more of these scales than it is possible to count as it swims past the observer – about 20 is the accepted minimum. Individual Gin-Rin scales on otherwise matt-scaled koi can look very attractive and do not detract from their value.

In the West, only Gin-Rin Go Sanke are benched Kin-Gin-Rin, although many other koi varieties have this type of scalation. In Japan, Kin-Gin-Rin "A" includes Go Sanke, while Kin-Gin-Rin "B" covers the rest.

A shimmering coat of reflective scales can lead the novice to fall for koi of otherwise limited attributes. Show judges in the Kin-Gin-Rin class, looking at a Gin-

Rin Kohaku, will first ask themselves "Is this a good Kohaku in its own right?" Only if they are satisfied that it is will they mark it highly.

Gin-Rin versus Fukurin

Some controversy exists over the status of Go Sanke said to possess "Fukurin" scalation, which is perceived by some as Gin-Rin and by others as a subtle "shine." This is an important distinction to make, since Grand Champions at shows are seldom drawn from Kin-Gin-Rin and "wrongly" benched koi can therefore upset entrants in two classes. Producers of these ambiguous fish claim that they use no Dia bloodlines. However, the arguments are set to continue for some time, especially as the breeders concerned say they will be spawning more and more Fukurin koi to compete at the highest level. From the hobby point of view, it is probably best simply to make the distinction between good and bad Gin-Rin. Whether Gin-Rin scalation improves or devalues Go Sanke is a personal opinion, but there is no doubt that it adds a new dimension to otherwise plain varieties such as Chagoi, Ochiba Shigure, and Soragoi.

KOI DEFINITIONS

Chagoi ~ Nonmetallic brown koi

Dia ~ Mutant scales that appear gold over red and silver over white areas of skin

Fukurin ~ Reticulated effect created by lustrous skin around the scales of (usually) metallic koi

Gin ~ Silver

Go Sanke ~ Koi from the Kohaku, Sanke, and Showa classes

Kin ~ Gold

Kin-Gin-Rin/Gin-Rin ~ Koi with highly reflective gold and/or silver scales

Kohaku ~ White koi with red markings

Ochiba/Ochiba Shigure ~ Blue-gray koi with a brown pattern

Ogon ~ Single-colored metallic koi

Pearl Gin-Rin ~ Reflective, slightly convex silver scales

Showa ~ Black koi with red and white markings

Sanke ~ White koi with red and black markings

Soragoi ~ Plain blue-gray koi

Tancho

Tancho are very much koi for the purist, and the Tancho Kohaku, in particular, appeals to the Japanese for its extreme simplicity of pattern and the symbolism it evokes. In Japan, the national bird is the rare Tancho, or dancing, crane *(Grus japonensis)*, which sports a round, red head marking. This reminds the people of the Japanese flag, as does the head hi of Tancho koi.

Virtually any koi variety can display a symmetrical head marking in isolation, but only Go Sanke with this characteristic – Kohaku, Sanke, and Showa – are benched Tancho. These can be in normal, Doitsu or Gin-Rin form, whereas a Tancho Goshiki in the West would go into the Koromo classification. For benching purposes (in Go Sanke only), Tancho overrides Gin-Rin. But for Go Sanke (Gin-Rin or otherwise) to qualify for Tancho status, the head hi has to be the only patch of that color on the fish. Those with separated head hi and red patterning elsewhere on the body are termed Maruten Kohaku, Sanke, etc.

The classic Tancho is the Tancho Kohaku, a pure white fish with only its head hi to set off the snowy skin. Traditionally, this hi is circular, of an even crimson,

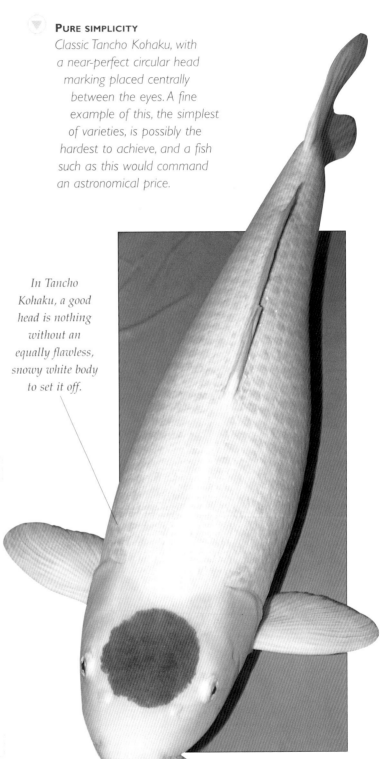

In Tancho Kohaku, a good head is nothing without an equally flawless, snowy white body to set it off.

KOI DEFINITIONS

Doitsu ~ Koi with no scales other than enlarged scales along the lateral line and two lines running either side of the dorsal fin

Gin-Rin ~ Koi with reflective silver scales

Go Sanke ~ Koi from the Kohaku, Sanke, and Showa classes

Goshiki ~ Koi with five-color pattern made up from red, white, black, light blue, and dark blue

Hi ~ Red

Kohaku ~ White koi with red markings

Koromo ~ "Robed." Red coloration overlaid with blue or black

Maruten ~ Self-contained head marking, plus red elsewhere on the body

Sanke ~ White koi with red and black markings

Showa ~ Black koi with red and white markings

Sumi ~ Black

HEAD-TURNING DISPLAY

In Tancho Showa, sumi intruding into the head hi is not seen as a fault. This fish would be a very passable Shiro Utsuri but for the patch of red. The V-shaped head sumi is typically Showa, as are the evenly marked pectoral fins.

HIGH-CLASS TANCHO SANKE

A hi-deficient Sanke or a Shiro Bekko with an added element? There is no such thing as a Tancho Bekko, of course. This is a Tancho Sanke of the highest quality, with subtle tortoiseshell sumi markings.

VARIATION ON A THEME

Unique Tancho markings deviate considerably from the plain circular spot, and this crown-shaped adornment falls into that category. However, from what can be seen of the koi, the body could do with more volume.

Do not confuse a stable, unique marking such as this with fading hi.

Heart-shaped head hi on a fish for a loved one, perhaps?

Right shape, wrong size. This Tancho mark is not imposing.

A flowery shaped Tancho mark is an acceptable variation.

If there is more than one hi marking, the koi is not a true Tancho.

Red lips (Kuchibeni) technically disqualify this koi from Tancho status.

Bilateral symmetry is a plus point in this unusual Tancho marking.

and placed centrally between the eyes. All other factors, such as skin quality and body shape, being equal, then the more perfect the circle, the more valuable the koi becomes.

Standards have been relaxed to a degree, so that Tancho Kohaku with oval, crown-shaped, heart-shaped, or otherwise interestingly configured hi are also held in esteem. However, symmetry, while not normally adjudged to be essential to the pattern of a koi, is important in the case of Tancho. If an imaginary line is drawn down the center of the head, the hi on either side should match up and not, for example, slip down over one eye.

Good examples of Tancho Kohaku are very expensive because, of course, it is impossible to

selectively breed fish with head hi only with any regularity. Many worthless Shiro Muji result from spawnings, and for every classic Tancho produced there will be hundreds more in which the head pattern is disappointing. More frustrating still, a near-perfect head can be accompanied by one or more small areas of body hi. The fish then falls between two stools and is neither a good Tancho nor an acceptably patterned Kohaku.

In Tancho Sanke, the head hi is complemented by sumi markings on the body and in some or all of the fins. The fish is essentially a Tancho Bekko, but this term is not recognized because Shiro Bekko never have any red. Although sumi occasionally intrudes into the head of a normal Sanke, a Tancho Sanke's hi should sit on a clear white ground, with the first sumi markings appearing on the shoulders. Many Bekko are thrown from spawnings of this tricky variety, but at least these fish – unlike Shiro Muji – have some commercial value.

The third type of Tancho koi is basically a Shiro Utsuri with head hi only. But once again, the latter variety should not display any red, which is why "Tancho Showa" is the only acceptable term for these koi. They are interesting in that the head hi is usually cut through by the sumi, either in strike-through (menware) or V-shaped configuration. The classic wraparound Utsurimono sumi and motoguro on the pectoral fins are bold features in their own right, so that rather than seeing these koi as Showa lacking hi, it makes more sense to view them as Shiro Utsuri with that bit extra.

Because good examples of all three types of Tancho koi are so rare, it has been known for fish to be "doctored" in their country of origin to heighten their value. Head hi is bleached or treated cryogenically to make it more symmetrical, while individual red body scales are removed the same way. If hi is lacking where it is wanted it can even be tattooed in – something for buyers to watch out for!

This heart-shaped Tancho mark is natural, but a few koi undergo the equivalent of cosmetic surgery to enhance what attributes they already have.

KOI DEFINITIONS

Bekko ~ Black markings on a white, red, or yellow base

Hi ~ Red

Kohaku ~ White koi with red markings

Kuchibeni ~ Red lips – literally "lipstick"

Menware ~ Strike-through sumi pattern on head of Showa, Utsurimono, or Hikariutsuri

Motoguro ~ Solid black coloration in the base of the pectoral fins on Showa and related varieties

Sanke ~ White koi with red and black markings

Shiro Bekko ~ White koi with black markings

Shiro Muji ~ White, nonmetallic koi

Shiro Utsuri ~ Black koi with white markings

Showa ~ Black koi with red and white markings

Sumi ~ Black

Tancho ~ Circular red spot on the head. No other red on the body

Tancho Sanke ~ Red on the head of a Sanke. No other red on the body

Tancho Showa ~ Red on the head of a Showa. No other red on the body

Utsurimono ~ Black koi with white, red, or yellow markings

❖ HEAD MARKINGS ❖

The near-unattainable, though ideal, Tancho Kohaku head.

Tancho Sanke – sumi stays well away from the head area.

Menware sumi through the head hi of a Tancho Showa is quite acceptable.

Oval Tancho marks are almost as valued as a perfect circle.

Doitsu

Doitsu (German-scaled fish) describes koi with no scales other than enlarged scales along the lateral line and two lines running on either side of the dorsal fin. In Japan, the Doitsu classification applies only to Go Sanke, while in Western shows there is no separate category for any German-scaled fish, with the exception of Shusui. However, the growing popularity of these virtually naked-skinned koi suggests that some revision may be necessary, so that Doitsu scalation can be recognized for what it is – an intriguing and challenging variation on the endless theme of Nishikigoi.

Even when grouped together with Asagi, Shusui are underrepresented at shows, yet other classes are crammed full of koi so diverse that judging one against another becomes very difficult. How do you compare a Kumonryu with a fully scaled Chagoi in Kawarimono, for example? Putting all Doitsu koi together in Western shows would not require any extra classifications, as Shusui could be included and Asagi could move to Kawarimono (from which Doitsu koi would now be excluded), joining several other old varieties – such as Soragoi and Kigoi – whose virtue lies in their simplicity. The crowded Hikarimuji and Hikarimoyo classes would benefit similarly from having their Doitsu representatives benched elsewhere.

Doitsu koi with their own names, such as Midorigoi and Kinsui, would rub shoulders nicely with most other koi of German table carp lineage. (Strictly speaking, the suffix "Doitsu" is added at the end of the variety, e.g., Kin Matsuba Doitsu, Hariwake Doitsu. But most koi keepers turn that around, i.e., Doitsu Hariwake. It is of no real consequence either way.)

Separating Doitsu fish from their fully scaled counterparts would be especially appropriate in cases where the two fish appear very dissimilar. For example, Kin Matsuba Doitsu lack the overall pinecone reticulation, which appears only on the Doitsu scales, while Ai Goromo Doitsu have clear hi, and only the blue/black dorsal and lateral scales give a

▶ **NAKED PERFECTION**
This Doitsu Sanke has attributes in abundance – a wonderful Kohaku-type pattern, well-distributed yet subtle sumi markings, and superb skin. The shoulder sumi is particularly well placed to draw attention to the flawless, striped pectoral fins of what is probably a female fish – and one with plenty more growing still to do.

This sumi overlaps both hi and white skin, a bringing together of the three colors of the koi.

The nose spot balances what would otherwise be a rather plain head.

SNAPPY DRESSER
This Doitsu Goshiki is a very clean-cut koi, which could be mistaken at first glance for a Sumi Goromo. It will be interesting to see if the pure white saddle remains that way as the fish grows, and whether the pattern breaks further.

Less is more – this white skin is the canvas on which the pattern is drawn.

INTEREST ALL DOWN THE LINE
A Doitsu Showa, whose sumi is delicately placed to draw the eye all down the fish. The somewhat one-sided head marking does not matter a bit, serving only to emphasize the pure white skin on the nose and shoulder. Perfectly balanced pectoral fins emphasize a full, but not overly plump, body.

KOI DEFINITIONS

Asagi ~ Koi showing a bluish back with reticulated scale pattern. Some red on cheeks, flanks, and pectoral fins

Chagoi ~ Nonmetallic brown koi

Goshiki ~ Koi with five-color pattern, made up from red, white, black, light blue, and dark blue

Hariwake ~ Two-colored koi with platinum base overlaid with orange or gold

Hikarimoyo ~ Class for all multicolored metallic koi except Utsuri and Showa

Hikarimuji ~ Class for single-colored metallic koi

Kigoi ~ Nonmetallic lemon-yellow koi

Kin Matsuba ~ Metallic yellow with pinecone scalation

Kinsui ~ Metallic Shusui with a gold luster

Kumonryu ~ Black Doitsu koi with some white on head, fins, and body

Midorigoi ~ Greenish yellow koi with mirror scales

Sanke ~ White koi with red and black markings

Shusui ~ Doitsu Asagi

Soragoi ~ Plain blue-gray koi

A REGULAR BEAUTY ▼

A Doitsu Hariwake with very regular markings and the requisite clear head. The variety is probably the most popular Doitsu metallic, and the dorsal scales of this one are regular and highly reflective.

KOI DEFINITIONS

Ai Goromo ~ White koi with red Kohaku pattern. Each red scale is reticulated in black or dark blue

Doitsu ~ Koi with no scales other than enlarged scales along the lateral line and two lines running either side of the dorsal fin

Go Sanke ~ Koi from the Kohaku, Sanke, and Showa classes

Hariwake ~ Two-colored koi with platinum base overlaid with orange or gold

Hi ~ Red

Kawarimono ~ Class for all nonmetallic koi not included in any other group

Kin-Gin-Rin/Gin-Rin ~ Koi with highly reflective gold and/or silver scales

Kiwa ~ Border of red and white at the rear edge of hi patterns

Kohaku ~ White koi with red markings

Maruten ~ Self-contained head marking, plus red elsewhere on the body

Shiro Utsuri ~ Black koi with white markings

Sashi ~ Overlap of red and white scales at the forward edge of hi patterns

Showa ~ Black koi with red and white marking

Sumi ~ Black

Yamatonishiki ~ Metallic Sanke

real clue to their lineage. And, given that the Japanese have wisely assigned Doitsu Go Sanke their own classification, would it not make sense to do this in other countries? At top show level, a Doitsu Kohaku would never beat a fully scaled koi of the same quality, but that does not make it any the less impressive a fish. Doitsu "A" for Go Sanke and Doitsu "B" for the rest would be one way around the dilemma.

All patterned Doitsu koi should have clearly defined markings. What they may lack is refinement. The Japanese still regard them as somewhat two-dimensional, and therefore vulgar, compared to their scaled counterparts. Yet without scales to diffuse the light, colors appear bright and sharp: a good Doitsu Showa, for example, almost seems lit from within.

The koi-buying public have no reservations about Doitsu koi, especially in Kawarimono, where their sales are increasing year after year. When you consider that any koi, except for Kin-Gin-Rin, can be produced in a Doitsu version, that is hardly surprising.

*These lateral mirror
scales are not present
in all Doitsu koi.*

*Not all Doitsu scalation
extends over the
shoulders, as here.*

▲ HEADING IN THE RIGHT DIRECTION
*This Doitsu Yamatonishiki could do with
more hi down its left flank, but the
Maruten head pattern is first-rate.*

▶ NO SCALES, NO PROBLEM!
*Doitsu Shiro Utsuri are rather rare, but with
no kiwa and sashi to blur the sumi, this fish
manages to combine the best of both
elements in a clean-cut, but still subtle,
pattern. All the sumi appears to be
through in this mature example.*

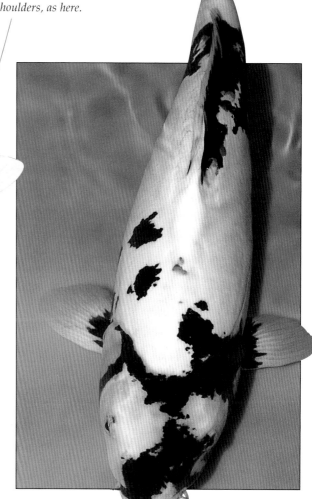

General Index

Varieties Index

Page numbers in **bold** indicate major entries, *italics* refer to captions and annotations; plain type indicates other text entries.

CREDITS

Practical photographs by Geoffrey Rogers © Interpet Publishing.

The publishers would like to thank the following photographers for providing images, credited by page number and position: (B)Bottom, T(Top), C(Center), BL(Bottom Left), etc.

Aqua Press (M-P & C Piednoir): 19(BR), 91(L, Peter Cole), (R)
Shunzo Baba (Kinsai Publishers Co. Ltd., Tokyo): 12(BR), 15(TL,C), 115(BL,R), 132, 137, 152, 157, 178, 184, 188
Dave Bevan: 76, 77, 86(TL)
Bernice Brewster: 85(T), 86(BL), 87(TL, CL), 88(TL, BR), 93(BL, BR), 95(CR)
Bridgeman Art Library: 12(BC)
David Brown: 48, 120(TR, C)
David Bucke: 82(C, BC)
Nigel Caddock, Nishikigoi International: 123(CL, BC), 126, 129(C), 131(L, R), 133, 135(R), 136, 138, 139, 141(R), 142, 143(R), 144, 145, 146, 147, 148, 150, 151(R), 154(R), 160, 161(L), 163, 164(L, R), 165(L, R), 166, 167, 168, 169(L, R), 173, 174, 175(C, R), 176, 179(T, C), 180(C, BR), 181, 182, 183(C, R), 185(L), 186(L, R), 189, 190, 191, (BL, C, R), 194, 195(L, R), 196, 197(T, B)
Derek Cattani: Copyright page, 10-11, 18, 21(R), 22(BL), 31(BL), 36, 37, 49, 55(T, BR), 56, 57(L, TR, BR), 81, 83, 92(TL, TR, CL, CR), 95(BC, BR), 98(T), 102(T, B), 107, 108, 109(T), 110(BL, BR), 111, 113(BL)
Christina Guthrie: 112(TL, CR)
Steve Hickling: 13(TL, TR), 58(TL, C), 68, 117(TL, TR)
Andrew McGill: Half-title page, 16, 127, 128, 129(TL), 134, 135(L), 141(L), 143(L), 151(BL), 154(L), 155, 156, 159, 161(TR), 171(L, R), 172(BL, BR), 177(T, B), 185(TC), 193
Stan McMahon: 89
Will Moody: 113(CR)
Tony Pitham (Koi Water Barn): 14, 17, 19(TL), 32(TL), 96, 97(T), 114(TL, TR, C), 116, 118(TL, TR, C), 119
Graham Quick: 53
Alec Scaresbrook: Title page, 34(TR)
Sue Scott: 21(TL)
Steve Worcester: 69(C, CR, BL, BR), 71(TL, TR, CL, BR)

Computer graphics by Phil Holmes and Stuart Watkinson © Interpet Publishing.

ACKNOWLEDGMENTS

The publishers would like to thank World of Koi, Oakley Road, Bromley, Kent, U.K., for their generous assistance with practical photography, both at the head office and at various pond-building sites. In particular, thanks are due to Steve Hickling for his expertise and unbounded enthusiasm for the project, to Mick Martin for writing and holding the fort while Steve finished his sections, to Billy Stone for his expert advice, to Matt Bird for taking on-site photographs and providing technical information, and to Kirk Jepson for demonstrating various practical techniques.

The following companies and individuals also helped during the preparation of this book: Tony Pitham and staff at Koi Water Barn, Chelsfield Village, Kent, England; NT Laboratories Ltd., Wateringbury, Kent, England; Tetra UK, Eastleigh, Hampshire, England; Tropical Marine Centre Ltd., Chorley Wood, Hertfordshire, England; Andrew Chatten and Chris Giles at Selective Koi Sales, Norwich, England; Andy Dixon of DKS, Lincoln, England; Mike Shaw at Evolution Aqua Ltd., Wigan, Lancashire, England; James Allison of Aquapic Solutions, Cheltenham, Gloucestershire, England; Steve Worcester for allowing photographic access to his emerging pond; Spencer Bell; Alan McDougal; Christina Guthrie, Koi Carp Magazine; Angela Rivers, Koi Ponds and Gardens Magazine; Geoff Kemp and Connoisseur Koi; Derek Henderson; George Rooney; John Peterson; Sally Wilson; Raymond Sawyer; Mario and Pauline Cavozzi; Pat Meecham; Ron Parlour; Denis Carter; and Richard Barker for providing visuals for some of the graphics.